Moody
BLUE

Moody BLUE

THE STORY OF MYSTERIOUS MARCO

BY JEFF HOLMES

First published by Pitch Publishing, 2015
Paperback edition, 2018

Pitch Publishing
A2 Yeoman Gate
Yeoman Way
Durrington
BN13 3QZ
www.pitchpublishing.co.uk

A CIP catalogue record is available for this book
from the British Library.

ISBN 978-1-78531-406-3

Typesetting and origination by Pitch Publishing

Printed in India by Replika Press

CONTENTS

ACKNOWLEDGEMENTS

My special thanks go to Claudio Minghetti, Marilena Rosatone, writer Jeff Holmes and to Pitch Publishing. This book first saw the light of day in Italy, with the help of Luglio Editore. The publisher, hailing from Trieste, took a courageous gamble with my story. The same applies in the UK to Paul and Jane at Pitch, and everyone else involved in the process at that wonderful publishing house.

And finally to the wonderful Rangers support – we almost made it!

INTRODUCTION

*'Each one of us has a pair
of wings, but only those
who dream learn to fly.'*

FOOTBALL has been my life since I was very small.
It has given me some of the most intoxicating highs,
and mind-numbing lows, but it still remains to this
day the one pleasure that I never want to lose. Despite
the pain it has caused, my passion for the game has never
diminished and I can say with hand on heart that it's the
place I still know better than anything else.

When I turned 40, I realised that a flame was still
burning brightly, and I wanted to do something about it. I
decided to take part in a coaching course to gain my UEFA
licence and, at the same time, develop a project that I like to
call 'revolutionary and incredibly ambitious', and which I
believe in with all my heart. An idea, formed exclusively in
my head and planned with extreme meticulousness. Ladies
and gentlemen, I give you a course designed specifically for
the striker. It's my hope that this is something which will

arouse the enthusiasm and curiosity of those who value the contribution of such a player. The course has been designed on the back of my own top-level experiences with the breath of the defender constantly on my neck, and the preying eyes of spectators trained on my boots.

Recently, though, this has been put on hold as I decided to document my life and career in print. If truth be told, not even for a moment of my 'previous life' would it have occurred to me to write a book about myself. Maybe because I'm quite a private and reserved person, but also because my professional career doesn't appear so important or outstanding to me, and I never felt the need to pass on its secrets to such a large number of people.

During pre-season, or in my hotel room on the evening before away games, apart from playing cards with my team-mates, I always maintained a passion for reading. Not exactly works of historical significance but mostly the biographies of professional athletes. Footballers, of course, but also tennis players, boxers, wrestlers, Formula 1 drivers, cyclists and rugby players – nothing was out of bounds. I've also had a long-held curiosity for the careers of well-known actors, politicians, and great and revolutionary men who made their mark on history. Thanks to my Scottish experience, I studied the English language at a higher level and started reading volumes that were in short supply in Italian libraries. Mostly non-authorised biographies – my favourites – that aren't simply pages filled with sport results in sequence, but highlight anecdotes, deep reflections, human weaknesses, major errors and uncomfortable truths on the life of the book's hero.

The first thoughts of putting my life down in print came when a Scottish journalist, Gary Ralston, called and suggested it would make an interesting read. The idea grew on me, and although Marco Negri was never the greatest, most talented, or best-loved player to wear the Rangers shirt, without doubt I've been one of the most enigmatic characters of Scottish football in the last 20 years.

My history is in fact quite curious and complex, especially in Scotland, where I left little in the way of interviews, whether in print or on TV. Of course, there are a couple of videos on YouTube or a few articles in the papers and sports magazines. The interest on some Scottish supporters' forums and websites has been quite bizarre, to say the least, but the reality is that nobody really knows how things went because I didn't ever speak about it to anyone on the 'outside'. That's why I thought that a book on my life and career might be a good idea: in fact, I was soon ready to throw myself head first into the project.

However, a lengthy series of unexpected hurdles appeared and slowed down the process until Gary decided to buy his plane ticket to Italy, complete with recorder and notebook, only to discover that I had been struck down with an extremely nasty form of labyrinthitis. I had lost all sense of balance and couldn't even stand up. It did occur to me that perhaps everything that happened during my time at Rangers really had brought on a massive headache! And not just that, but that period produced the coldest temperatures in the UK in the last 50 years, and completely paralysed British airports for a few days. It was the winter of 2010/11, and it was a nasty one.

With this in mind, and wrought by desperation, Gary and I decided to try and use the internet to get the ball rolling and started speaking via Skype. It was a real bind, hard to explain, and only served to complicate matters as problems with the line seemed to arise every five minutes. Our main issue was that every time we lost the connection, we would invariably lose track of what we had been saying and would always have to start again from the beginning. We managed to overcome most problems and my journalist friend advised me to write down a couple of chapters, just to see how much I had to say, and to see how the story would pan out. I enjoyed those weekend appointments and was confident something interesting would come of it.

Unfortunately, during the Christmas holidays, I received a phone call from Gary to tell me that the first draft of the book was at risk as a sad, unexpected and sudden episode had taken place in his personal life. Understandably, he had to take a step back as his priorities had changed. At that moment I decided to abandon all notion of writing my story. Or just about, because my brother stepped in and persuaded me to keep on writing, and jot down snippets when they came to mind. I simply watched again the film of my life and, spontaneously, tasty particulars started to form in my mind – situations that I thought were lost and forgotten, when they had merely been hibernating in a distant corner of my memory. Once again I threw open the doors of that abstract wardrobe, curious to see what joys I would come across in the deep recesses of my mind.

I must admit I had real fun writing this book. I hope you experience the same emotions while turning the pages. What initially appeared to be a difficult journey turned out in the end to be a pleasant stroll because it soon became natural writing about myself, especially as I described my experiences with the same intensity used while living my life – and with complete honesty.

I also reckon writing a book represents a great way for an ex-footballer to make sense of what he has just lived and experienced, and with that in mind I would recommend that more pick up the pen and start scribbling. Giving up a career such as football is incredibly difficult and nothing prepares you for it. Everything changes with the flick of a switch. You give up the camaraderie of the dressing room, training, technical meetings and actually playing. Sadly, I've known many colleagues that found themselves lost once they had kicked their last ball. In the blink of an eye, they had moved from a totally privileged position, a status that gives you control on everything and everyone, to a world of confusion and negative emotions. The feeling of not being useful anymore is potentially destructive.

At this time, and almost without realising it, you can fall into a world of temptations, and more than one of my former colleagues have destroyed an apparently solid relationship with their wives through choosing a much younger girlfriend, perhaps because they wanted to feel young again. Others have thrown themselves head first into risky adventures, just to feel one last time that adrenaline rush that only professional football brings. And just a small number, fortunately, have been seduced by drugs.

According to Ralph Waldo Emerson, an American man of words, 'The non-examined life is not worth living.' I have to agree with him, as through a book such as this, you can accompany the author on his journey, before summing up the life just lived. And, of course, it is a wonderful legacy to leave to children, parents and best friends.

'For a man, there's no greater glory, until he lives, than to accomplish undertaking with his feet and hands.' So, if it's true I was a success in my chosen field, I would have to conclude that the Great Omer was accurate with his words. I can only hope I do not disappoint with mine, as for me, he has been a tremendous source of inspiration.

WITH A LITTLE HELP FROM MY FRIENDS

Gennaro (Rino) Gattuso

Marco and I have always had a great relationship, and one built on trust and real friendship. But out of all the experiences we have shared on the field and in everyday life, I like to remember one episode that still makes me happy even though many years have passed. We met each other in Perugia while the team was fighting for the Serie B championship. It was season 1994/95 and I was still a young man. Even so, I was part of the main team, albeit on the periphery, but was determined to make a career in football. Marco, on the other hand, was already the 'prince bomber (striker)' of the *Grifone*. That was just the start of our relationship and the first time our paths had crossed, but even though I was a good bit younger, he looked after me, and that was something I really appreciated.

I left Perugia and joined Glasgow Rangers and, if the truth be told, it was incredible when he joined me at Ibrox. Once again we teamed up and continued our friendship. We lived not far from each other in Glasgow and would travel to training together at Ibrox. When we weren't training or playing football, we would spend a lot of time together, whether that was just the guys or with our girlfriends.

One episode that I still remember clearly came during a match against Hearts. We won but, and this was a rare occurrence for me, I managed to score two goals. It was a tough game and after the final whistle, we trooped back to the dressing room. I was really tired, but obviously delighted, that first of all we had won the match and obviously there was extra special pleasure at scoring two goals. I sat opposite Marco and I looked over at him and his eyes said everything. I wanted to share the magic of my goals with him and the look he gave me was pure gold. He had a tear in his eye and he was so happy for me. Marco didn't say much, but he didn't have to.

To be honest, he wasn't the type of guy who just dished out meaningless compliments on a regular basis, but the look he gave me that day was sincere, and even today I hold that look and expression with great affection, and it is up there with my best memories in football. That was, for me, an extraordinary moment, and a gesture that was worth much more than a thousand words!

Michael Mols

When I joined Rangers, I didn't know Marco at all. They told me he was also a striker and sometimes moody, but when I first met him, my first thoughts were that he was 'Model Marco' and not 'Moody Marco'. His love of Italian fashion was legendary, and then there was his long hair!

It's always possible when a new player arrives at a club, and he also plays in 'your' position, that the player who is already there can take the attitude that it's you against me. Not Marco, though, as he was one of the first, together with his wife Monica, to help me settle in at both Rangers and in Glasgow. He shared his love of the city with me, as well as the good Italian restaurants, and also showed me where I could shop, although in this case, it should have been where I shouldn't shop!

He even invited me over to Italy for a holiday, and this told me so much about his character and mentality and the way Marco was then, and still is today.

After our shared experience in Scotland, we lost a wee bit of contact, but whenever we see each other again it's like nothing has changed. The best thing about my time at Rangers and in Scotland wasn't only the football and winning prizes, but the friendships I made – and still have, and I'm so proud and happy to call Marco my friend!

A strong friendship doesn't need daily conversations, and doesn't always need togetherness, as long as the relationship lives in the heart, and that means true friends will never part.

Marco Materazzi

When Marco asked me to relate an episode of our relationship and deep friendship for his book I answered immediately, 'Are you sure? In this case, perhaps I should write another book!'

To be honest, our friendship has always been the real deal. Moreover, after knowing him as well as anyone, I prefer to remember him not as the 'sad bomber' (a definition given to him by those that are in the business of handing out descriptions that don't properly describe their subjects), but as an authentic 'breed bomber' instead (just take one look at those records that he still has in Scotland).

I can assure you, that if you're not a striker with the capital S in British football, then you have very little chance of scoring the amount of goals that he did.

I'm sure that just one slice of bad luck stalled his career at European level, because this was a man who was born to score goals. But Marco has always been characterised by a big heart; he helped me a lot and I will always thank him for that. When we played together in Perugia under the coach, Giovanni Galeone, it was an incredibly difficult time in my career. Never mind, because Marco was always there for me, and we became very close. To the point that once, even though he decided not to talk to journalists, he made an exception and publicly dedicated one of his many goals to me. He did so to give me the boost that I obviously needed at that time. He was telling me not to give up, and I am so glad that I listened to him! I can tell you something else. In 'our' world, a gesture like that isn't so common.

Alberto Zaccheroni

I am so flattered that Marco asked me to contribute to his memoirs. I had the absolute pleasure and good fortune of being able to coach him for an entire year at Cosenza. When he arrived at the club, I already knew of the super technical qualities he had shown in Bologna the year before, during the only two weeks that we shared. He went on to show his quality for the remainder of that season.

I coached a lot of big-name footballers but, unfortunately, some of them didn't reach the heights their talent deserved. Take a look at my CV and you will see some of the names I have worked with, but I have to say that the name of Marco Negri should be up there with the very best of them. Not for the obvious talents that he had, but for what those talents should have achieved in football. When

I talk about class strikers, Marco's name always comes up. I firmly believe that the opportunity to be up there with the great names, not just of Italian football, was taken away by the now infamous injury. Seriously, it was one of my biggest regrets in football that I did not see Marco play in a truly great team. He certainly deserved to.

PROLOGUE

THEY tell me that Rottenrow Maternity Hospital in Glasgow welcomed thousands of tiny babies into the world for more than 150 years before closing in 2001. Little did I know when I stumbled through its doors on the evening of 5 January 1998, an ice patch clamped against my right eye and team-mate Sergio Porrini following in my wake, that the career I had always wanted to father was destined to remain unfulfilled, along with my ambitions of leading Rangers to ten in a row.

We must have looked an odd couple, Sergio and I. His car had been parked hurriedly and haphazardly at the kerbside, something I'm sure hospital staff had grown accustomed to over the years as expectant mums and proud dads-to-be raced towards the welcoming lights of its entrance. For them, a whole new exciting adventure in family life lay sometimes only a matter of minutes away. For me? Just pain that would last a whole lot longer than the contractions of labour.

After only six months in Scotland my English was still fractured but competent enough as I hurried up to reception and made a frantic request to see a doctor. The lady behind the desk didn't need to see the injury, never mind my trademark facial growth, to know I wasn't one of her usual patients.

'I'm very sorry sir,' she explained, genuinely sympathetic. 'This is a maternity hospital. The nearest accident and emergency unit is at Stobhill. You must go there. Do you need directions?'

To be honest, she would have been as well offering us a map to Timbuktu. Bloody squash. Bloody Porrini. Not only had I chosen to play a game I barely knew, but my partner, a good friend, just happened to be the fiercest competitor I'd ever met in any walk of life. Now this. Sergio may have known his way up and down the right side of a football field, but the geography of Glasgow was still, for the most part, alien to him – and me. We had raced away from the Livingwell leisure club in the shadow of the Hilton Hotel just ten minutes previously, my eye already closing after being struck by a squash ball during only my second attempt at playing the sport.

We knew the city centre well enough and Sergio headed for George Square because he had seen a signpost there for a hospital on a previous visit. It was early evening and the festive lights still twinkling around the city's most famous piazza were nothing compared to the fireworks of red, blue and green going off inside my head. Bloody squash, I told myself again. To think, I had only taken it up because I reckoned the speed and agility required on court would be the perfect athletic supplement to someone who thrived on using a similar range of skills in the penalty box. Instead, it led to arguably the most bizarre injury in the history of Scottish football; certainly one of the most talked-about.

We had clearly made a mistake with our choice of hospital, but surely that would be the last mishap in this whole affair. After all, what could possibly go wrong in the life of Marco Negri? It was a black eye, just a bit of bruising and temporary blurred vision, right? We have a saying in Italy, 'You have gone from the top of the stairs to the floor of the stable.' Nothing could push me down that low, could it? After all, I was leading the rock star lifestyle, my career panning out as I had dared to fantasise as a kid growing up in Italy.

I had already scored 33 goals in the first half of the season with my new club Rangers and although I had serious issues with assistant coach Archie Knox I enjoyed working with Walter Smith and my multi-national team-mates and life in Scotland was beautiful as the supporters took me to their hearts. My girlfriend, Monica, had joined me in Glasgow and we thought nothing of heading to Paris when time permitted and there were even Saturday nights out in London after games where, much to my pleasant surprise, there was also recognition from English football fans. I was a serious contender for the Golden Boot and, most importantly, ten in a row beckoned as a record milestone for Rangers and in the process I could become the first Italian to win the Scottish championship. There was even talk of a call-up for Italy and maybe, just maybe, the chance to push my way into Cesare Maldini's plans for the 1998 World Cup finals in France.

My team-mates included the wonderful Paul Gascoigne, who took me to see Oasis in concert and introduced me to the Gallagher brothers. At that stage of my existence, I knew exactly what Noel Gallagher meant when he wrote he was going to live forever.

Surprisingly, perhaps, as I turned on my heels at Rottenrow there was little pain, only a kaleidoscope of colours going off behind my battered eyelid and a gnawing fear that it might be a little more serious than I first imagined. With the gynaecologists otherwise engaged, it was on to Stobhill. Really, we knew the directions we had been given meant next to nothing when we emerged from the maternity hospital with only a vague notion to head north to the fringes of the city but Sergio, thinking quickly, hailed a taxi and told the driver to lead the way to accident and emergency so we could follow behind in his car.

Thankfully, we were seen straight away, but the doctor was a student whose calming bedside manner masked a chronic inability to diagnose the true extent of the problem. At that moment, the only thing on my mind was the Aberdeen game at Ibrox in three days' time. She told me the injury did not look so serious and that with eyedrops and rest she was confident my recovery would be complete. Sweet words, but some hope. Sergio dropped me home, where Monica was waiting. Clearly, misery still sat heavily on the shoulders of Sergio, despite assurances I could never be angry with him for an accident that was a one-in-a-million occurrence.

There may have been an issue with my right eye but, like almost everyone in life, my vision in hindsight is pretty much perfect. In truth, my choice of sport was fine, my playing partner less so, although let me stress absolutely no blame is attached to Sergio for what happened then and afterwards. His concern at the time was genuine and his remorse sincere. I was in the wrong place at the wrong time. But, and isn't there always a 'but'? I long ago became comfortable with English 'but' have still to come across a word that's so small and yet can lead to phrases and sentences that mean so much.

The culture in Italian football is different to Scotland in many ways, not least the structure of the professional working week. Wednesdays are always tough in Serie A, the hardest of the week, including morning and afternoon sessions. In Scotland, it is usually a day off for players, but when I moved to Rangers in the summer of 1997 I still could not shake off my upbringing. Wednesdays were for work, not play, so when the weather was nice I would go for a jog around the countryside near my home in Milngavie and if it rained, I would take a trip to Livingwell, usually with Sergio, to exercise and work in the gym. The squash courts were intriguing. It was not a sport I knew well, but I had played tennis as a kid and squash was attractive because of the speed and mobility it demanded from its players. As Christmas beckoned that year, we gifted ourselves a present of court time.

It never even occurred to us to wear safety glasses. No one else did and, besides, there was nothing in the terms and conditions at the side of the entrance door to the court that demanded their use. By sheer coincidence – what else could it have been, huh? – but within 24 hours of my accident a poster appeared on the wall advising all players to wear eye protection. Our first adventure passed without incident as we played for over an hour and honours were even at one game apiece but – and there's that word again – I should have realised with Sergio it was always going to be more than just a bit of light-hearted fun. My team-mate did not reach two Champions League finals with a club of the stature of Juventus without having a tremendous will to win and it was an aspect of his character that dominated his personality off the field as well.

Sergio was a terrific professional and it was always about the winning. If you played him at cards or a game of pool, he always had to win. On the rare occasion he didn't succeed, he would come in the following day and challenge you at something else until finally emerging victorious. That's great for football, but it causes too much pressure in other areas of life. He was the wrong choice of playmate for squash because it should not have been a game in which winning became everything and yet with Sergio that was impossible.

Our games quickly took on a more competitive edge than they should have. In the second week, during our second game – only the second of my entire life – the scores were evenly poised and I had moved to the front of the court, trying to reach one of Sergio's 'floppy' shots. Sergio was behind me, so I stole a glance at his position and in that fraction of a second I lost contact with the ball and by the time I turned back to the wall it was too late. At a speed that felt like 100 miles an hour that sphere of hard, hot rubber cannoned off the concrete and straight into the centre of my eye.

Later that evening, after returning from Stobhill, the plans of Monica and I to have dinner were shelved, not least because the fridge had already been raided for the best piece of beef to place over my eye. The words of the student doctor should have offered at least some consolation and comfort but, instead, fear began to grip when I looked in the mirror and saw the pulpy mess my eye had become. In addition, my mood was not lightened when I lay back on my bed and watery blood began to flow from the corner of my eye like the tears I would later fight for real as the true impact of the injury took its toll on my life and career.

At Ibrox the next day I turned up looking as if I had gone 15 rounds with Mike Tyson and although my right eye was badly swollen, bloodied and bruised, even I could see the anxiety on the face of Walter Smith, still smarting from our 2-0 defeat at Celtic Park a few days earlier that had cut our lead at the top of the table against our biggest rivals to just one point, when it could have been seven. He clearly feared a bad week was about to get even worse with the loss of his in-form striker. A return visit to Stobhill was immediately arranged by the Rangers doctor, this time to see a leading eye specialist, who confirmed my retina had become detached. The squash shot was so powerful and landed with such ferocity it had thrown my eye back into my head until it bounced off the membrane that separated it from the brain. The retina had become dislodged and attached itself to the membrous gel. Sadly, the cure would not be found in the finest and most tender cuts of sirloin.

Suddenly, things had stepped up a notch. Laser surgery was arranged within a week, after the initial swelling had gone down, and the retina was re-attached and re-aligned with the eyeball in as painful a procedure as you could imagine. There were fears I could lose the sight altogether and if my eyes had been blue, not brown, my vision would almost certainly have been devastated by blindness as lighter coloured eyes are genetically more delicate and not as capable of coping with trauma. It had the potential to impact seriously on my life, not just my career. To add insult to injury, a couple of days after that squash game I was called upstairs at Ibrox to the office of financial director Douglas Odam. A fax had just arrived from the Italian Football Federation, asking me to prepare for an invite in the forthcoming days from Maldini to join the national squad for a friendly international. The follow-up document never arrived. They say good news travels fast. Bad news regarding injuries clearly travels faster.

However, at that stage all I could think about was Rangers and a return to playing and yet the specialist diagnosed a month on the sidelines, which I knew would stretch to at least six weeks by the time match fitness was taken into consideration. After all, he insisted on absolutely no physical activity whatsoever for at least a month to give the eye the best chance possible of healing – and even then he caveated that statement by warning I could face difficulties with my sight by the time I reached 50. There could be no training, he warned sternly, not even work in the gym or on the exercise bike because even those exertions could have potentially disastrous consequences for my sight. I was ordered to wear dark glasses and was even banished to the spare room at home, lest a stray elbow from Monica in the middle of the night cause any damage.

The injury could not have come at a worse time, for me or Rangers. By the beginning of February, only three goals separated us from Celtic at the top of the table, and Hearts had also joined the fray, just eight goals behind after 23 games played. At a time in the campaign where I should have been adding to my goals tally and pushing us towards the magical tenth title, I had become an ambassador for the Scottish tourist industry. In reality, I wanted to return to Italy immediately after the laser surgery because, for the first time since I had joined Rangers, my working environment had ceased to become enjoyable. My teammates were nothing but supportive and encouraged me back to full fitness – and let that put an end to the tiresome rumours that my injury had been inflicted after a training ground punch-up. A couple of newspapers even suggested there had been a flare-up and to hear some of the more outrageous stories the only personality at Ibrox with whom I did not engage in fisticuffs was Broxi Bear. Nonsense – and not the first time tall tales would be fabricated about me, but I shrugged it off as part of the modern day alliance between the media and sport aimed at boosting and publicising both sides of the relationship. So long as it did not encroach into my personal life, I was happy to let the gossip wash off my back.

Still, visiting Ibrox became very difficult. At that time, before the construction of Murray Park, the players reported to the stadium every morning before being bussed to the training ground, but there was nothing for me to do. Remember, even entering the gym was forbidden. It became a lonely environment and walking around Glasgow in the depths of winter with sunglasses on, like Roy Orbison, certainly drew me to the attention of people more than usual. Rangers fans sent cards and offered good wishes for a speedy recovery. Celtic supporters placed their palms over their eyes and laughed whenever they saw me in the street, or feigned blindness as they groped in front of me with imaginary white sticks.

In my heart, I wanted to return home for the month. My head had been in the clouds because so much had happened to me in the past six months, almost all of it positive. I needed to ground myself again among the familiar and the everyday of home – family, friends, old sights and realities, not the wonderful, crazy existence of Glasgow. However, even flying was forbidden as the cabin pressure would have played havoc with my eye and as driving was also a no-no it would have been unfair to ask Monica to sit behind the wheel for two or three days as we made our way through England and across mainland Europe. Instead, we struck a compromise of sorts that involved spending around half a week at home and the other half exploring the fantastic new country we had come to call home. Every second day we headed north, south, east or west – to the Highlands and islands, Inverness, Stirling, Edinburgh, the romantic old abbeys and castles and remote distilleries. It was a way to know better the place we would be living for the next three years. The photographs in our family album today still testify to some wonderful days away but the problem for Rangers is the memories I was making for myself were suddenly all off the field, not on it.

The decision to stay away from Ibrox was not taken at any formal meeting between myself and Walter Smith, which may surprise some people. However, Walter trusted me as a man and as a professional to behave appropriately and to do the right thing for myself at that time, believing Rangers would eventually reap the rewards in the closing stages of a season that would also represent his last with the club after 11 years. He knew that if I couldn't train, I had to take good care of my emotions. He understood this mentality and never said anything about it. He wanted only the best for me.

We spoke closely about it the week after I returned to the team, a 1-1 draw at home to Dunfermline on 7 February. Walter had taken the squad to Puerto Banus in southern Spain for a few days of warm weather training and we had a man-to-man discussion in which he told me he was very happy with me and my contribution to the team. Walter was good that way, I was sure our relationship was great. However, that month out injured would prove a watershed in my time at Rangers and, in truth, my entire career. Suddenly, I was perched precariously at the edge of that top step, looking down at the stable for the first time in my life. How could life change so dramatically? Four weeks previously I had been flying high. I was at the right club, I'd taken my career to the next level and everyone in Europe knew my name. Even the newspapers back home were so intrigued about this goalscoring phenomenon they had been calling my mother for the lowdown on her boy.

I was at the peak of my career and intoxicated with the success of it all.

The blunt truth is I was rushed back to first-team action far too soon after a month of inactivity, but there could be no grudges to bear. In my time away we had defeated Aberdeen and Motherwell in the league, but lost 2-0 to St Johnstone and had managed only five goals in four games, which was the Ibrox equivalent of a striking famine after an astonishing 69 goals in the first half of the campaign. Walter was under pressure, the team was under pressure. Ally McCoist had struggled for most of the season to that point with niggling injuries and would not make his comeback until March. I was never the most naturally athletic or physically fit player. I really had to work at it and needed the equivalent of an abridged pre-season training programme before I could capture top form again. It was time the team could not afford to give me, so I had to make do with those few days of hard work in the sunshine of southern Spain. Sadly, my fitness and sharpness were not up to scratch, which was underlined with just three goals in the next two and a half months.

There was another more serious problem that developed in that time too, which highlighted my darkest and most dreaded fear. My eye operation would have been considered an overwhelming success for anyone else in any other walk of life, but it left a legacy no football player, certainly not a penalty box poacher like me, would ever have wanted. My eye surgeon in Scotland did a great job, confirmed to me later by other eye specialists in Italy who told me I could not have been treated better. However, the injury with the squash ball had left me with difficulties with my peripheral vision, a terrible shortcoming for someone like me, who really only came alive in the 18-

yard box and relied on razor sharp reflexes to steal crucial half metres on central defenders. I had to see movements and commitments to tackle out the corner of my eye and plan my own positioning accordingly, but instead there was only a blur. It was especially problematic with crosses and passes delivered from the right wing – yes, even with Brian Laudrup on the ball, turning defenders this way and that. I had never focused too much on my abilities as a goalscorer before, believing my instincts to put the ball in the net were animalistic, and something with which I was born. Suddenly, the gift had been taken away and I was being asked to adjust and turn my head in the process, which cost me the split seconds that determine the good goalscorers from the great.

To add to it all, my right pupil had also lost its ability to react instinctively to light. In darkness, the pupil grows bigger and when the eye is introduced to brightness it diminishes in size. However, my pupil had developed difficulties balancing light – and still faces those challenges today. It was a significant issue for a footballer, especially as we were playing a lot of midweek games at that time under floodlights. My right eye was being asked to work at a pace with which it was no longer comfortable and the result of the efforts it was making was an increase in tiredness, blurred vision and more frequent headaches. Issues with focus led to slips in concentration, all of which took a toll on my ability to contribute as much to the team as I had done before.

My downturn in form coincided with the return to fitness of Ally McCoist, who was not only determined to win the 11th championship medal of his Rangers career, but prove he could still be an asset for Scotland at the World Cup finals. There was no way Ally and I could play together because we were two penalty box predators and that balance in the team would not have been good. Walter, more desperate than anyone to win ten in a row, trusted 100 per cent in the players who had been with him for several seasons before and if it came to a choice between McCoist and the 'new' Marco Negri, Ally would always be the winner. It was a decision I found difficult to accept, because I had scored so many goals that season, but other things were beginning to prey on my mind at the same time.

The eye injury was bad enough but Monica and I began to have difficulties in our relationship, which is no great surprise for any young couple. In Italy, we saw each other once or twice a week, but now we were living together for the first time in a new country and there were inevitable highs and lows that come with living in the pockets of one another 24 hours a day. On top of all that, I began to receive two different sets of pretty disturbing letters, one claiming to be from a Celtic fan, the others from a couple of Rangers supporters. The Celtic fan rounded on me for being a Catholic representing a Protestant club and the Rangers followers claimed I could never be a true hero to the fans because of my religion. I was already beginning to feel emotionally fragile and being placed in the middle of a sectarian sandwich in an argument between two extremes about which I knew nothing, nor cared even less, did little to help my state of mind. All I knew was that when I signed for Rangers, Walter Smith had advised me not to make the sign of the cross on the pitch, which I viewed as a polite and unobtrusive request, but as it was something I had never done in Italy, I certainly wasn't about to start it now.

It seemed to be one thing after another and I yearned to have Walter Smith reach out to me like a father in a way he did with Paul Gascoigne. I admired Walter's man-management of Gazza so much and I knew he could be good for me. I needed something from him, but it didn't really happen. If only he could reach out to a player who had scored so many goals for him in so few games we might have grasped that Holy Grail of ten in a row. Unfortunately for me, for Walter and for Rangers, there was a barrier to that ever happening. You will find out his name later in the book.

I

FIRST STEPS

MILAN was around a decade away from becoming the fashion capital of Europe when I was born in the city's main hospital, the Mangiagalli e Regina Elena, in October 1970. I'm told Italy's second-most populous city was still a bustling and vibrant metropolis but that didn't prevent my father, Angelo, deciding to move the family north-east to Monfalcone when I was just 12 months old. His decision to relocate was taken on the basis that it would be good for the family, and his own job prospects, so it was goodbye 'Mia bela Madunina' (the unofficial anthem of Milan) and nice to meet you 'Rocca', a ruined fortress that dominates the town of Monfalcone.

Monfalcone is as close to the old Yugoslavian border as it gets, and just a few miles north of Trieste. But unlike Milan, which is landlocked, Monfalcone is at the head of the beautiful Adriatic Sea, so while we may have moved just 250 miles to the east it was like switching to a whole new country, such was the dramatic change in landscape. It was the ideal place to grow up, with lots to see and do. As a kid you make your own entertainment, but there was a huge US Naval shipyard on our doorstep, while we just had to open the door of our flat and there were great schools, medical centres and awesome sports facilities. The sea and beaches were reachable even by bicycle, and there were snowy mountains, where you could ski, within a 90-minute drive of the centre of town.

My father has always represented the classical masculine figure, the strong and important axis around which my entire family revolved. A typical Milan citizen of many generations, he started work at just 15, and found himself in Puglia, miles from home, where he decided to join the Italian Navy. Apart from fulfilling his many naval duties, he distinguished himself in marine sports activities, achieving medals in rowing as well as football. On his release from the Navy, he started a professional football career with AC Fanfulla, a Serie C side. He was an attacking midfielder with clever feet but his career was brought to a shuddering halt when he developed serious knee problems, which may have had something to do with the strict manner in which he always ensured his children did the best they could at school. On the other hand, even though he would often work long shifts and was usually tired by the time he arrived home, he would still pass the evening playing with me and my brother.

My mother Maria is a very sweet, fragile and sensitive person, with a real passion for cooking. She was born in Piove di Sacco, about 25 miles south-west of Venice, and brought up in Domodossola, before moving to Milan. She met my father in a dance hall when she was 20 and they soon fell in love. They often spoke of their romantic meeting, which I 'now' find really sweet. She had been working in the Olivetti typewriter factory but when my brother Alessandro and I came along, she dedicated her life to her husband and children. With my father working from early morning to late evening, she gave up work, and while that must have saddened her to a certain extent, she never once showed it and was always extremely cheerful and positive.

Dad, despite his strong moral values and having his head firmly attached to his shoulders, was an unsuspecting spendthrift. The family still talk about the time he spent his entire salary on a brand new camera. It was Christmas, and savings were pretty low in the Negri household, so I can still imagine the discussions my mother and father had about it. My mother is still the complete opposite and the most careful saver I ever met, although we didn't ever go without.

Like most siblings, Alessandro, who was the eldest, and I were always fighting. I suppose I was a typical 'second son', forever instigating trouble but always coming off second best. His favourite sport was basketball – which he was pretty good at – but my passion was always football. He is left-handed and I am right, and he was around 12 when he started forging friendships with other kids of a similar age in our neighbourhood. I wasn't too happy about it at first because I was happiest playing around with Alessandro, and inevitably we started moving in different circles. Our frequent conflicts were usually born out of petty little things, but I suppose it was an unconscious way of keeping our sibling rivalry intact.

Growing up, Alessandro and I were of similar build – but one thing I learned quickly was to never go near his wardrobe. His sweatshirts, trousers etc were strictly off limits and I didn't even get them when they didn't fit him any more. As we continued to grow and develop, our relationship changed somewhat, with Alessandro spending the bulk of his time studying at university, while I began to follow my dream of becoming a footballer. It was only when we started moving in different directions that I began to really look up to him. I consider my brother to be very intelligent and hard-working – qualities that allowed him to fulfil, with merit, an enviable position in a well-known, worldwide industry. He has achieved so much by showing great personal strength, intelligence and a strong, fighting character.

As we grew apart, we became even closer, and for years now he has been the first person I get in touch with if I have any problems. We get on very well and I can't remember a single verbal clash or difference of opinion since we were kids. Despite the obvious geographical distance, we have a very tight relationship and it's one that I value so much. I might have opted for a more high-profile career, but never once has he felt envy towards me. I have always felt proud of the fact that I achieved many goals in life, and these are the exact same feelings that I have for him, his work and his private life.

My childhood was divided equally between school and having fun with friends. When I was six, the family moved to a bigger apartment, which had a large tarmacked courtyard. We became friendly with two other boys from our block – who were also called Marco and Alessandro, although on this occasion Marco was the older of the two! We became good friends and in the winter months, I took up basketball. My brother was already playing to a very good standard but when spring arrived, I went back to football, and in the afternoon we would all play in the yard. The matches would last hours and it would be the 'Marcos' against the 'Alessandros'. These games were fiercely contested and, to all intents and purposes, were like small-sided derby matches, where the need to win was all-pervading. Sadly, they were usually brought to a premature end as the neighbours regularly complained that the constant thumping of the ball against the garage doors was driving them mad. Eventually, the council got involved and we were banned from playing games there before 4pm.

When we weren't being chastened by our fellow tenants, there was one more danger to our matches – the private villa with the scary drop at the front of the building. The wall that separated the two buildings was so high that one misplaced shot could've ended the game. From that moment, we knew we had just one minute to run around the block and ring the bell of the neighbours' house to ask for our precious ball back. If it hadn't taken the drop, then their boxer dog would have ripped it to shreds. That would have signalled the end of the 'season', until we could afford a new ball. At other times, our cup final would end when my exhausted father clapped his hands from the bathroom window and we would have time only for the 'golden goal'. Then it was a quick wash, a few minutes watching my favourite cartoon *Goldrake* – about a super robot – and then dinner.

My father had golden hands and a big heart, and he created our own personal basketball park in the yard. We had a high basket with scoreboard, iron and net. It was only then that hands replaced feet and Alessandro and I would enjoy regular matches. I might have had the upper hand over him at football, but in terms of basketball, the shoe was on the other foot. We had a great rivalry, and again the matches were fiercely competitive. I would inevitably end up defeated, but always possessed the greater desire to improve and compete with the type of spirit that would help save face – and bring the occasional victory.

There is no question I felt more comfortable with the ball at my feet, but as far as I'm concerned, I never felt destined to be a top footballer, like a kid at say four or five years old who you can just tell has the look and qualities of a future star. And I didn't ever support any particular team when I was a kid. Not even the great Zibi Boniek or Michel Platini pulled me towards the black and white of Juventus. There were no posters on my bedroom walls or football shirt doubling as pyjamas. At the start of my career, I didn't have one team in particular that I supported (although that has changed now, because Glasgow Rangers will always be my number one), which is probably why I had difficulties understanding the mentality of the typical football supporter: the one who has a tattoo of his favourite team and takes annual holidays to follow that team despite awful weather or a furious girlfriend. Mind you, in recent years I have come to better understand this mentality, and grown to fully appreciate their passion.

It was amazing to see supporters in Scotland going about their daily lives from Monday to Friday and then transforming into crazy fans at the weekend, singing loudly with giant hats on, like at the Munich Beer Festival, and sitting next to their little son, who was already draped in club colours and doing everything his father did.

I remember watching a television interview with a Celtic supporter, who made up a story about a serious family problem just to get a couple of days off to go and watch his team at the 2003 UEFA Cup Final in Seville. Celtic were up against Jose Mourinho's Porto, and this fan was willing to do just about anything to see his team attempt to lift their first European trophy since 1967.

However, his trip ended in disappointment, and was well documented in the Scottish press, with pictures galore of the fans having a ball in the Spanish sunshine. And here comes the good part, because our friend was unmasked while directing the Celtic choir, perched on top of a crash barrier. Unfortunately for him, his boss reckoned he wasn't sick at all and fired him on his return. Maybe his boss was a Rangers fan who gleaned double satisfaction from the fan's desperate situation. A couple of years later, he got another job and appeared once again in front of the cameras with the photo that lost him his previous job. Asked if he would have changed anything about the past, he answered, 'Yes, the result!' That's the passion I mean when I talk of football supporters.

When I was growing up, dad never pressured either Alessandro or I into practising any sport in particular. My main reason for leaning towards basketball at one point was down to the impressive facilities of A.R. Italcantieri of Monfalcone. They also offered training sessions during the cold winter months in a warm and safe environment. Alessandro and I were encouraged by dad to practise sport because it was healthy, but especially as a release valve for two restless kids. We had a lot of fun with loads of other kids, and reaped the rewards of the discipline that taking part in a team sport brings. We learned to respect the coach, and anyone in authority, and I grew up loving sport in general thanks to this kind of encouragement and mentality. Tasting the adrenaline of the challenge, living the happiness of the victory or the disappointment of defeat, as well as the desire of revenge, was drummed into me from a young age. There was always the need to keep improving, and show the type of determination that you need to achieve your goals, but most of all, to enjoy the shared experience of achieving something with your friends. That's why afternoons passed so quickly. The word tired didn't exist, nor were there any kind of huffs or moods. We went to sleep satisfied, thinking about what we did and what we would do better the next day.

Following the same philosophy we started playing tennis. We built a net in the yard, with the manhole covers defining the boundaries of the court, and we would watch how the professionals played and attempt to copy them during our games. Today it's all different. Children don't take advantage of the simple street teaching and the rules that come with it. They're not free to put their imagination into practice. Once, you only played if you were good or if the ball was yours. Otherwise you would go in goals or, even worse, just watch. Now, everything is done with the help of a coach or teacher: football camps with the teacher, skiing with the teacher, tennis and golf with the teacher. Everything is straight from the textbook, which brings a real lack of entertainment or competition. I'm certainly not suggesting that teaching is useless. I'm doing it now but in the 1980s there was a different way of doing things. For example, I learned to play tennis with a racket that was just about hanging together, whereas today kids are brought up to believe that boots sponsored by Zlatan Ibrahimovic have the magical powers to score thousands of goals. Unfortunately – or perhaps fortunately – we know that's not true.

When a child is starting out in any sport, money is nothing compared to passion, devotion and sacrifice. Sadly, there is little talent being nurtured nowadays, especially in Italy, because there are no playgrounds, yards, or streets that proved a source of inspiration for many generations. But there are also many new dangers generated by the sick world in which we now live. Whereas kids were always out playing when Alessandro and I were growing up, many parents are now alert to the dangers that their children face from unscrupulous predators.

In summer, though, our exciting little world was transferred from the city to the stunning gulf of Trieste and, in particular, the happy and colourful Marina Julia. It was a time we looked forward to for months. We would meet in the yard immediately after lunch, each of us with his bicycle and the inevitable ball attached to the luggage rack. We would then pedal and chat all the way to a part of the beach that was just ten minutes from home. We were well aware of the rules of the road. Never ride four deep, always in couples, so that drivers could pass easily, although there were always the angry ones who would honk their horn and shout at us as they passed. In fact, it was a game of ours to count the number of 'curses' we got before reaching our destination! We would then lay down our beach towels and get the ball out. All around was empty beach – as nobody wanted to get hit on the head with our ball or breathe in the shifting sand.

It became our personal beach soccer field and we constructed goalposts with pieces of wood. Sometimes other children would join in and only when we were exhausted, and I mean really exhausted, would the final whistle sound and our reward was a relaxing dip in the Adriatic. We would then buy an ice lolly from one of the many beach bars with the few coins we had in our pockets and, change permitting, enjoy a game of table football to round off the perfect day. That said, the table football could last an eternity because we soon discovered a way of keeping the lever opened, without the owners knowing, and have endless balls to play. It was then a case of collecting our meagre possessions and cycling home. Then, as usual, it was a quick shower, dinner and we would reconvene to pass more time together in the yard. It was bliss.

II

TEENAGE KICKS

THE first fundamental change in the life of 'young Marco' was the switch from elementary to primary school. A new sector of the school was dedicated to learning German, which wasn't too bad an idea considering students weren't interested in learning it voluntarily. So, in the absence of a show of hands, 30 names were put forward and mine was one of them. My father reluctantly accepted it, but only after convincing the headteacher to give us free textbooks.

The bigger problem for me was leaving behind old classmates, as we had become very close. In their place came 29 strangers, although one of them, Andrea Pasian, lived less than 150 metres from my house. Right from the start, he was fun to be around, although he had little interest in studies. Before I met him, I had some doubts over whether to choose football or basketball as my vocation, but Andrea convinced me that football was the way forward, and at that point he was considered one of the most promising talents in the region.

We practised a lot at school, which gave me the perfect opportunity to hang out with my best friend. During the second year of primary school, I joined my first football club, A.R. Italcantieri of Monfalcone, and enjoyed training regularly under the guidance of head coach Mario Pilutto – and we even played for a real championship.

School wasn't a big problem for me as I managed fine in almost every subject, although the same couldn't be said for Andrea, with his daily visits to the headteacher a highlight for him. Rather predictably, he was turfed out of school at the end of the year, although we continued to be a great team on the football pitch. We played every Sunday, which also gave our respective parents the opportunity to get to know one another, and we are all still great friends to this day. Andrea and I matured together and shared a common goal, and we were determined we would achieve that goal in the same team.

At the time, Andrea was definitely the more likely to succeed. He was a technically gifted and fast defender, and a guy who possessed boundless energy, although perhaps a bit too much at times. He had a natural gift and although he did have many good opportunities, he didn't always get the break that you sometimes need to make the grade. His father had a bakery and Andrea, from the age of 14, would be up at the crack of dawn to help him. Saturdays were his busiest day, so he was always grateful for his football the following day.

We were still virtual newcomers in our second season, but Pilutto knew us well and our team was the strongest in the province. We had Stefano Trevisan in goals, Andrea rock solid in defence and me playing in midfield. We won many games and had a lot of fun in the process, which are the magical ingredients as far as I'm concerned. At the end of the season, the three of us were invited to take part in a trial match for Udinese. We were joined by a full-back called Daniele Guerin, who achieved infamy for wearing two left boots during a match. When he told me he had packed his kit bag in haste, I couldn't stop laughing. He had refused to own up in case he was dropped! Udinese were in Serie A at the time and had some fantastic players, including Brazilian stars Zico and Edinho. We were also asked to take part in a trial match at Triestina, who had just been promoted to Serie B, thanks mainly to the goals of the great striker 'Toto' De Falco.

When we arrived at Udinese for the trial, it was very busy and dozens of young lads – complete with colourful kit bags and boots – were milling around like toy soldiers, and accompanied by a crowd of impatient parents that looked like they didn't really want to be there. Everyone had to wait their turn to be called forward and when 'Negri' was called out, I wasted no time in getting into the changing room and within a few minutes, I was out on the field and in my comfort zone. There was no anxiety or fear. I was there to have fun and it wasn't important if I knew my new team-mates or not. To be honest, I didn't fully understand the importance of that opportunity, and maybe that's why everything went so well. Really, it was perfect, and in the end, Italcantieri decided to send me to Udinese, who were well known throughout Italy for looking after their younger players. Trevisan had been spotted by the Udinese goalkeeping coach and rightly chosen, while Guerin was also recruited. Inexplicably, only Pasian wasn't chosen despite his obvious qualities.

Our side won the trial match easily, which meant Pasian didn't really get an opportunity to show his qualities, as the ball was more often than not up the other end of the park. With the benefit of hindsight, that was a negative turning point in his career, even though Triestina chose him some years later, which was of little benefit to him at the time of the trial. As soon as we finished third grade, Andrea moved into his dad's bakery full-time. Compared to the hours of a professional footballer, he worked round the clock, but never once showed a grain of envy towards me, even though he was the more talented between us – and I'm not ashamed to admit that. I have always seen in his eyes a sincere pride for what I achieved, almost as if the goals I scored were in some way also netted by Andrea.

I was on my way to the Udinese youth team, something which would develop into a pretty lengthy stay, between 1984 and 1988. I don't mind admitting that it was one of the most challenging periods of my life. We all have to make sacrifices if we want to achieve something noteworthy but it was still difficult. I had just started high school, Michelangelo Buonarroti, in Monfalcone, and it was really tough, where no one and nothing was forgiven. I was also scheduled to be in Udine two afternoons a week for training, which was something new to me – and exhausting.

Now, I can look back and see that it was the first important stage of my career. At that point, I had the chance to get closer to my dream at an age where I could learn things really quickly and improve day on day. And my personality, not only on the field, was changing thanks to the type of experiences, both good and bad, that reality is constantly offering. My self-esteem was also growing, which I put down to a confidence in my natural abilities.

Nevertheless, I had to be careful because it was too good an opportunity to waste, and I knew it was a marathon and not a sprint. Nothing is assured at that age, and you have to keep your feet firmly on the ground, especially at training. There is sometimes a tendency to accept that you've 'made it' when you are invited to train with a big club, but nothing could be further from the truth. The last thing you want to do is assume you are better than the others. Looking back, I think I managed that side of it very well, and with a lot of humility. For this I really should thank my father for always being by my side. He offered stable support when I needed it, but always in a bashful and silent way, without inducing pressures of any kind. Extremely different from the 'coach/parents' who shout and bawl at their sons from the side of the park, like furious dogs behind a fence, perhaps in frustration that they themselves didn't make the grade, and maybe now living their lives through their children.

My best memories of that period are of dad fussing over me when I got home. While waiting for dinner to be ready he would take my training bag and carefully clean my boots, to preserve them and so I would get the best from them. After cleaning, he would plaster them with seal fat to keep them soft. It became an almost sacred ritual that made me understand how much he cared about what I was trying to achieve and that he was proud of me.

When fans started to ask for my autograph, I had another dilemma. I knew you wrote your name, but how would I write it? Problem solved as I chose my father's signature. I liked it. It was fast, elegant and, most of all, I thought this little gesture would please him. It was like a family mark.

However, the first day of training at Udinese wasn't a happy day at all. It was August, school hadn't started and the excitement of the days ahead slowly morphed into an anxiety and fear in tackling a new situation. Only the kindness of my mother's words comforted me sufficiently to give me the strength to overcome my insecurities. When I got to the field, everything, as if by magic, passed in a flash. Not that it was easy, not for a moment. I wasn't yet 13 and took the train from Monfalcone to Udine (a one-hour journey) with a heavy heart. Then, at the station, I had to jump on a bus to the training field. I should point out here that the training ground was situated within the confines of a former madhouse, Sant Osvaldo. The people who were still there weren't dangerous but they did have some serious mental problems.

At the time, a few psychiatric hospitals that were no longer in use were still open after becoming protected residences. As I walked to training I would pass someone who pretended to drive using an imaginary steering wheel; someone shouting directions already given by the coach or screaming 'Tang!' when the ball hit the post; someone running after the balls which left the field and someone continually asking the time. So the atmosphere was quite unique. After training I would grab a quick shower and catch the bus to the train station, hopefully in time for the express to Monfalcone where, two hours later, I would find my father waiting in the car. When we got home, there was just time for dinner before an exhausted Marco slumped into bed.

When school started, and I was also training, my mother would bring me a light lunch to the fences of the 'Buonarroti', where an exchange of school bag for training bag would also take place.

I recall one trip to Udine that was full of excitement. We were forced to stop because the road ahead was closed due to an accident and the bus driver, under pressure from passengers desperate to get to the train station on time, decided to take an alternative road that, he insisted, would rejoin the main route further up the road. Unfortunately, though, we got stuck in a tunnel and couldn't go forward or backwards. I was sitting at the back of the bus and it was like watching a film. The driver jumped out and started to deflate the tyres to lower the height. In the end, his course of action was successful, but we had to stop at a petrol station to fill up – and missed our connecting train, but when I eventually got there I had a big story to tell.

After a settling-in period, I started studying early in the morning and afternoons when I didn't have training. Some years later, I was asked how hard it had been to become a Serie A player and I've always answered that my life wasn't tough. It actually felt rewarding because I was always well looked after and revered. When fellow players suggest that in some way their life was 'hard', it always makes me laugh. Just think about all those people that work every day of the week and are 'rewarded' with a well-deserved, but modest salary. By playing football I had the chance to earn a lot of money and fast, and to enjoy the moments of excitement that only the adrenaline of a match, a noisy stadium, a goal and victory can offer.

I've been privileged, and helped so much because of the career I chose. Many footballers don't really have to think for themselves because they're spoiled and pampered by a world that sees them as simple and perfect. The negative part is that you can easily be surrounded by fake friends that want to exploit your notoriety and wealth. On the other hand, if you're a mature player with a special personality on field, it doesn't mean you're the same in everyday life. In addition, the managing of personal relations isn't easier due to your young age, and in other cases the distance from your family and feelings of jealousy a footballer can create can be a real issue. So, I dealt with genuine sacrifice during this period, but it was nothing different from boys my age all over the world striving to make something of themselves. I can look back now and insist I always gave 100 per cent without knowing if I would be rewarded with an enjoyable and successful career.

But the journey was lined with a great many potential pitfalls, just waiting to gobble you up should you choose the wrong path at any time. There were myriad temptations and distractions, the need to earn a living wage, as well as the things that were out of your control such as injuries or a coach who didn't rate you. Looking back, I think I managed my teenage years with a good level of maturity and approached everything with moderation.

Don't get me wrong, sometimes I envied my mates who were able to pass their afternoons doing things that 16-year-old boys did, especially if they didn't have to be up at the crack of dawn to study, but my passion for football helped me over any physical or mental tiredness. Rarely did I go to school unprepared and never once did I skip training, neither for snow nor a missed train. The alternative was to move to a college in Udine where some of my team-mates were staying, although I never took this option seriously as I was too attached to family, friends, and routine.

That year turned out to be very important. School was going well and I discovered the right way to do so many things, including how to handle my football ability. It was my good fortune to have met such a well-prepared coach as Umberto Picco. His methods were based on the daily care of the little, but important, things. I improved rapidly and during that season became prolific in front of goal, even scoring more than the rest of our strikers put together –

and I was a midfielder! I learned to play 'with' and 'for' the team. I still remember one of the first statements the coach shouted at me, 'Negri, don't run with the ball, pass it. Make it roll, the ball doesn't sweat!' That made me laugh but it turned out to be such a valuable lesson. The ball could actually run, roll left and right without feeling tired or getting injured, so I made *it* do the work.

At the end of the season, we won the youth championship and I was delighted to accept the top scorer award. We were then invited to take part in important tournaments in other regions, and it was a great experience. I spent many days away from home, for the first time in my young life, but everything was organised in great detail, and I felt just like a pro. We had a lot of fun but never once lost focus of our goals. In the mornings we would visit a place of historical interest, while matches were played in the afternoons. For us they were always like finals. It was win or bust. It was then back to the hotel for a meal and then off to our rooms (there were five or six of us in a room – with no TV). Sleep was at a premium as we would inevitably discuss the matches we had just played, and how we could improve for the next round or competition.

After we had exhausted talk of tactics, we spoke about music – and at that time, the most fashionable groups were Duran Duran, Spandau Ballet, U2 and Simple Minds – but in the end, the final discussion was always about girls. At that age, some were more mature than others, and they would inevitably have 'the floor' and regale us with tales of first loves. Those who didn't have any kind of experience naturally didn't want to feel left out, so they would invent adventures that in the end were even more interesting. The others would listen intently and even if you knew the story was contrived, you never interrupted, and listened to find out how it all ended. Then, one by one, we would fall asleep, tired from another intense day.

The following year I moved on to the elite category, the National Allievi, with older mates, who were stronger and more prepared. It was, without any doubt, the strongest and most talented young team I had ever been a part of. Sadly, though, I found a coach that didn't believe in my potential, so while my studies continued without many problems, the football was tougher and full of obstacles. My team-mates seemed exempt from criticism and, at times, I seemed invisible to the new coach. Mind you, I didn't help the situation myself. One day after training, he asked, 'Who wants to go get my car and bring it here?' I offered but sadly bumped his new Audi on a tree! During the ensuing months, my character developed far more than my technique. I tried to use each match as a means not to enjoy myself but to demonstrate to the coach he was wrong about me. That season, we reached the semi-finals of the championship but lost to Fiorentina, and finished third. I played a big part in the final games, and contributed some good performances and a few goals, so in the end I was pleased with that.

It was then I realised the importance of winning and the sweet taste it brought. A lot of my team-mates moved up a grade, to the level just below the first team, and it soon became clear that Udinese were relying a lot on that group going all the way to the top team. But instead of joining my mates, I remained in the same category but with a new coach, and a real determination to prove myself worthy of eventual promotion. But with a new coach come a new position in the team – that of winger. Until then I had been used as a central midfielder, but Valentino Leonarduzzi, a former Udinese midfielder, was convinced I had the talents to play out wide. Maybe because of his unrealistic expectations of me, as I was one of the 'veterans' of the category, or because the positional change wasn't my favourite, it turned out to be a pretty tough season. It worried me that I still didn't have a precise identity as a player, and I didn't see any improvement due to long periods of unexplained apathy. I had also grown around ten centimetres in a few months and was looking more like Popeye's girlfriend, Olive Oyl, than a future athlete.

I suffered my first bad injury towards the end of the season, which required an operation on my meniscus and a recovery period spent in the bedroom of our new villa in Staranzano, which was close to Monfalcone. I decided to use the rest period to study in a bid to improve the bad marks I had received in a couple of subjects. In the end it worked a treat and I passed them all, although I had to ask for a little help from some friends. For example, I took part in a student exchange programme and spent a fortnight in Munich. The result of this trip, to aid my German, was that the girl who accommodated me considerably improved her Italian, while my German was perhaps worse than before!

On the eve of my fourth year at Udinese, I was given the news I had craved. I was being moved up a level, but the announcement was tempered by the fact that once again I had a coach, Marino Lombardo, the former Torino player, who simply didn't rate me. I had to face a harsh reality. We were at an age where physical fitness could make a big difference. Some already had the build of an adult athlete, while others, like me, were still waiting for complete maturation. But even though it wasn't an easy period, I remained in love with football and would never, ever miss training.

One big plus point for me was that my father had secured a new job with a telecommunications company in

Udine, which meant he would pick me up, which allowed more time to study. He would also take me to training when he could, but on one occasion a tyre exploded and we jumped out of the car at high speed, and ended up in among the trees. Miraculously we escaped with little injury and I took my training bag and still reached the nearest bus station in time. The only times I didn't train in my entire career were during heavy storms, as I was frightened of lightning, although this happened no more than a handful of times.

After summer training, the coach suggested I move to another club, where I would play more, so off I went to Pro Gorizia where the president, Giancarlo Pozzo, was the brother of an Udinese official. He told me that if I wanted to be a professional footballer, I could do so in the blue and white of his club, but first I had to prove myself, and if I did so, I could come back the following year and play for the club. His suggestion was about as appealing as a cold shower. I didn't think he was being honest with me. I wasn't his kind of player, end of story, and that hurt a lot. I was just 16, and had been brought up to tell the truth, but his approach was frosty and I didn't care much for it.

Throughout my career, there have been times when that moment has come to mind, especially when I tasted success at a good level. I'm talking about the 'sliding doors' effect, and how things would have been so different had I not followed my instinct. To be honest, I never seriously considered his proposals, and my parents weren't even aware of them. Sadly, some of my friends took his advice and failed to achieve their potential. Many other footballers had just made the wrong decision at the wrong time. When that happens, though, coaches should be experienced enough to notice what is happening and have the ability to rescue a young player from the scrapheap. I've already mentioned the many pitfalls of the teenage years so it is crucial that young players are nursed through it so that talent isn't lost to the game. It's important to recognise when there's a jewel that has still to be polished, and that episode really disturbed me. In fact, from that moment, I decided to always respect the coach, but without giving too much importance to some of the key decisions he would inevitably make.

And then, midway through the season, Lombardo moved on and the new coach had more faith in my ability. It was the breakthrough I had craved – and it would pay handsome dividends, even though our tilt at the championship ground to a premature halt when we failed to make the national finals. Instead, I received the unexpected – and amazing news – that the new Udinese coach, Nedo Sonetti, wanted me to join the first team to train until the end of the season. And moreover, I got called up for the last match in Serie B against San Benedetto, but remained on the bench.

I can still recall the emotion I felt when the coach called and told me with his Tuscan accent, 'Boy, get the bag ready because tomorrow you're going with the first team.' And how proud I was when I pulled on the club suit for the first time. I looked and felt so elegant with jacket and tie, even though it was a size too big as Udinese had given me the suit of a suspended player – a man-mountain centre-half!

So, it really was an unexpected way to end a season of turbulent highs and difficult lows. Now, I had an opportunity to move one step closer to achieving my goals, and from that one unexpected call, I realised all my sacrifices had been worth it.

III

MARCO NEGRI: PRO FOOTBALLER

I WAS on a high during the close season after getting the call-up to the first-team squad at the end of the previous campaign. 'Dreams really do come true,' I thought. I wasn't yet 18 but I was part of the staff at Serie B side, Udinese and it was a happy teenager who left home for his first day of training in Ravascletto under the watchful eye of coach 'Sergeant' Nedo Sonetti. The Tuscan tough guy was a hard man to please but we soon discovered that if one of us needed help, he was there for us. Ravascletto may have been better known for its skiing but I was determined my career would be going in only one direction – and it wasn't downhill.

Sonetti's main qualities were the energy and spirit he was able to transmit to his players before a match. He was such a fantastic motivator, although I will always be grateful to him for giving me the chance, and ensuring my physical preparation was perfect. He also picked me for our five Italian Cup matches, including the derby match against Triestina.

But the big one for me was the first league match, in Calabria against Reggina, managed at that time by the great Nevio Scala. It was September 1988 and the memories and experience of the whole occasion will live with me forever. Mind you, I had a bit of a wake-up call before the match had even started. I was a substitute, and was out warming up with the rest of the squad, running up and down the touchline – feeling a mixture of excitement and fear – when I stopped to do some stretches. It was at that moment the home fans decided to unleash the full range of their fury. They were full of hate and baying for blood. I suddenly wondered how the hell I was supposed to go out there and play football when the majority of the crowd just wanted to eat us! I was about to find out, and with half an hour remaining, Sonetti told me I was going on for Daniele Pasa. Suddenly I forgot all about the opposition fans because this player, with number 15 on his back, was just about to make his professional debut. I was the happiest man in the stadium. Fear had been replaced by adrenaline, and my first touch came the moment I ran on to the park. We were 2-0 down at the time and despite getting a goal back, my debut was a losing one. But it was also the start of something special and my season continued in a positive way and before long, training with the first team became the norm. It was just the start, but I was determined to work my socks off in an effort to make the grade. I had to improve both athletically and tactically, while listening to every little snippet of advice from my more experienced team-mates. I even learned new jokes to use back home in Monfalcone and just tried to get on well with everyone.

I quickly understood the rules of the dressing room and the balance I had to strike between enjoying the experience and knowing my place. The only real problem in the early weeks was school: training became a daily routine and Wednesday was also harder due to the double session. Sometimes, I would also train with the second team just to retain my sharpness, but all this meant I had little time to study and continue to make an impact in the classroom. I spoke to my teachers, because it was my last year and the all-important exams were coming up. Football might have been important, but so too were my studies, especially as I had put so much into my latter years at school. My teachers were sympathetic but made it clear I would receive no favours. I had a dilemma, and was advised to enrol in a high school in Udine. After a fortnight there, I was called in by the headteacher and advised to change schools because of poor attendance, which was down to training and matches. I couldn't be in two places at once and felt the timing of my big break could have been better. I had the chance of a lifetime with Udinese, but on the other hand I knew how important it was to my parents that I continued to study, and had been told just how precarious a career in football was. My mother and father knew I needed something to fall back on.

In the end I decided to leave school. It was the first big decision of my life, and it didn't go down too well with my parents, especially my father, but we talked it over and they both insisted they were 100 per cent behind me. Mind you, my biggest embarrassment was seeing dad wake up really early in the morning – as he had done for 40 years – while I didn't even have to set my alarm, as training was always in the afternoon, except on a Wednesday. My only job was to have fun for a few hours on the football field, and I was well looked after. But knowing only too well the impact my decision had on my parents, I was determined to take it as far as I could on the football field.

I managed just three appearances in the league that first season but continued to work hard and genuinely felt part of the team. I also knew the coach rated me highly, which was important, as was the acceptance of my teammates. Even with a couple of appearances under my belt, and with bonuses, I was easily taking home the same pay as my father, but still felt something was missing in my life. That gap was soon filled when I bumped into an old friend, Gabriele, who worked as a temporary secretary at a private high school, and after chatting for a while, a plan soon formulated in my head. I had a few weeks off training and was told there was a chance I could take my exams after all. I spoke to my parents about it and the smile returned to their faces. I dived head first into my studies, with more than a little help from friends such as Giorgio, Andrea, Gianluca, Paolo, Fabio, Daniele and Max. They had already passed all their exams and were only too happy to help a friend in need.

During that period, I inherited the motorbike of my dreams from my brother. After years of using either the Califfo Atala or Fifty Malaguti (both Italian 50cc mopeds) I was now the proud owner of a Honda NSF 125, a 'beast' in comparison to my previous machines. I was in love with that bike and during the summer I was out on it all day, every day, and only returned home when the fuel light started to flash. Occasionally I would use it to get to training, but had to be careful to park it out of sight as the club had banned us from using motorcycles. And I admit that apart from the feeling of freedom you get from such a machine, doing something that was banned definitely had its merits!

From June to September the bike was important because all my friends had one, which meant you could easily reach the beach without stopping in the traffic, looking for a parking space, or keeping the air conditioning on. Feeling the air flowing through your hair, since helmets weren't obligatory, was also a great feeling, not to mention the great appeal for females...

If those were the roses, naturally there were thorns. On one occasion, I was returning home after picking up some notes for my studies, when I was almost wiped out by a driver trying to jump the traffic queue. I was close to a set of lights, and the right lane was already occupied by a line of cars, while the left was out because of an ambulance turning the opposite way. I took the middle lane, just as this crazy car driver came roaring up. I saw it coming but there was little space and I had to keep my nerve and make myself as small as possible. The car hit my bike – bending both pedals – but I managed, just, to stay on, although it gave me a real scare, and I soon realised why the club didn't want their players running around on motorbikes. That night, I spoke very little and lay in bed, eyes wide open, and alive to the fact that the situation could have been so much worse. I knew, though, that I had to get straight back on the bike or I would soon be too frightened to ride it.

But the sight of the twisted pedals soon brought it all back home and I never again felt safe on a bike. I used it for a couple of months, as it was my only means of transport, but the amazing feeling I once had riding it never returned. Not even when some Harley friends tried to re-ignite my enthusiasm for two wheels. But I believe things happen for a reason, and falling out of love with my dream machine freed up the time to really get stuck into my studies, and I passed my exams – even if it was by the skin of my teeth, and a mark of 38 out of 60. For me, though, it was like winning a title in the last minute of the last match thanks to my goal. Sure, it had definitely helped that I had come across my old Maths teacher, a big football fan, and he had little hesitation in helping a 'friend' in need. For quite some time, that piece of paper was the thing I was most proud of, and I could see in my father's eyes all the pride he felt. Personally, though, it brought to an end a tough chapter in my life. Now it was time to concentrate solely on the football.

The start of the 1989/90 season brought a new challenge, and one I was relishing. I was farmed out to Serie C side Novara, which was normal for a young guy like me. Novara were ambitious, but played around 280 miles from my home in Monfalcone. It meant being away from friends, family and normality, but I knew it was something I had to overcome in order to keep progressing in the game. The overriding factor was that moving short-term meant I would get to play regularly. I was told it was an obligatory stop for a burgeoning talent, which is the polar opposite of nowadays, when talented teens are more or less offered a top-team place straight away, regardless of whether it's in Serie A or the lower divisions.

The most important challenge for me, though, was to handle being away from home for the first time in my life. Novara is also in the north of Italy, but on the opposite side of the country from Monfalcone, where the language was more Friulian. In Piedmont, though, where the capital of the region was Turin, it was completely different. I won't pretend it wasn't tough but this little man was forced to stand on his own two feet and manage his own life. Of course, my first contract and £488 in the bank each month certainly helped. Oh, and the club paid my room and board.

That season, Novara had been constructed solely to win the championship. It was an ideal environment for me, but it would have helped enormously had I been able to get my driving licence. I was unable to sit the practical exam after driving my dad's Lancia Delta a bit too 'boldly'. I still recall vividly getting a bit too carried away with the accelerator and the look of disappointment on his face. He had been taking me out for regular lessons. In fact, we had covered around 3,000 miles of the Udine–Monfalcone route and I knew every inch of tarmac on that stretch. Our coach, Adriano Fedele, who was also Friulian, would drop me off on a Sunday and pick me up again on a Tuesday morning, just in time for the start of training. Fedele was one of the main reasons I accepted the move, although he dropped a bombshell at the start of the season when he told me he was quitting. There were quite clearly problems at the club between coach and board, issues that I had no knowledge of. I was gutted for Fedele, and myself, but I was fortunate that one of my new team-mates, Alberto Diodicibus, immediately took me under his wing and was very generous with advice. He acted like a big brother and, above all, lived just 35 miles from me, which ensured I had a seat in his family Volvo when we were travelling to and from Novara.

Meanwhile, Fedele was replaced by the unforgettable Angelo Domenghini, an Italian footballing legend. He had been a European champion in 1968, and one of the heroes of Mexico 1970, but was also an exceedingly bizarre character. He is the only man I know that would smoke in the shower, something I wouldn't imagine would be easy. He had perfected the art of keeping his cigarette completely dry with one hand, while soaping himself at the same time with the other. 'Domingo' was permanently tanned, thanks to the weekly ritual of the lamp, and coupled his perfect colouring with some rather natty salmon sweaters. He was living proof of the talents of the magical coach Helenio Herrera, as well as the original 'number 7' par excellence of Italian football – perhaps even more so than illustrious successors such as Franco Causio and Bruno Conti. He was a guy who did not refuse invitations to parties or cocktails in trendy bars.

One afternoon, I was in the dressing room getting changed for training when one of his backroom staff told me the boss wanted to see me. Of course I was nervous and was trying to recall anything I'd done wrong, or right, for that matter. It was a few weeks into the season and we hadn't exactly got off to the perfect start. The team had underperformed, as had I, but I certainly wasn't alone. I knocked on the door of his office and entered. It was like walking into a Turkish bath, although instead of healthy aroma steam, there was only a blanket of thick smoke. He didn't waste any time with formalities but merely chucked me the keys to his BMW and ordered me to put it through the car wash. I was relieved that I wasn't in trouble but thought it worthwhile pointing out that I didn't have a licence. 'Can you drive?' he asked. 'The car wash is just opposite the stadium.' I didn't see any point in arguing about insignificant details, like 'I don't have a licence gaffer', so I got the job done, and missed a tough training session in the process.

I was back in time for the final part of training, and it was a real eye-opener. He summoned the club goalkeepers to the edge of the area – and then put them through their paces. He took a dozen footballs and lined them up at the edge of the 18-yard box. He started taking shots at each keeper in turn, and it looked as though each shot had been measured with a slide rule, because in turn they were low to the left, and the right; in both top corners; straight down the middle. To the bitter end, with seamless continuity, he put on quite a show for his players. I had never before seen anyone kick with such a level of simplicity, but unerring accuracy. Some of the players mockingly cheered as the keepers failed to save the bulk of the shots but I remained silent, observing this footballing genius with a mixture of respect and awe.

Domingo was a genuine superstar; a world champion in all respects, regardless of the fact that the 1970 World Cup Final had been all about Pele and Brazil. Although still being a champion and a man with the most incredible CV, as a coach he was quite modest, but sadly he failed to give us the boost of enthusiasm and energy we needed. I played many games under him, always on the right wing, but without excelling, despite being summoned to the national team for my age group. On the other hand, I learned some great life lessons, like living in a house with other people, paying bills and generally keeping my life in order. I had a very enjoyable time at Novara and would accompany my team-mates to some swanky parties in nearby Milan, which would inevitably be patronised by players from both AC and Inter. We would also frequent – when the budget allowed – the casino of Saint-Vincent, where I would place a small bet as my budget was all but exhausted after paying to get in!

I also witnessed, for the first time, the problems that can arise in the dressing room, and heard the complaints of supporters and attacks in the press. I felt the disappointment of numerous defeats and, most importantly, of a lost play-off that led to relegation. That led to problems with our wages, but these were situations that taught me a lot about professional football, and its many pitfalls. Don't get me wrong, it can be a rewarding profession, but it's not without its problems. Fortunately, young players accounted for the bulk of our team, which made up for the absence of my family and I genuinely did enjoy my first real experience of professional football. What next, though, for Marco Negri?

IV

I'M IN THE ARMY NOW

UDINESE had been relegated and that meant at least a season in Serie B for the players and supporters – and also a recall for me. I was looking forward to getting back and making an impact on the first team, but I hardly had time to pack my belongings when the phone rang again, and this call meant pre-season training would be something very different – and the boots I'd be wearing wouldn't be brightly-coloured Nikes. During the months of July and August, instead of working out on the training ground, I would be marching and running with a rifle on my shoulder. That's right, I had been called up by the military to complete my National Service – and there was no getting out of it, so it was goodbye Udinese and hello Barletta.

I was incredibly fit at that time but still had to follow a strict programme of military exercises. I was stationed at a barracks in the north of the country, in Milan, and there was a broad smile on my face when I was told I would be a soldier from Monday to Friday morning, and could then join up with Udinese at the weekend. While it was great news for me personally, I knew it would still make the job of getting into the team that bit harder. I wasn't able to train during the week, which meant the coach didn't see me until the regular Friday afternoon session, but the military was an Italian way of life so I certainly wasn't the first young player to find himself in this situation.

It wasn't the best way to fight your way into a competitive team, certainly not one that was determined to gain promotion back to Serie A in just a single season, but I immediately saw a glimmer of hope in the shape of our new coach, Rino Marchesi. He was a real gentleman, and Diego Maradona's first coach at Napoli. He was also the last mentor of French great Michel Platini, while both were at Torino. I will never forget his favourite saying, 'We must try to win without taking the risk of losing.' Then I discovered Marchesi and my father had been good friends growing up, and suddenly thought, 'This could work in my favour,' but how wrong could I be. For some reason, he decided he didn't even want to take a few moments out from his busy schedule to see what I was capable of.

We were due to play a pre-season friendly at Arezzo and the changing room was the smallest I had ever been in. Once changed, I moved out on to the field to give others a bit of space – and that was my first mistake. While I was out stretching and warming up, our right winger, Luca Mattei, developed a muscle problem and withdrew from the team. But instead of using me, as a like-for-like replacement, he looked around the dressing room and spotted a lad that normally played in a completely different position. 'You will be playing on the right wing,' he told him. Okay, so I wasn't there in front of his eyes but surely he knew what players he had available. He quickly went down in my estimation. Had I remained in the changing room then I'm sure I would have been in the side, but if that was how he picked his teams then it was a big let-down. I vowed there and then to work as hard as I could and make myself impossible to ignore. If I wanted to succeed in football then I would have to do it all by myself.

Meanwhile, I adjusted to life in the military barracks and enjoyed it as best I could. I was surrounded by a good bunch of boys and we would play cards, sneak out at night to go dancing and share our tales of home. And then, in March of that year, war broke out in Iraq and the dynamics changed almost immediately. Suddenly, we were in a confused state of 'permanent alert'. We were ordered to beef up security and search everyone and everything meticulously. Anyone entering our barracks would get the full once over. In fact, one of my friends took the orders literally and was punished for a month for interrogating the commander's wife and rummaging in her shopping bags. In reality, we weren't allowed to use guns so our potential efficiency in the case of a real emergency was questionable. Within a few days, though, the situation had returned to normal and we got back to playing cards and dancing! It had still been an exhilarating couple of days.

And then came the call from Udinese. Marchesi had quit just a few weeks into the season. The team hadn't enjoyed the best of fortunes on the park and the manager had decided to walk, which was a strange decision to say the least. To be honest, it didn't change much for me. Our new boss was Adriano Buffoni, who I felt was a good appointment for the club. I had been training as a midfielder, which was doomed from the start, as my natural instinct was to get into the box as often as possible, which led to us often being a man short in the middle of the park. Then, it happened. The new coach decided my talents might be better employed in an attacking role. Had I found my salvation? After all, I had the good fortune to train alongside Abel Balbo, a quality striker who had arrived from Argentine side River Plate, and a future star of Roma. I still look upon him as the complete centre-forward – he had the lot. We also had Francesco Dell'Anno in our ranks, and at that time he was an incredible talent. He was a massive inspiration for me, not only in terms of the way he played the game, but also for his infectious personality.

Sadly, though, results didn't improve enough and we were soon out of the promotion race. It also lost the coach a lot of credibility and authority in the eyes of the more experienced members of the dressing room. It was at this time, ironically, that he started to appreciate the significant improvements I was making. I tried to spend as much time as possible with future Inter Milan star Dell'Anno, because I soon realised I had a very special colleague at hand. He was known as the great hope of Italian football, even though he was still very young. He had made his Serie A debut in the colours of Lazio while just 17, before losing his way a little, although it was great testament to his strong character that he managed to get his career back on track.

It was clear Buffoni had 'lost the dressing room', and he recalled me to the team a couple of times, but even then it was all stop-start, and I was in and out. On one occasion, when everyone expected me to play from the start, I was left sitting in the stand, one frustrated young man. Before the game that day, each player in turn came up to me and offered words of comfort, which was a clear demonstration of their displeasure at the coach's decision. The following Tuesday, during training, instead of celebrating a good, solid 4-0 victory over Messina, Buffoni decided instead to scold the team for their show of solidarity. He said it showed a careless attitude and sloppiness in their pre-match preparation. Not that it affected the final score, though.

In a strange sort of way, Buffoni had given me a new lease of life by playing me in a more advanced position, while my time spent as a winger had also given me a greater understanding of the role. Playing striker brought with it a fresh enthusiasm on my part and for the first time in my career, I genuinely felt I could make a breakthrough into the first team – and stay there. I knew if I wanted to score goals on a regular basis, I would need to follow my instincts and develop a predatory streak. It was within touching distance and I had to continue to work hard. But the feeling I thought had vanished, was returning. I was enjoying my football again and starting to rediscover the thrill of the 'swollen net' and a goalkeeper with fists clenched in anger. I was able to awaken the unique and almost indescribable emotions only a striker feels when the ball leaves his boot and flies past the despairing dive of the goalkeeper, and straight into the back of the net. You hear the roar of the crowd – which is a mere whisper compared to what you experience inside your head – and the mix of adrenaline and satisfaction is exhilarating.

But the flip side is that when you go through a goal drought – like every striker does – it can lead to you feeling down and in the throes of loneliness. Then the goals arrive and you feel unstoppable, infallible and able to score from all positions, in all kinds of way and in every single match. At this point I was in love with the game and, more importantly, I fell in love with scoring goals. On the last day of the season, I played the entire match. In the second half I had a great chance, but hit the crossbar with a header. Then, in the dying moments – and at 2-1 down – I controlled the ball in the area, slipped past the centre-half and sent in a shot. Unfortunately, it hit the post, but fell kindly at the feet of Balbo, who tapped it into the empty net. We had rescued a point and, immediately, our players ran to the Argentine to congratulate him on the late equaliser.

Just one Udinese player didn't follow on, but instead turned and looked up to the stand. That was me. I was glad we had salvaged something from the game but also disappointed at missing the chance. I was searching for my father's face, desperately looking for some emotional help.

The season was over but I was still 'attached' to the military for a while yet. Mind you, I was able to enjoy a boot camp for a week at the beautiful seaside town of Marina di Romeo, in Ravenna. During the day we would train hard – and at night party equally as hard. As long as we were back in our tents by a certain time there were no tough military rules to adhere to. Mind you, one of our 'sorties after sunset' almost ended in tears when we came across a group of smugglers, loading up a boat with crates of contraband. We were walking along the beach on our way back to the barracks when we noticed a boat on the sand. It looked suspicious, but then we saw a whole line of people carrying crates from a nearby truck. We stared for a while but when they spotted us, and let out a menacing scream, we ran off like frightened rabbits – and we were supposed to be defending the country!

The day before we were to be discharged really must rank as the day I did one of the stupidest things in the history of stupidity. We were looking forward to lining up and meeting the commander before receiving our official discharge papers. Beforehand, we decided to go down to the beach for one last party. Someone – not me – came up with an idea for a game, and certainly not one for intellectuals. He wanted to see who could dive into the shallowest water – head first – from the greatest height. Wanting to prove myself as the most stupid of this happy brigade, I took far too big a risk, jumped in and promptly dislocated my shoulder. Sadly, no one believed I was really injured and it descended into farce.

On arrival back at the camp I went straight to see the military doctor. He took one look at my anguished face, another at my shoulder joint, six inches lower than the other, and immediately put the shoulder back in place. My shriek, allied to that of his aggressive moves, froze the gang completely. Now they believed me and I was declared the champion! There was no sympathy from the duty officer, though, as he decided I would spend the night in the tent like everyone else and wouldn't travel back to Bologna until everyone else was ready to leave next morning. Despite a scary amount of painkillers, I didn't sleep that night. The next morning I was in agony and my arm was put in a sling to restrict movement.

My final morning in the military was certainly not shrouded in glory. Because of my injury, I was named 'Eagle 4', along with three other companions, and ordered to patrol the perimeter fence of the barracks, to ensure that no civilians came into the remote area. I wasn't best pleased and instead of marching slowly around the fence all day, I lay down in the shade of a pine tree. I then turned down the volume on my walkie-talkie and, cheered by the chirping of birds, decided to rest. I woke up nearly three hours later with the commander screaming at me through the handset. Our patrol was over for the day and he was in a hurry to get back to the command centre in Bologna. Everyone was already on the truck, packed and ready to go, while trooper Negri was snoring pleasantly in the sunshine. What a complete fool! I was forgiven only because of my shoulder but, probably above all, because it was the last day of my military career.

V

HEADING FOR MIDDLE ITALY

I SHOULD have been able to relax and unwind during the close season by heading off somewhere nice on holiday, but because of my gross stupidity – and the shoulder injury suffered as a result – it was a case of gym, gym and even more gym. Mind you, two things contributed to a record-breaking healing process – youth and an incredibly hot summer – and I was ready for the start of the new season. I had returned to Udinese, fit as a fiddle, and raring to go. As usual, we had a new coach. This time, the man in charge was the well-educated and 'witty professor' Franco Scoglio, a very fair man. It was such a tragedy when he died during a live sporting broadcast in 2005. Despite the new coach, the team was almost the same as the season previous, but this time came a directive from above – promotion to Serie A was a 'must'. So the pressure was on from the start.

I trained with fresh enthusiasm and banged in a few goals during the pre-season friendlies. My team-mates were now seeing the real Marco Negri – not just a young boy who had casually arrived in the team on a whim. The coach wasn't known for his promotion of youth, but I could see that I was definitely catching his eye – and for all the right reasons this time. Mind you, I was still quite far down the pecking order for a regular start, and I knew that. We had Balbo, ex-Bologna striker Lorenzo Marronaro and even Marco 'Nippo' Nappi, later likened to a seal by the presenters of an Italian comedy show for the time he ran the length of the field balancing the ball perfectly on his head during a league match. Nappi was a funny guy and one day he lay down on the grass and balanced the ball on his forehead for what seemed like an eternity. I was impressed.

Then my room-mate came on the scene. Emidio Oddi, a lightning-quick defender nearing the end of his career, was a likeable guy and recognisable by a huge moustache, which wasn't exactly in fashion, unlike his superb range of skills. His party piece was to kick the ball cleanly in the direction of a door, which it would then enter without having touched the ground – and from a distance of around 30 yards. One night, after the team meal, Oddi – a former protégé of Nils Liedholm and Sven-Goran Eriksson – approached me and said he was there to take the place of Scoglio, adding that he had taken note of my technical ability, as well as my commitment, attitude and grades. Apparently the team needed someone else who could play on the right wing, and the coach knew I had fulfilled that role when I was younger. Oddi said it was a chance for more game time as the forward position was already fully covered. I took a risk and declined the offer.

I was too much in love with scoring goals, and considered myself an out-and-out striker.

I waited for my chance, and I waited, and waited, but by Christmas things were looking bleak. I sat on the bench, trained hard during the week, but still the opportunities were few and far between. One issue was solved, mind you – my first contract, which I signed in haste. And then it happened. Ternana, a team from Group B of Serie C, started to show an interest in me. They made it clear they wanted me, and that I would get game time. I had a decision to make. Udine was near my home, and all the people I love. I felt comfortable there, but it was clear that my chances were limited. On the other hand, Ternana, who played in the Umbria region of the country – which is in middle Italy, and not far from San Marino – were offering a chance to play most weeks, and they were a fiercely ambitious club.

I was 20 years old, so I had to play football if I were to make the grade, and I wasn't going to do that by training all week and sitting on the bench on a Sunday. I spoke to my parents and also to people within the game that I liked and trusted, and decided it was time to take to the stage and try to woo the audience. I wasn't going to Ternana to fulfil a similar role to that at Udinese, I went there to further my career and give everything I had, although it wasn't long until I realised Umbrian fans were looking upon me as the missing part in their promotion-chasing jigsaw. It was the first time I had felt any weight of expectation on my young shoulders.

Ternana had shelled out £800,000 for me, at that time an almost unthinkable price for a young player yet to prove himself. How much do you pay for a good young prospect? I don't know, but it just seemed an awful lot of money.

One thing was for sure, though, I wouldn't wilt under the pressure of expectation. With the benefit of hindsight, I'm proud to say there isn't a chairman around who was wrong to sign me. One thing I always gave was value for money. Indeed, all were able to sell me on for a very decent profit, except, of course, at Rangers, although we will visit that a little later.

My spell in Umbria was valuable in more ways than one. I became aware of how to cope with pressure, and to learn, in earnest, how to sign an autograph. Whenever I was in the town centre, fans started to recognise me and I even became something of a semi-regular on the sports pages of newspapers. It was a bit strange, at first, seeing my photo and articles telling my story and of my hopes and ambitions for the future. And then it happened. Nike offered me a sponsorship deal, even though I hadn't scored a professional goal. I was made up.

But I had to forget all of that and concentrate on my job. I didn't have the luxury of watching and learning from the more experienced players any more. It was a struggle just to get into the team, so I worked hard, which was something I never had a problem with. Novara had been a good experience for me but there hadn't been so much pressure there. I was looked upon as the kid. They hadn't paid me well and perhaps not a great deal had been expected of me in return. So, welcome to the world of pressure Marco! No more would one good performance be enough to have people talking about me. I needed to do it every single week.

Anyway, the pressure wasn't a problem – although the start I made to my career in Umbria was. A dip in form had coincided with my arrival at the club and one of my first games with Ternana took me on the long and difficult journey to Licata. We headed off on the Saturday for the game the following day. As soon as the game was over, I had made plans to fly home to see my family, and put money in an envelope for my mother. This, I put in a second bag, which I had made up so I could replace the club blazer, tie and trousers with my 'civvies'. Rather foolishly, I left the envelope with the cash in my suitcase that was to go through customs. The money, while not an absolute fortune, would have allowed my family to live comfortably for a year – but it never got there. Once we arrived at the Hotel Agrigento, I soon realised that a 'kind' airport baggage handler had relieved me of the envelope. I was absolutely furious. How dare some stranger go through my belongings – and how dare he take what wasn't his?

As if that wasn't bad enough, we arrived at the Licata stadium on the Sunday morning and I was informed by the coach that I wasn't in the team – for technical reasons! Whatever they were I don't know, because he didn't bother explaining them. We lost 4-1, which simply compounded an awful weekend, although it was far from over. When we landed at Trieste Airport, just one step from home, I was told by my team-mates that when they returned to Terni they found their cars had been damaged. Apparently my car had been quite badly vandalised. This disgusting act had been committed by so-called 'fans' of Ternana, angry at their team's bad result. I'll tell you something, they weren't half as angry as me.

The Monday morning simply put the tin lid on what had been the weekend from hell – and the final chapter in a sad tale merely helped me put in place a decision that I would carry with me my entire career – and that was disdain for the journalistic profession. I opened a newspaper to read the report on our game and it wasn't very pleasant. It was critical and hard-hitting, which was, I suppose, fair enough as the team had played badly and lost heavily – but then came the personal bit. I was the subject of a vicious and brutal attack. They called me 'a bad purchase', 'a nag' and 'a bin'. I thought to myself, 'How can they do that?' Just the week before they hailed me as the club saviour. Now, seven days later I was the scapegoat – and I hadn't even played.

Reporters from several different papers seemed to focus on me, rather than the game, which I found baffling. It hit me hard. They were making it personal – and I had hardly started my career. They weren't interested in focusing on someone's technical performance; they just wanted to bring you down. I soon realised just how much power the media have, quite literally, in their hands. The pen is mightier than the sword, they say, and I was soon in agreement. Up until that point I didn't know a lot about the media, so when it came, it hit me hard. I decided to get my punch in early, and vowed there and then I wouldn't play ball with them. Looking back I now realise it was a decision taken without the benefit of maturity, but it was my way of dealing with what I perceived to be their negativity. I would never speak to the media again, and if they decided to criticise me, at least I would've given them reason to do so.

I also stopped reading the sports pages of newspapers and started concentrating on my game. The thing I never managed to accept was how a journalist could praise me for a good performance, and then the following week, write nothing but negative stuff about me. I thought, 'Let them write about me if I have a good or bad performance.' That was fair enough, but when they got personal, and delved into my background, they crossed the line. It seemed some journalists had no problem slating you in their paper, and then have the cheek to call you the following day acting as if nothing had happened. Was I missing something? Their power sometimes worried me. They could make or break players by writing certain things, which the supporters might take as the truth.

But I have also known team-mates who have talked 'on the quiet' to reporters and that was something else I despised. What is said in the dressing room should stay there. It's not for public consumption. I have known coaches to believe that their dressing room was bugged, as stories were appearing in the press that could only have come from the inner sanctum. Some players, fearing for their position in the team, would also have spoken to a 'sympathetic' reporter and the next thing a story appears in the press putting pressure on the coach to return this or that player to the team – and we all know how much 'weight' the supporter carries in Italy. I only ever did my talking on the field and I hope supporters appreciated and judged me only by these actions.

Another aside to this little tale is that I always found it incredibly boring having to respond with clichéd phrases, and worried more about what 'had to be said', rather than my real thoughts on the game. Perhaps my real thoughts would have made uncomfortable reading for some within the dressing room, including myself, so it was maybe best left unsaid. For many observers, though, it was an odd choice, but it did allow me to get on with my career without worrying about being misquoted in the press, or some things being 'lost in translation'. It was something I started in Italy, and extended to my career in Scotland. Perhaps I overdid it, almost categorically avoiding reporters and all print media. I am convinced the world, in general, is made up of individuals and not groups of people, and it is for this reason that today I find myself with just one Scottish and one Italian journalist to thank. The only reporter I ever trusted in Italy was Daniele Benvenuti, a man who became my friend, and Jeff Holmes in Scotland. It was these guys who encouraged me to embark on this wonderful journey, and it was advice I'm glad I heeded.

But I digress. The most pressing issue was to make something of myself at Ternana. I recovered from the weekend from hell and worked hard on the training ground. I was rewarded with a starting jersey for a tricky match in Reggio Calabria. When the half-time whistle blew, I was satisfied with my performance – although not with my boots and, in particular, the left one. I had ripped it during an altercation with an opponent and as I walked back to the dressing room, my big toe was poking out. I felt more like Goofy, the wacky friend of Mickey Mouse, than a professional footballer. It was a scorching hot day and the pitch was brick hard. I couldn't play on with my boot like this but due to the pitch I couldn't wear my other boots, which had aluminium studs.

I asked my team-mates for a loan of a spare pair of boots, and it turned out that the only guy who took the same size was Marco Mazzoni. I tried them on and they weren't the most comfortable but I borrowed the left one and when I ran out for the second half, many people in the crowd must have thought I was trying to start a new fashion. But it wouldn't have mattered what I was wearing when the stadium clock struck 75 minutes because that was the moment I stopped the ball with my right boot, 30 yards from goal, and hit the most beautiful shot straight into the back of the net – with my left boot. Not only did the goal give us a valuable win, but it was also my first as a professional footballer, and how I enjoyed it – and against the same team I had made my pro debut as a raw 17-year-old.

That victory seemed to spur us on and we could do no wrong. Personally, I was glad I had repaid the faith shown in me by the coach, but the team was much more important than the individual.

Our next big challenge was looming – and that meant a journey into the lion's den. Acireale were second in the league – behind only the mighty Ternana – so the game had everything and if the build-up was intense, it was nothing to the actual match itself. As I said, football fans in Italy are as passionate as anywhere in the world – but the fans at Acireale were something else. They howled and screamed at us, the referee, in fact anything that didn't have their colours nailed to it. The atmosphere was horrible, probably the worst I have ever experienced – and I played in some terrifying places! Our Sicilian opponents were convinced they only had to turn up to win. Just before kick-off, as the captains were exchanging pennants, I noticed two white hens walking around on the pitch, draped in the red and green of Ternana. It was like 'here are the chickens, now we're gonna pluck you!' And then, just before kick-off, Sandro Cangini, the most talented, but craziest member of our team, took an almighty kick of the ball and hit one of the poor hens. Feathers fluttered everywhere and the bird lay dead on the spot where it fell. That shocking incident seemed to whip the Sicilian crowd into a frenzy. They were shaking the fence violently and trying to get on to the pitch. They were too far gone, but despite their crazy antics, we won the game with a goal in the dying moments. We had shown immense character and personality, but after the final whistle, the predictable manhunt started and all along the narrow and dark corridors, which led to the dressing rooms, we were viciously attacked by home fans who had managed to infiltrate a restricted area. I was one of the first players showered and changed and walked out to the team bus, somewhat apprehensively. I immediately lay down in the seats on the back row of the coach (my usual position, a tactical choice to keep out of view of everyone and everything). I waited a good 20 minutes before my team-mates started to make their way on to the bus and all the while I had to put up with insults from a handful of Acireale thugs, who couldn't accept defeat. I sketched a smile to try and defuse the situation but they continued until everyone was on the bus.

Our masseuse began the ritual of 'counting heads' but I knew everyone was present and motioned for the driver to leave. As soon as I heard the engine spark into life I took all the money I had out of my pockets, about £200, and waved it at the local fans, who became crazier than ever. Maybe it wasn't the cleverest thing to do as the coach hadn't actually started moving away. The fans went berserk and started slamming their fists against the windows and the sides of the bus, kicking at the access doors and spitting on the windows. The bus started to spin dangerously under the pressure of the crowd while, inside, 30 heads turned towards me. I was recognised as the chief culprit and called every name under the sun – and in quite a few different dialects. The manager, who looked terrified, ordered me to close the curtains and, above all, not to incite the mob any more. I did as I was told but slid my hand under them and flashed the finger in a true gesture of defiance!

Only one person on the bus saw me do this – the driver, who had the benefit of his rear-view mirror, and he glowered at me. There was now the potential for a mini-riot, and only a heavy police escort allowed us to reach Catania Airport without further trouble. We had gained two vital points and not even a mini blip in form could prevent us from securing promotion to Serie B, and it was said I was the central figure in quite an adventure. The only team-mate who couldn't celebrate completely was Cangini, the killer of hens. In fact, within days of that dreadful incident, a complaint had arrived from bosses at the World Wildlife Foundation – and not without justification.

VI

MEETING GAZZA

SUPPORTERS celebrated our historic promotion throughout the close season and Umbria was a good place to be. The coaches decided to step up training in a bid to gain a second successive promotion, this time to the promised land of Serie A.

A number of talented new faces – big names and youngsters with promising futures – arrived at the club. The push was on, although for me it was time to go under the knife and get a problem knee sorted out. My right one had been giving me trouble and it was decided the close season was the time to deal with it. I was a quick healer so I wasn't far behind the rest of the players in terms of pre-season training, but as the new season grew closer, the first murmurs of discontent began to resonate in the corridors of the Libero Liberati Stadium.

It was said the directors had bitten off more than they could chew in signing the new players, and that there were serious cashflow problems. I had just signed a new three-year contract, and was looking forward to my first bona fide season in Serie B, but it seemed some of the players we had brought in – such as striker Sandro Tovalieri, from Ancona, the talented playmaker Pietro Maiellaro and goalkeeper Joseph Taglialatela – had been more than the club could afford and meetings were going on behind the scenes to sort things out.

Personally, I was fit and ready to play thanks to the surgical skills of Professor Giuliano Cerulli, in Terni, and I scored against AC Milan in the second leg of our Italian Cup tie. Sadly, we had lost the first leg 4-0 in the San Siro, and fared little better in the following match, but on a personal level I was delighted to score against a defence featuring the likes of Mauro Tassotti, Paolo Maldini, Franco Baresi and Billy Costacurta, who was marking me. I'll just mention, very quickly, that the second leg, or, perhaps, the second 'set', ended 6-2 – to Milan!

I suppose it's a gross understatement to say our season could have started better. Apart from a 2-1 win over Lecce, in which I scored, we struggled to pick up points and were soon hovering around in the Serie B basement, but strangely I was enjoying my football and the challenge of playing regularly against guys in the higher division was one I relished. Throughout my career I was always able to rise to the occasion, but I was only one player and perhaps it came as no surprise when the coach was sacked, which really disappointed me, as I was close to him.

Franco Liguori was the new man in the hot-seat, and he hardly endeared himself to the players when he decided to bring along a megaphone to his first training session! He then decided we needed time to reflect, and sent us off to think about recent performances. It was quite a culture change from the normally mild-mannered Roberto Clagluna, who liked to laugh and joke at sessions.

But Liguori was a local hero and he was sent in to sort us out. He seemed permanently angry, and his face would have seemed incomplete without his trademark scowl. As a player, the Neapolitan had been tipped for a bright future in the game – and an important role with the national team – but was badly injured after an incident involving Bologna's Romeo Benetti. The bright star of Italian football was never the same again.

Of course, I had my concerns about working under such a grumpy man, but I needn't have worried because our relationship lasted just a few days. I received a 'tap on the shoulder' from the president of the club, Rinaldo Gelfusa. Here was a man who had a Marlboro cigarette pressed permanently against his lips. Mind you, he never seemed to puff on it, instead preferring to allow a long line of ash to build – sometimes up to two centimetres – before it would simply fall off the end. He was a kind and fair man and didn't even remove the cigarette when he spoke, but somehow it always remained in place. He explained that the club was struggling financially, and that he could no longer afford to pay salaries. He said I was one of his most saleable assets and the need to 'cash in' was great. It was necessary for the club to move me on, although I was happy at Ternana – despite the new coach – but I was also aware the money could help save jobs. It was a dilemma. I also thought of how our fans would react. Would they think I was deserting a sinking ship?

After giving the conversation some serious thought, I decided to go. The first team in for me was Cosenza, another Serie B side who played a few hundred miles to the south. And then I discovered that Lazio wanted in on the deal, and had asked for a future option on me. The total cost of the transfer would be around £1.3m. Lazio were a top, top team and their interest gave me a massive boost. I was even invited to the Olympic Stadium, in Rome, where I met the coaches and the great Dino Zoff before a match. I was asked to play in a future friendly game alongside Lazio's new signing, the one and only Paul Gascoigne, a £5m purchase from Tottenham Hotspur. 'Gazza' was still recovering from an awful cruciate ligament injury picked up while making a wretched tackle during the 1991 FA Cup Final at Wembley against Nottingham Forest, but he was on the mend and that was the main thing.

I watched Lazio in action that afternoon from the main stand, sitting not too far from Gazza, and the attention on him was overwhelming. After the game, he walked on to the pitch to take the cheers of the supporters who, by this point, were in an absolute frenzy. He went under the North Curva to wave to supporters, while all the time dozens of paparazzi preceded him and documented his every step. He then walked over, voluntarily, to the pit, which was used as part of the 3,000m steeplechase course, forcing the photographers to 'snap' him while walking backwards. They weren't looking where they were going and were concerned only in getting the best photos possible. Then, one by one, they started falling into the pit, which was one of the funniest things I ever saw. You could see everyone in the stands breaking into uncontrollable laughter and immediately I was impressed by the ability of this unpredictable British midfielder to improvise on the field, and that was without his boots on. I was intrigued by him but could never have imagined what the future held for us both, and that I would one day become a team-mate of this loveable madman.

But that was Lazio, and I quickly warmed to the people at Cosenza. It was a demanding environment, but everyone was warm and friendly. I started the majority of early games on the bench but I had grown up and when things weren't going our way I wasn't slow to let my team-mates know. It's always difficult moving to a new club during the season, where you are more or less expected to hit the ground running. There are many problems to overcome, not least getting to know 25 new people straight away, when they only have to get to know you, and discover how your new team plays the game. But it is you who must fit into the existing group, and anything you showed at your last team is by the way. Sure, each pitch is roughly the same size and the ball is always round but there is still much to get up to speed with, and there is no time for initiations.

I also had to learn to fight for a jersey, as there was plenty of competition for places at Cosenza. In the past, if I had been on the bench I had always accepted the coach's decision, if I thought it was technically and tactically the correct decision, or if I recognised that the guy in front of me was a better player. This time, though, I was ready to fight tooth and nail to pull on the red and blue shirt.

My new coach Fausto Silipo was the man I had to convince. It was also important that the fans were onside and I couldn't wait to get started for my new team. But if I thought I was coming to Cosenza with a new found maturity, then I was sadly mistaken. With the benefit of hindsight, I now realise I still had an awful lot of growing up to do. The undeniable immaturity made me deal with this new experience in the worst possible way. As well as indulging in some childish behaviour – such as going around the dressing room with my pay cheque stuck to my forehead in an attempt to make some team-mates, who were perhaps paid less despite many years in the game, jealous – an episode occurred which I am still deeply ashamed of to this day. During training, I had a massive blowout with Ugo Napolitano, one of toughest defenders in the Italian game and a living Sunday nightmare for unfortunate opponents. A real tough guy; one that, if cut by an opponent in the heat of battle, would savour the taste of his own blood with his fingers, before looking menacingly at the man who had hit him, and who was about to suffer the full consequences.

To be fair, though, Napolitano had been kicking lumps out of me on the training ground and I was pretty much fed up with it. There is only so much any man can take, and after the umpteenth boot on the calf, I stood up quickly and, without thinking, spat in his face. It is something that even to this day I find hard to write. What transpired was like a scene from the cartoon *Tom & Jerry*. Sadly, I was the frightened mouse being chased all over the pitch by the furious cat. I ran zig-zagging around the field trying to escape the clutches of this man mountain. He was only a couple of feet behind and was yelling 'I'm gonna kill you' in Neapolitan dialect. Some of my team-mates looked on open-mouthed, but others, wishing for the fun to continue, started goading him, while the coach genuinely feared for my safety, which was pretty much what I was doing.

The fact I am able to tell this tale means he didn't catch me, and we eventually managed to sort it out within the sanctuary of the dressing room. By 'sorting it out', I mean I issued a grovelling apology which thankfully he accepted.

There was no justification for my action, no matter the levels of frustration I was feeling at being used as his personal plaything. Such a vile response is certainly not a part of me and I knew instantly I had crossed the line – big time. That incident coincided with a period in which I was feeling homesick. I couldn't wait until we played in the north of the country so I could enjoy a few days at home. Staranzano certainly wasn't New York, but to me it was home, and was still where I felt most comfortable. My team-mates knew I was feeling down, and decided to try and cheer me up – with a little help from our friendly local restaurant owner.

I arrived with three mates for lunch and the owner told me a couple of ultras had been in that morning looking for me. I didn't pay too much attention to what he was saying. He brought over our coffees, and just as I went to take my first sip, I saw this suspicious-looking guy enter. His face was partially hidden, and he had dark glasses on. The first thing I noticed was a sparkling gun in plain view at his waist – and it was pointing in my direction. I didn't even have time to realise it was the landlord in disguise as I was under the table in record time. On my way down I dragged the tablecloth, cutlery, glasses and plates with me and began to scream in desperation. It was only when I noticed I was the only one to hide from this crazed gunman, and began to hear the laughter of diners, that I realised I had been the victim of a disturbing but ultimately very funny gag.

On the field, the season ended even worse for the team as we failed to gain promotion to Serie A. It had seemed well within our grasp but we failed to reach out and take it, which was so disappointing. And disappointment on a personal level soon followed when Lazio dropped their interest in me. As if that wasn't enough, there was also a serious deterioration in the condition of my right shoulder. I had suffered quite a few blows to the already-damaged joint which, if you remember, was a consequence of that ill-fated dip in the sea. The muscle was quite worn and had even dislocated itself while I was sleeping, so you can just imagine how it felt during a match. The resulting pain had become unbearable and, above all, was affecting my performances on the field.

I took advantage of the close season to try and sort it out. I turned once again to Professor Cerulli, who knew me well after my knee surgery. He was regarded as the 'guru' of upper limbs by the football fraternity and later on, I would work with him at Perugia but, for now, there was only shoulder pain on my mind. The surgery wasn't easy as it was divided into two phases. As a taster, he slipped three ten-centimetre-long needles into the injured shoulder. It was a delicate op, and that was the most painful. I had my arm immobilised by stiff bandaging and the heat was terrible, and I couldn't even go to the seaside to cool down or have a refreshing shower. I was in such despair that I decided to have my hair shaved off and anyone who knows me, knows how much I love my hair! I spent my days lying on the couch trying to read or watch sport on TV, but evenings were a real nightmare. The needles were sticking out two inches from the shoulder and I could only sleep on my back, which isn't my usual position. In the mornings, my mother would inevitably find me sitting in a chair, and slumped over the kitchen table with my head propped up on a stack of pillows.

I had to put up with this for a month, before going back to hospital in Terni to endure the second part of my ordeal. This involved pulling out these foreign objects with a simple clamp, as though my shoulder was a piece of wood. The post-treatment physiotherapy was very important – and intense – and I was given exercises to ensure I regained maximum mobility before going under the knife again. This time, Professor Cerulli inserted a screw directly into the bones before reinforcing the 'scaffold'. Everything went perfectly well and, finally, I was able to rest. A few weeks later I returned to Cosenza and began my rehabilitation which, it was expected, would be a lengthy one.

Unfortunately, though, the coach, Silipo, seemed reluctant to change anything about and it looked as though I would remain on the edge of the team once I was fit and ready to play again. That was in November, but just as I was available for selection, the whispers started that Bologna, once a real powerhouse of Italian football, wanted to sign me. Sadly, they had fallen from grace, and were now playing in the league below Cosenza. Was I interested? Of course I was, but I didn't want to be seen as leaving a team where I hadn't proved myself to that club, its supporters – and MYSELF.

Bologna – with seven league titles on their roll of honour – were desperate to get back to the hallowed land of Serie A. I had a real decision to make, but armed with the knowledge that my career needed a vigorous shake, I decided to take the plunge and move on – and it was a great decision. I was introduced to the head coach, Alberto Zaccheroni, and it was love at first sight!

Bologna played their football in a gorgeous and charming stadium, set within a beautiful city, which was populated with friendly and funny people. I felt immediately at home, and just knew I would be happy in my new surroundings. I was 23 and it was time to make an impact on the game. I felt a real desire to prove myself with Bologna as my career had stalled somewhat. It was time to get this show back on the road. I met the players and found them to be a really special, strange mix of youngsters, with bags of exuberance and energy, and experience, those who had been over the course many times before.

One of the most bizarre characters I met in the dressing room at Bologna was Cristian Bini. They say goalkeepers are just a little crazy, but they got it wrong with Bini – he was a big bit crazy! I arrived during a short break in the season and we had arranged a challenge match against a touring Russian side. We played them at the Renato Dall'Ara Stadium and it was an extremely cold afternoon in February, just before the city carnival was due to take place. We were in the tunnel, waiting to be introduced on to the field, when Bini winked at me. Despite the biting cold, I noticed he wasn't wearing gloves. On closer inspection, I saw that his hands were massive – and very rough. And then I noticed they were also made of plastic! The type you buy in the joke shops when you want to scare your little sister. It was the most incredible thing as I would come back to defend corners, and Cristian would be organising the defence and pointing to everyone to tell them where they should be – and no one seemed to notice his massive Frankenstein hands. I was in stitches and he played the entire first half wearing them – and made some brilliant saves!

I was only at the club for a few days when the phone rang in my hotel room. It was my agent, Tiberio Cavalleri, who informed me that our captain, Marco De Marchi – who was also his client – was on his way to pick me up. The defender had been a central figure during Bologna's glory times, under the tutelage of Gigi Maifredi, before following the coach to Juventus, where he was a team-mate of Roberto Baggio, and together they had won the UEFA Cup. At 28, he returned to his adopted city, knowing that it was a step backwards, but in a bid to help the club move forward again. The new president, Giuseppe Gazzoni, had convinced him good times lay ahead.

I met Marco in the lobby of the Jolly Hotel and we walked to the nearby Brasserie. It was a rather famous restaurant in the shadow of the iconic twin towers, and popular among the city's sportsmen and women. It helped that it was managed by Ivo, a big Bologna supporter.

As we walked along Independence Street, Marco started to tell me all about the club, which was great, before moving on to the local traditions, and then how I would have to behave to be loved by the supporters, the rules of the group and its ambitions to return to Serie A in a couple of years. It soon became clear that Cavalleri had ordered him to 'programme' me in record time, and soon one of the most charming streets in Bologna had become, for me, a kind of Stations of the Cross.

I decided I would pretend to listen to the sermon, and contribute vague positive comments now and again. In reality, I was peering into the shop windows and watching the beautiful shop assistants that I would hopefully get to know at a later date. We had a lovely meal and it was clear we got on well together, but that was as far as it went. I was my own man and was big enough to understand certain things without having them drilled in to me. We became good pals and would go for dinner, visit clubs and watch basketball matches, and after attending a concert given by Eros Ramazzotti, he took me backstage to meet the singer with whom he had become friends while at Juventus. On another occasion, he dragged me to Milan to watch a recording of a TV programme, before we met the lead actor, Alberto Castagna, in his dressing room.

They were good times and Marco was friendly, generous, always cheerful and genuine. He was the classic 'good guy next door' and at Christmas we were invited to the theatre and, dressed as Santa Claus with white beards on, were asked to hand out gifts to schoolchildren. After this, we kept the Santa outfits on and strolled downtown – and soon became the two most unlikely Santas of the year. It was a blast going into shops where friends worked, and we inevitably made fools of ourselves and generally just took advantage of being dressed up as Santa – as nobody could see our faces. I had never obtained so many women's phone numbers in a single afternoon, and definitely not with such ease.

But then our fantastic relationship came to a brutal end. One afternoon, Lele Oriali, World Cup winner in 1982, and sports director at Bologna, asked if he could have a word with me. He immediately told me the club would not accept any more unprofessional behaviour on my part. Quite aggressively, he added, 'I know you go out often...' He spoke with authority, and was a professional and elegant person, but also with the expression of a real tough guy. I interrupted him at once, and countered, 'I always train with commitment and never miss a session. I work hard for the team on the pitch, and thanks to my goals, we have moved to the top of the table. Against Pro Sesto, a match we won 5-1, I played the entire 90 minutes with a dislocated shoulder – and scored. And now you talk to me about professionalism!'

Oriali didn't wait long to answer, and said, 'With you, however, goes De Marchi, and he now has an ass worthy of a bride.' He continued to put down poor Marco, despite us both knowing he no longer had the metabolism of a 23-year-old. I stopped him in his tracks and said, 'Then speak with him and not me.' At that moment, I lost my partner in crime but certainly not a friend and an amazing captain.

Things were definitely going well on the park, and the goals were starting to flow. As a result, more and more supporters were asking for my autograph, and I was getting noticed everywhere I went. One day, I decided to have a bit of fun with my new fans, although I would never have done this to children. I started to produce a doodle that reproduced the signature...of Zico (and, I must admit, I was pretty good at it) or Johan Cruyff, and sometimes I even copied Pele's moniker. While signing the ball, shirt or autograph book, I would imagine the face of the fans who, sitting admiring the autograph at home, would suddenly discover an illustrious but false signature on the item.

One day, we were at our training centre and before entering the changing room to get ready, I scribbled an autograph on a ball which had already been signed by my team-mates. I opened the black permanent marker and signed...Beppe Savoldi – all-time hero of Bologna FC. Who knows why? There was no reason for me to do so, but I just did. Maybe it was because since arriving in the area, I had often heard of the famous goalscoring striker with the moustache. This time, however, I was rumbled. The supporter noticed straight away and let everyone know. The next day, *Corriere dello Sport* ran with a page lead story with the headline, 'Negri is already signing as Beppe Goal', which was quite embarrassing, to be honest. It had only been a bit of fun but the tone of the newspaper story suggested I already thought I was the next Savoldi, and nothing could have been further from the truth. I did score goals and, if I say so myself, I was playing well. One which stood out was a vital strike against Pistoia, a spectacular overhead kick, which helped us reach the play-offs at the end of the season.

Earlier, and shortly after my arrival, Zaccheroni had been replaced as coach by Edy Reja. The team struggled, which was a big disappointment for a team like Bologna.

But we worked hard and racked up nine consecutive victories, which ended only in front of 30,000 fans in the derby against Spal. I contributed a goal and an assist but it wasn't enough to maintain our record. Mind you, we were still enjoying a rich spell of form which, I suppose with the players we had at our disposal, was expected of us. We had many players with Serie A experience, including De Marchi, Ivano Bonetti, a league winner with Sampdoria, Luca Cecconi (ex-Pisa), Franco Ermini (of Ancona), Rosario Pergolizzi (Ascoli) and Paolo Sacchetti (Reggiana). It was just incredible that we didn't achieve promotion that season, when at one point our lead seemed bulletproof.

When it came to the play-offs, which the supporters loved, we were both physically and emotionally drained. We were drawn against Spal – who else – and lost the home leg 2-0. Despite playing far better in the second match at Ferrara, we were reduced to ten men and simply couldn't get the goals we required. We regained some lost pride from the first game, and the home fans were certainly worried, but ultimately we failed, and it was a bitter pill to swallow. We had come up short, and that aggregate defeat left our Serie B dream in tatters. An entire city was in mourning. On a personal level, it was easily the biggest disappointment of my career to date.

My one-year loan deal was up and I prepared to return to Cosenza. Then I read in the press that the new coach, Renzo Ulivieri, a true Tuscan, hadn't been too complimentary towards me. Asked by reporters if I would be part of his first-team plans for the forthcoming season, he responded by saying he preferred players who spent their evenings relaxing on the couch at home, watching television. It wasn't the greatest thing to read, but my time at Bologna had given me back my swagger, and the goals had convinced me I could make something of myself in this game, so it was a different Marco Negri that walked back through the players' entrance at Cosenza on the first day of pre-season training.

VII

TEARS FOR GIUSEPPE

MY GOALS at Bologna had given me the perfect springboard and I was highly motivated and confident ahead of the new campaign. Initially, though, pre-season training was tougher than normal, thanks to a bout of tendinitis. The condition was more annoying than anything else, but it was never going to prevent me from getting fit. Mind you, I probably spent the biggest part of the summer months acting as detective, trying to find out if the club was economically sound enough to make it through the season. I'd heard quite a few whispers but it seemed that Cosenza were okay financially, and that allowed me to relax a bit more and enjoy the build-up to the new season. My first choice would have been to remain at Bologna, but that was out of my hands, and I decided to knuckle down and work as hard as I could for the coach, Alberto Zaccheroni, who at least wanted us to play the game in the proper manner.

I was training hard and preparing for the new season when I received the devastating news that hit me like a ten-tonne jackhammer. Giuseppe Campione, my talented Bologna team-mate, was dead – killed tragically in a road accident in Ferrara, a city he had moved to when signing for *Rossoblu* at the tender age of 15. I was in complete shock. Just two days beforehand I had spoken to him on the phone and we had been talking about the new season – and now he was gone.

At that age you live each day as if it were your last; you feel invincible and immortal. All of a sudden I realised the reality was sadly very different. Giuseppe had made many sacrifices to become a professional footballer. Still a boy, he had left his home town of Bari to seek his fortune and wore that red and blue jersey with great pride. Giuseppe was a fantastic striker, quick, explosive and technically gifted, possessing a venomous shot but also great in the air and with great mobility. He had a strong personality and, although still young, was already playing like a veteran and ready to take the next step up in quality.

While I was at Bologna, I noticed on the club bulletin board one day that there would be no more 'Saturday retreat', which meant the club would not be putting us up in a nice hotel before home games. We had to report to the ground of our own accord but because I had yet to find a semi-permanent home, I had no alternative but to stay in the hotel the night before a match – and that's when I discovered the club had one set of rules for one player, and another for the rest. That player was Giuseppe, although it was impossible not to love him. And then I discovered the reason why he had been singled out. The previous week, he hadn't heard his alarm and turned up late for the pre-match meeting – with a huge grin on his face.

As I was staying in the same hotel, Giuseppe and I became big friends, and we developed a Saturday night ritual. After our evening meal, we would head up to my room to watch the Serie B preview programme – armed with a big bag of sweets. We had liquorice, and chocolate-covered peanuts, lollipops, candy bar eggs and chocolates.

We were like a couple of grazing cows, with the jaws going tenfold in front of our 'private cinema'. After the football came a classic Italian film. Fortunately, the PlayStation came on to the market just a few months later, otherwise the lights would have gone out much later than 3am, which was pretty scandalous on the eve of a big match.

Although he had a room of his own, Giuseppe fell asleep on the other single bed in my room, with the tacit understanding not to get up early for breakfast. Mind you, that didn't prevent me being awakened by the annoying ring of his mobile phone and, by the noise of him groping around in the dark for the phone, falling off the bed and knocking over bottles and cans. It would quite often be 5am and I would be screaming at him, and then he would look at me with those big doe eyes before whispering 'Oops'. It was impossible to get angry with him. When *Championship Manager* was released we became big rivals, and enjoyed many games of the computer favourite. And I can still remember him belting out 'That's Amore' (the old Dean Martin classic) in the shower at the end of training each day. He also had his own personal wardrobe in the dressing room, which allowed him to come in with a certain look, however questionable, and then leave dressed in a completely different way. Mind you, the day he wore the unforgettable, and just as unlikely, combination of tracksuit and cowboy boots was the day we stopped taking his sartorial elegance seriously!

We performed together on the microphone at the local karaoke club in the crowded centre of Bologna, and joked with fans during a series of special dinners held at the club (I would go only if he did). Campione was a special guy, light-hearted, sympathetic and generous. He was respectful towards his parents, friends and comrades, although something of an extrovert. I knew him for a few months but we shared many jokes (our favourite was going to the central station and laughing and sometimes even lightly slapping the faces of travellers looking out the windows of departing trains) and much laughter and even though he was always ready to have fun, he also lived life the right way. What a tragedy, and a terrible loss.

In the years that followed, I tried to stay in touch with his family, especially his mother, who understandably never got over the loss of her son. I decided to wear a white cuff on the left forearm in every match, as a mark of respect and as a way of giving my friend the opportunity to be with me on the field. It was my final gesture to the one who was born to play football, but who was cruelly taken from us before he could receive the rewards he deserved.

Ironically, in the months to come, I found myself playing out what I called the magical 'drunkard season'. A period in which everything goes perfectly, and you find yourself constantly in the right place at the right time. I felt I could score in every game and, for such a young team, we achieved some great results, but slumped to the bottom of the league through no fault of our own. A few missed payments by the club saw us docked nine points, and we weren't a happy bunch.

But there was another shock in store just before a game against Acireale. Zaccheroni called me and Aldo Monza into his office. Aldo was the heartbeat of the team, a fantastic midfield player with the heart of a lion. He was also my room-mate and we were very close. The coach informed us that the club had 'urged' him to change his approach to the match. They wanted him to be a little less cavalier. To me it stank of the simmering discontent between coach and board, but if they had wanted Zaccheroni to change his tactics to suit them, they had picked the wrong guy, because 'The Zac' would bend for no man. He was telling Aldo and I because he wanted allies in the dressing room – and we, like the entire team, were 100 per cent behind him. We were fighting a relegation battle, and I wanted us to do that together.

But there was another issue on the horizon for yours truly, and it was something that disturbed me greatly. It wasn't just the players, coach and directors who were unhappy with our league situation – but the bosses of the curva, our supporters, who had a reputation for sorting out club problems in their own irrefutable way. In fact, they organised a meeting and came to our pick-up place to meet the team. This was a normal occurrence in southern Italy, when things weren't going too well, but it was a strange coincidence that everything had occurred within a few hours. First, the pressure on the coach from the board, and now the request for a meeting by the fans.

For one reason or another, I had been put forward as team spokesman. Perhaps it was because the supporters and I had never enjoyed much of a relationship and I had done a few things to wind them up. The boss of the ultras 'invited the whole team not to give up', which was expressed in quite an aggressive manner. In addition, all the players – although at this point everyone stared at me – had a duty to step up their efforts and commitment, and show a real attachment to the jersey, otherwise there would be serious consequences. We were told in no uncertain terms that if Cosenza were relegated, there would be reprisals. It wasn't a vague threat, but a concrete promise, and I've recounted it here as politely as I could. I likened the situation to that of the hostage, already terrified, and to whom the bad guy shows the gun to let him know he isn't bluffing and that, indeed, things will get to the point of no return if he doesn't get his way.

The following Sunday, I missed a penalty during the first half but, fortunately, 15 minutes from the end I scored the winning goal, silencing the moans and groans from the terracing and stands in the process. You could see the relief on the faces of my team-mates, who didn't quite fancy the 'consequences' from the ultras. Above all, though, that goal helped us on our way to a positive spell of form in which we moved smoothly up the table – despite the obvious handicap of our points loss. At the end of the season we avoided relegation, and there was relief all around – for a number of reasons. The Zac was delighted and embraced every single player – many times – when it became clear we were safe.

Personally, I was also a relieved young man. I was 24 but already felt like one of the team's elder statesmen. For me, the season had started with a lot of negative vibes, as I had made it known that I wanted to stay at Bologna, but by the end of the campaign I was happy at Cosenza, and delighted for the players, coaches and supporters that we had been able to enjoy the last part of the season. I think I also changed as a person. When things weren't going well, I became particularly grumpy, edgy and moody. I was never able to detach Marco Negri the player from Marco Negri the person. My two lives had never before travelled in a parallel manner but definitely overlapped that season. I had enjoyed a good campaign and was happy. I was also able to appreciate Cosenza's wonderful climate, the hospitality of the people in Calabria, the warmth and affection of the truly unique fans and the pride of that land for the beauty of its nature. From the mountains of Camigliatello Silano, where I went skiing in the winter months, to gorgeous views of the sea where I ate the most delicious fish and where I tasted the best ice cream in the world, it was a stunning part of the country.

That was a bonus, but the most important thing was always the team. In the season just finished, I had struck up a fantastic relationship with my team-mates, and we had come to understand each other. We had a great dressing room and I think they knew I only wanted to play for Cosenza, not myself. Something else that pulled us together was the club's financial problems. At times, they were struggling to pay salaries, but we remained a tight-knit group.

On one occasion, a training session was abandoned because the coaches said we weren't putting enough effort in. They simply left the ground and Aldo and I decided we should play a game of football with a difference – and it must have produced one of the most bizarre sights ever seen on a training ground anywhere in Italy. We played 11 v 11, but on a shorter pitch, and sitting down 'Swedish style'. He laid out a few simple rules, but basically we were to play a match while acting like giant crabs! No one opted out, as we saw it as a great opportunity to revisit our childhood for an hour or two. A number of supporters would watch us train regularly and they got a real eyeful that day. At first they looked bemused, but were soon cheering and laughing at the sight before them. It was perhaps the most bizarre exercise I have ever taken part in, but boy was it good fun. And it turned out to be quite an omen as 48 hours later we beat the dreaded Cesena FC thanks to a double from Mr Negri – although that victory also had repercussions for yours truly.

Cesena, in the region of Emilia-Romagna, is a truly historical part of Italy and I decided it might be a good idea to 'divert' the team bus to the old town so we could do a little sightseeing of our own. We enjoyed ourselves but it was pretty late in the night when we got back to the team hotel. The coach wasn't happy and was sitting bleary-eyed at the front door. He immediately threatened to sack the poor driver and punish the players, but we soon got back in his good books by getting some good results on the field.

I finished the season with 19 goals, which included just the one penalty, probably because I was a disaster from 12 yards, but it ended disappointingly for me when I broke a bone in my foot, due mainly to the incredibly tough head of the Pescara goalkeeper! Apart from that, I had enjoyed a fine campaign, with my goals inevitably attracting attention from other clubs. But a striker cannot do it alone and I had the likes of Francesco Palmieri, the great Gigi Marulla and Luigi De Rosa to thank for some great assists. I had improved many parts of my game but, above all, I had discovered 'the way to goal'.

My contract had run out but the infamous Bosman ruling – whereby a player in such a situation can find himself a club for free – had not yet come into play. My value was determined by a number of factors such as age, goals, salary and others. Cosenza decided I was worth £2.1m and they had the right to hold out for such a fee. Soon, I had a couple of options. Atalanta were the first to show an interest, and they were a viable proposition, as they had an enviable record of always looking after younger players. And they played in Serie A. Mind you, despite playing one league below, I was also interested when Perugia came in with an offer. They had a good side, and looked set to dominate Serie B. Both sides made very generous financial offers to me, but I chose Perugia. I wasn't sure I was ready to lead the line in the top league and believed that one more season in Serie B was the way to go.

I might have decided Perugia was the club for me, but that didn't stop the Umbrian board moving mountains to get my signature on a piece of paper. I jetted off to New York on a pre-season holiday with friends – and the directors of Perugia followed suit! One of them admitted they were so frightened in case I changed my mind they arranged a meeting in the palatial Plaza Hotel. They wanted me to sign a binding pre-contract agreement that would give them peace of mind, or 'greater tranquillity' as they put it. I was to meet them at the Plaza for breakfast, but when I turned up casually dressed at the hotel, which is in the heart of Manhattan, and sits on the periphery of Central Park, I almost wasn't allowed in.

The setting was straight out of a classic American film but I was on holiday, and arrived at the foyer wearing shorts and sneakers, and with a rucksack on my back. 'May I help you, sir?' was the polite but strict request of the uniformed concierge, who appeared almost out of nowhere. He might not have said as much, but his intention was clear – I would not be entering the grand breakfast room any time that day. Only the arrival of the breathless Perugia director, Ermanno Pieroni, flanked by my lawyer, both looking sharp in a suit and tie, brushed away any misunderstanding and, between bites of muffin and a sip of cappuccino, I signed the most important autograph of my young career.

So without hesitation, I went back out into the Manhattan street to meet my friends, and gave them a satisfactory grin – as if I had just robbed a bank and everything had gone smoothly, waving in the air something that to passers-by may have seemed a trivial sheet of paper but, instead, was my copy of the contract, which, I must admit, looked good with a sprinkling of zeros on the bottom line. Negotiations between Cosenza and Perugia lasted throughout the summer and with the Calabrians still sailing in dodgy waters, financially speaking, it was a relief when it was sorted out. It was good knowing that my transfer fee had helped solve some of their cashflow problems, even if they had tried to stall the deal for more cash, and insisted I would be going nowhere if Perugia didn't 'pay up'.

After returning to Italy from New York, there was just one place I was heading for – home. I wanted to spend time with my family and didn't give my diet a second thought. After a few weeks, my waistline certainly wasn't that of a professional footballer. My mother was a genius behind the stove and I was living proof. And due to my foot injury, which still hurt, I couldn't train to keep the pounds off. Mind you, it didn't prevent me becoming a regular at Lignano Sabbiadoro, a local nightclub.

One night, I was on my way home with good friends Gabriele and Max when we saw the most amazing thing. We noticed a strange object flying in the beautiful dawn sky, diamond in shape and dark in colour. We pitched up at the best vantage point and watched as it travelled along smoothly before turning on itself, just over the hills of the Carso. We were certainly tired, but I assure you, completely lucid. We were parked on the edge of the motorway and jumped out to observe this phenomenon. Seconds later we were in the company of other lucky witnesses who, in turn, had parked next to us to watch this UFO open-mouthed. It's a shame mobile camera phones didn't exist at that time or we could have documented the sighting, which remained unexplained despite the strong opinions of some experts.

Sadly, much more real was the problem over my transfer to Perugia. I had believed it was all sorted out, which apparently wasn't the case. Cosenza were still holding out for top dollar and we were getting mighty close to the start of the new season. One night I received a call from Roberto, the playboy kitman of Cosenza. He told me the club was in dire straits, and that only my fee would save it. He said he had a wife and children to support and was afraid of losing the job he loved so much. It soon became clear he thought I was the one holding out for more cash, and that my actions were jeopardising the future of so many employees. In fact, he even went as far as to warn me not to do anything 'u'ciuto' ('stupid' in Calabrian dialect). I decided to do something about it, because these people did not deserve such worry. I called my agent immediately and told him to stir things up because I was tired of waiting. I told him that if Perugia had not taken the decisive step within the week, I would rip up my contract and tell everyone what was really going on, which wouldn't have been great PR for the Umbrians. It worked a treat and all the obstacles that had previously been put in place magically disappeared. I was finally on my way to Perugia.

VIII

MY PERUGIAN DREAM

I WAS looking forward to my first day at Perugia's Pian de Massiano training complex. It was time to prepare for the new season and dispose of the extra 'baggage' I had accumulated due to a mix of my mother's home cooking and the niggling foot injury that had limited my mobility. But even I couldn't have predicted the furore that accompanied my return. My future team-mates mistook me for the kitman, and one even ordered me to bring him a pair of socks for a game that was just about to begin!

My identity was only revealed when Gianluca Atzori, who had played alongside me at Ternana, walked into the changing room. Mind you, when he hardly recognised me himself, I knew it was time to knuckle down and work twice as hard as the others. But when I did, my foot became painful, and that slowed me down considerably. This led to an unpleasant argument with the coach, Walter Novellino. He was always meticulous in his preparation, but perhaps his downside was the way he spoke to his players. He insisted there was nothing wrong with me, and even ordered me to have an x-ray – just to prove *his* point. But he crossed the line the day he verbally attacked me in front of my team-mates.

We were in the dressing room when he suddenly let rip with a verbal volley. He screamed, 'Negri, you are no longer on holiday. You are not even trying! When do you think you are gonna come back?' I'd had enough of his ranting and replied, 'I have four years to get back in shape, exactly the length of my contract.' It was the start of a deterioration in our relationship.

I did step it up though, and worked incredibly hard on the training ground – and was soon on a par with the others. One of our first matches was a home tie against Luton Town in the Anglo-Italian Cup. During our pre-match meeting, the coach was going over positions and tactics at the hotel and I knew I was in line for a start, although I was disappointed when he told me I would be part of the wall when opponents were taking free kicks. It was something I simply didn't like, because I knew there was always the potential to catch a whack in the face from a free kick taken by someone with the power of Jorg Albertz! Candidly, I raised my hand, pointed to the exact location on the board where I wanted to be and returned to my seat. My team-mates looked amazed, but I made my position loud and clear, and said to them, 'I simply cannot risk ruining my pretty little nose!' Novellino couldn't believe it, and when we started making our way out of the room, one of my team-mates overheard him say nervously to one of his staff, 'Does Negri think he is the new Gianni Rivera?'

Rivera was the one-time golden boy of Italian football, and a hero at AC Milan. Novellino had played alongside

him at the San Siro and knew the great man very well.
I also knew the coach had spoken to our main striker,
Paolo Baldieri, before the match and asked him to take my
place, and that was despite our medical staff insisting that
Baldieri wasn't fit. Apparently he was *that* annoyed by my
'mutiny'. He eventually, albeit reluctantly, abandoned the
idea of calling on Baldieri and I played from the beginning.
We won 4-0 and I scored twice. I won the man of the match
award – and never went anywhere near a defensive wall.

Our form wasn't so good in the championship though,
and we weren't playing as well as we should have. And
in the absence of good results, it's always the coach that
carries the can – especially when the big boss is Luciano
Gaucci. Of Roman origin, he had purchased Perugia when
they were in Serie C and promised supporters that within
a few years he would take them to the top level. He had
invested a lot of money but, until then, it hadn't been
enough to make the leap. So, he tried to reach the promised
land of Serie A by other means, and they weren't always
on the right side of the line – like giving a racehorse to a
referee. And not just any old nag, but a thoroughbred.
His little plan was discovered and he was banned for a
while, although the team also received a harsh penalty.
He was really generous when things were going well, but
became bad-tempered and irrepressible (which is why we
called him 'Luciano the Hurricane') when we lost, or if we
weren't progressing the way he demanded.

To be honest, my first few months weren't brilliant.
My effort could never be questioned but the end product
wasn't always there – and the president wasn't slow in
pointing out his disappointment. Once he came bounding
into the dressing room in the middle of a coaches' meeting
and, taking the floor, began listing everything that he

thought wasn't right. And then he started on me. In an unmistakably high-pitched voice, he screeched, 'And as for you, dear Negri, I remind you that I bought you and, moreover, I give you a lot of money, in order for you to make the difference on the field. But I'm asking for us, not for the opponents.' I wasn't best pleased and spent many days in my own bubble if we lost a match.

But nothing Gaucci did could surprise me, even the following season when he burst into our dressing room at Napoli (we were trailing at half-time) and 'shooshed' the new coach, the great Nevio Scala, who was in the middle of explaining how we would rescue the situation. He started screaming and shouting about how the side nearest to us in the table were winning, and that it would mean certain relegation if we didn't get the victory. It was crazy, because there were still seven games remaining. If we didn't win the match, he said, we would not see our families until the end of the season. 'I'll have you living on bread and water!'

In the second half, Milan Rapaic made sure we got a draw when he knocked in the equaliser with his hand, a gesture that provoked an avalanche of controversy during sports broadcasts and in newspapers. He was fiercely condemned by journalists who insisted it was not in the best interests of the game. Perhaps Milan, a Croatian, was driven by despair at the thought of remaining in some Umbrian hotel for the rest of the season. Meanwhile, we celebrated as if we had just won the World Cup.

I was never one to get over-excited by the prospect of team meetings, although I recognise they did have their place on occasions, especially if the team was perhaps demotivated, tired or apathetic. But when there was meeting after meeting, just for the sake of it, there was no benefit whatsoever. On one occasion, though, when the team was going through a rough period, Gaucci organised a game of Fair Merchant, only this time the prizes weren't worth just a few lire, but expensive jewellery, watches and valuable paintings. I could hardly believe it, and stood there open-mouthed as the game began. Somehow it just didn't seem right, although I remember Gaucci getting very excited, and wearing a grin of Cheshire cat proportions whenever someone won a prize. Maybe he thought that throwing about expensive items would motivate us for the next game when, in reality, it would have been enough to let us go home to our families to improve the collective mood.

We were due at Cesena for a match, but I was out because of my injured foot, which had started playing up again. I decided to go to Rome to watch Zaccheroni's Udinese take on Lazio. The plan was to watch the match and then go out that night. I reached the city in the afternoon and hooked up with Marco Materazzi, and we wisely used his scooter to get to the Olympic Stadium to avoid the heavy traffic. However, our evening plans were dashed when one of the directors called to tell me that we had lost at Cesena, and as a result, Novellino had been dismissed and that I should join the rest of the team at a hotel on the outskirts of Perugia. The hotel was very modest, without even televisions for its guests, and I was told this was our punishment for losing to Cesena. Gaucci made his grand entrance and proclaimed to all that we were in a 'hotel for truckers' due to a lack of commitment. This remark severely pissed off the owners, who threatened legal action.

Meanwhile, the team was in disarray and we were under the temporary control of Giovanni Galeone, one of the best coaches I ever worked with. He was also a histrionic character with a passion for wine. As a younger man he played for Ponziana of Trieste, a few miles from my home, and was also with Udinese. During practice matches after training, the prizes were slightly more humble than Gaucci's jewellery and paintings. This time, we had pizza up for grabs – and the occasional bottle of champagne – although the coaches always got more than their fair share! Mind you, every time Galeone attempted to open a bottle of champers, he would aim the cork at a specific target, although in nearly 18 months I don't ever remember him hitting it – unlike myself, as the goals weren't too far away.

As a coach, Galeone was the epitome of organised. He was complete, prepared and competent. The mood of the team changed immediately and he helped us find a winning identity, which in turn allowed many players to show their individual potential. Massimiliano Allegri, a talented midfielder, previously of Pescara and Cagliari – as well as a future star of AC Milan and coach of Juventus – was a case in point. He blossomed under Galeone and was the real driving force of the team. We started to play with fresh desire and turned in some wonderful performances, winning both at home and on our travels. Above all, though, we were playing with a smile and having fun. This period coincided with my return to full fitness and suddenly I was reaping the rewards. I scored 18 times in the league, almost all important goals, and often scored late on in games when the game was evenly poised. It was a decent return considering I had played the first couple of months of the season almost on one leg!

A couple of weeks before Christmas we were at Salerno, and I scored with around five minutes of the match remaining. I had to be really flexible to get to the ball, and felt an unnatural twisting of my left knee, although I finished the game. It was only when we were travelling back in the team bus that I started to feel the joint deteriorate. Sadly, an MRI scan highlighted the complete rupture of the lateral meniscus and also a partial tear of the posterior cruciate ligament. It was a bad injury to get, but I bravely, or foolishly, decided to play against Avellino at the Renato Curi Stadium the following Sunday. The knee was a mess and I looked like a 1970s Soviet player with my showy white bandage, but I played and scored the winner in a 2-1 victory.

The following week, of course, my condition had deteriorated, and I was out of the game in Venice. Two days before Christmas, I had surgery in Perugia and Professor Cerulli removed the crushed meniscus and cleaned up the affected area. Regardless of how well the op went – and it was a big success – I was out for the rest of the season. My dad drove down to Perugia and took me home to recuperate. My phone didn't stop ringing with well-wishers, although when we reached a cafe not far from Monfalcone, dad stopped to refuel, and for a cup of coffee. The calls continued, and we immediately worried about a 'peaceful' recovery and rehabilitation.

The phone rang again just as we sat down to coffee and dad and I just looked at one another. This time it was Renzo Lucchini, a physio at Perugia. I knew he would be calling for an update every day, but told him my parents lived in an area with very little mobile phone reception. Thinking on my feet, I gave him the phone number from the receipt for the coffee shop and told him this was my home number. Thankfully I was untraceable for a few days, and when I turned on my mobile again, I had 40 or 50 messages from Renzo. I called immediately to tell him how much I was improving, and was explaining how

I didn't need my crutches when he suddenly exploded with rage. 'I do not care about your knee,' he screamed. 'There is a revolution going on here. Gaucci said he is firing all of us. He wanted to hear from you, but when I told him I did not know anything because every time I called I always got a motorway cafe, he exploded with rage.' To this day, I still smile when I picture his face as he calls that number for the umpteenth time and asks, 'Is Marco there?' 'No, but we serve lovely coffee!' It must have driven him mad.

I returned to Umbria as soon as the leg could withstand a five-hour car journey but not before having celebrated New Year's Eve in a nice club with friends, and the ice of the champagne bucket on my knee. There was no messing around by the medical staff and I was on the bench for the home match against Brescia, just ten days after the operation. Perhaps it was a record of sorts, but there was no getting away from the fact that I wasn't 100 per cent fit. Newspapers heaped praise on Professor Cerulli – who was also our team doctor – for my rapid return to action, although I know the club medics were just relieved that the threats of 'Luciano the Hurricane' had calmed down, and their jobs were safe – for the time being at least.

But I wasn't happy with the knee and, unknown to everyone at Perugia, I headed up to Bologna, a journey of almost three hours, to see Dr Gianni Nanni, club doctor at the Stadio Renato Dall'Ara, with whom I had a fantastic relationship. I rated him the best in his field. He spotted the problem straight away and told me I had to rest, or risk a second operation. I listened to 50 per cent of his advice, and began to follow his advised exercises, starting off with those in a swimming pool. I played in the next game, but with little success – until I again popped up late on to score what proved to be the winning goal. Ironically, it was against Bologna, and Dr Nanni sat incredulous on the bench as I celebrated the late strike. As soon as the final whistle sounded, I made for the visiting bench to greet him. He said to me, 'Had I known it would end like this, I would have operated on you immediately!' Looking straight at me, he added, 'Congratulations Marco.'

It was this type of result that had us on the verge of promotion as the season neared its conclusion. The people of Umbria had waited 25 years for this and when it eventually arrived, the feeling of contentment was second to none. I was a Serie A player, but thanks to my own efforts and not as a result of a transfer or loan deal. It felt good.

The final match was against Verona – at home – and victory would have made promotion a mathematical certainty. I invited all my friends from Monfalcone. Some arrived in Perugia the day before, and it was great to see them again. The match was a sell-out but I made sure they all had gold-dust briefs for the big game. I was certain we were going to win, and wanted to share that joy with friends and family. Mind you, the game proved more difficult than I thought, and it was then I experienced the real pressure of having to win a game, and it wasn't much fun – at first. Once the game started though, I forgot all about that pressure. We won 3-2, and I scored twice – and right in front of those I had known since I was a child. It was the greatest feeling in the world and I milked it for all it was worth. My first goal was an equaliser, while Max Beghetto set up my second. We led the Venetians 2-1, and it was written in the stars that we should win – and seal promotion. In the dressing room after the game, I escaped the water balloon fight (with cold water) and went out to greet my family and friends, wearing just underpants and a pair of trainers. It was an incredible evening.

Seven days later, the season would officially be over – but we weren't waiting a week to party. Marco Materazzi and I – without taking a shower, and with me still wearing the number two shirt I had swapped with opponent Diego Caverzan (an old team-mate at Udinese) – jumped on his scooter and made for the old town, where the party had already started. We had sprayed our hair blue and fitted in nicely with our supporters. A whole city had been holding its breath for 90 long minutes and now it was time to celebrate, and the scene was incredible. The roads were jammed full of cars and scooters, tooting horns and waving flags and cheering. Everyone was heading in the same direction – Central Plaza IV Novembre.

Marco and I had wanted to experience the delirium up close and personal and he drove while I sat back with a flag in my right hand and one of those annoying horns in the left. On two wheels we moved quickly and got side by side with the excited fans to exchange euphoric glances. After a few seconds some of them recognised us in disbelief and asked us to drink with them. We were handed two gigantic bottles of wine. Others threw their arms around us without even recognising us. It was fun and exciting, and I was proud to have contributed to that gleam in the eye of so many people.

Much less fun, however, was the dinner organised by the club, to which Materazzi and I arrived on the scooter a few hours later. It was our promotion party, but it had the feel of a gala dinner for a literary awards evening. Mind you, when we entered the hall in just our shorts, half the guests rolled about laughing, while others covered their eyes and sighed. Marco and I were determined to continue the 'street festival' theme although the stadium chants didn't go down too well in some quarters. We drank a lot and danced to the rhythm of the Samba. It was also confession time, and the perfect moment to tell all the little stories of a glorious season. At midnight we had a diving competition in the outdoor swimming pool of the hotel La Villa, our base on the eve of home matches. We had all contributed to promotion and it was great to see the entire first-team squad let their hair down and enjoy the evening.

I remained in Perugia over the next fortnight and fully enjoyed the hero status afforded us by a grateful city, and this was never better illustrated than during a night out which ended in me driving my car along the full length of the pedestrianised Corso Vannucci, in the historic city centre. As I neared the end of the street, I noticed the police car behind, and they 'invited' me to pull over. 'Okay sir, licence and registration documents,' said the cop in a firm voice. Then, when he recognised me and my team-mate, Roberto Goretti, he handed back the documents, shook his head and muttered, 'Never in 20 years of this job have I seen crap like this,' and started walking back to his car. In a low voice, however, and in a moment of utter stupidity, I turned to Goretti and said, 'Hey honey, it's thanks to us that after so many years you can get to watch Juventus, Inter and Milan at the Curi.'

Not even a second passed before another uniformed colleague got out the car and started walking towards us. I thought, 'That's it, now I'm really for it.' The young officer poked his head in the window, didn't shout at us, but merely asked for a couple of autographs. 'But of course,' I replied, visibly relieved – 'as long as it's not on an official report,' and so ended a glorious season in Perugia!

IX

THE PROMISED LAND

S ERIE A is a world apart, and pretty exciting I must say. You are playing with the best young Italian footballers and performing regularly in magnificent stadiums, and then there is the opportunity to test your skills against opponents who until just a short time before, you were admiring only on television. During the summer months, and despite the fact that my name had been linked to some of the top clubs in Italy, I was happy to remain with Perugia.

For me, it wasn't the right time to move clubs, get to know new coaches and team-mates, and try to acclimatise in new surroundings. It was a jump in class and remaining with Perugia was my best option. It offered the best chance of success, both collectively and individual. I was really looking forward to such an exciting challenge and to prove to everyone that, at the age of 25, I deserved my place among the elite. There would be no relaxation – this was the season that could make or break me.

I had worked hard to get to this point and developed a strong mentality, but most importantly, I had a real striker's instinct in the penalty area. I came alive the moment I got near the box and was capable of scoring all manner of goals – and I didn't need ten chances to score. I suppose it was a different story off the field. I was considered a rather strange character, crabby and grumpy despite my soft French 'r' in my tone, more a lone voice than a black sheep, and haughty and solitary. I was the 'silent voice' when it came to reporters, even if their complicity could have helped further my career. I certainly wasn't shy when there was a bit of fun on the go, or on nights out, although I can guarantee this never affected my performance during a match. I would describe myself as a simple guy, very lucky, spontaneous and instinctive, and certainly not a man with a motive.

Up until my second season with Perugia, any friendships I had formed at my clubs were not as deep-rooted as those from my childhood. I might have gone months sometimes without seeing my friends from home, but when we met up again it was simply a case of 'business as usual' and we picked up where we had left off. Team-mates were like work-mates. We saw each other almost every day and there were some you preferred to others, but that was just natural.

Another reason I hadn't formed many lifelong friendships with fellow players was because I had changed clubs every 12 months at the start of my career. Certainly the best way to achieve good results was to be united with team-mates, and that was never a problem for me. I was happy to sacrifice personal goals for the benefit of the team. We had to help each other in times of difficulty, setting aside any problems, including jealousies, friction or personality issues.

In my first season at Perugia, I had bonded with very few team-mates, but became good friends with Marco Materazzi and Gennaro Gattuso. Marco and I hit it off straight away. The son of a famous coach, he grew up following his father on business trips, and quickly nurtured a love for football while cultivating the dream of one day becoming a professional. In Umbria he had the chance to be part of a good team chasing promotion and, in those days, he still operated as a left-back. He was tall but very thin and the tattoos would come much later, but even back then his jokes weren't the best! He already expressed a dogged determination to prove he was a good player regardless of his surname.

His relationship with Galeone, however, wasn't great and he was poorly treated. In fact, he almost never played and suffered for that. Off the field, however, we had a lot of fun and, after an early evening game (I wasn't playing due to a knee injury), we had a great night out at a club in Riccione, and slept for a few hours in a convenience store car park in his crumpled red Golf. When we awoke, we had an impromptu kick-about in the town square, which just happened to be getting resurfaced, and we were forced to avoid a conga-line of lorries and red-hot asphalt! In the afternoon, we drove up to Milan and watched AC play at the San Siro, but my mind drifts back to the enjoyable hours spent in the car singing along to the radio, laughing and joking and generally just having a great time. Mind you, we didn't always fool around, and often shared many stories that were both deep and personal.

Our friendship became strong and finally I realised that, despite the way he came across, Marco was a sensitive and fragile guy, regularly looking for attention. More importantly, he wasn't handling the situation at Perugia at all well. In fact, there was a genuine danger it could seriously compromise his career, so it was important he had the right coach at an important time in his life. I'm convinced that he truly became complete when he met his future wife, Daniela, a very sweet girl. Marco knew instantly that he had someone special and immediately started a beautiful relationship. Our friendship, in the meantime, remained solid and we kept in touch, especially if either of us experienced difficult moments or when, with his great disappointment, he was loaned out to Serie C side AC Carpi. He was a bit down so I dedicated one of my goals to him. I remember telling a journalist the goal was for Marco – even though I hadn't spoken to a reporter for three years. I wanted to show how much Marco meant to me and to let him know I cared about him.

As a result, we've seen a lot of each other in recent years and caught up quite a bit when I was in Glasgow and he was at Everton. Our paths seldom crossed after that until I met him by pure chance ten years later on a white coral Caribbean beach in the archipelago of Turks and Caicos. By then, of course, he was a World Cup winner and we were staying in adjacent hotels. I am very proud of what he achieved. He has won everything there is to win, but I know even that pales into insignificance to the wonderful family he has around him. That, more than anything, has brought him serenity and happiness, which is very important for someone who lost his mother when he was so young.

I have great memories of two loyal and sincere young lads, a little cheeky, but united and able to mix and match every day. I remember an episode in Cesenatico where Marco had an appointment with a physiotherapist, Germano Chierici, of whom I had heard much about. I decided to go with him, and two of Marco's other friends came along. One was Giulio, an undercover cop and big fan of the *Grifoni* (Perugia), and a good person to know. The other was Toni, a sympathetic Palermitan who had lived in Umbria for many years.

On the way back, we stopped for some fish, and after eating, Giulio, who was driving, decided against taking the motorway, which was clogged up with roadworks. Marco and I were sitting in the back of the car, chatting and quite relaxed, when I noticed a large truck immediately behind us. I started to wind up the driver by 'showing him the horn with my hand' (in Italy, people 'do the horn' when they want to be nasty. It means your wife is cheating on you). Materazzi's head was masking my hand so Giulio couldn't see me. The guy behind completely lost it and started to tailgate us. He was pumping his horn and flashing his lights. Giulio tried to play it cool, but didn't know that it was now Materazzi's turn to give the truck driver the middle finger, while using my head to conceal it from our driver. This made the truck driver even madder and he tried to pull alongside us in an effort to give us a real fright.

Giulio, totally unaware of our actions, put his police flashlight on the roof of the car and pulled the guy over. We could see the look of terror on his face. Giulio got out the car and motioned for the truck driver to do the same. Once he had shown his documents, he started to point to us in the back seat and only then did Giulio realise what had *really* gone on and immediately directed his inquisitive eyes towards me. Marco and I tried to protest our innocence as the trucker climbed back into his cab, cursing these four crazy undercover cops, but Giulio was having none of it. The trucker got a ticking off for dangerous driving and we were scolded for our childish actions, although the episode ended with much laughter.

Another player who would become a good friend started to show real signs of promise during my second season at Perugia. Gennaro Gattuso was very young but despite being part of the youth team, showed up well whenever he was asked to join the first team. His main qualities at that time were strength, grit and determination. He was just 17 but already well-structured athletically – he certainly had more muscles than me – and his desire to make it to the top was there for all to see. I had never seen a boy of his age demonstrate such clear ideas about his future and, in training, struggle, sweat and fight for every ball as if it were the most important of his career. He never once complained about anything, but equally he didn't give an inch, or ever hold back in the tackle – even during bounce matches. He had such a strong personality but not once did I see that quality cross the line into hateful arrogance.

Rino's father had taught him a lot, but I think most of his energy came from a desire to succeed – something you either have inside or you don't – and knowing he had made a big sacrifice so young to leave his family behind in Calabria to travel to Perugia. Everyone could see what a great prospect he was. He possessed a football maturity well beyond his years, and had the perfect build for the great player he would eventually become. But he worked exceedingly hard to become that player.

There is an eight-year age gap between Rino and I, which is a lot, but we always got on well, both at Perugia and Rangers. We didn't hang out with one another at Perugia but we had a great relationship in the dressing room, and I used to tease him a lot. One day I said to him, 'Always stay committed because, while you may not be so cute, if you ever become a famous player, perhaps a nice girl will want to get to know you more.' His usual disconsolate reply was, 'Maybe…' One day he said to me, 'Marco, there is one girl that follows me everywhere, from the boarding school to the stadium, to my youth team matches and even when I go for a walk. It's a nightmare!' I was confused, and asked him why the situation was so bad. He replied, 'She is a fucking monster!' He started to laugh out loud, and I was doubled in two.

On another occasion, he asked me for a lift to his boarding school and, along the way, I handed him some of the letters I received from fans. I told him to open the ones from the ladies first, and he couldn't believe what was inside. The first one included some pretty lingerie and I told him that I would twirl it around in the dressing room until Gigi Tufo, one of our physios, would be so embarrassed that he would ask me to stop. It was always a funny sight.

Rino started reading one letter in particular, in which the sender had used lots of 4s. To better explain the gag, it was like if an English girl sent a text message, using the number four in the context of 'be4' instead of before or '4you' instead of for you. Every time Rino read the message, he would read the proper number 'four'. I tried not to laugh at the start, but I couldn't contain myself. I could see he was confused and eventually said, in a loud voice, 'Chissù tutti sti cazze ics?' ('What are all those fucking 4s?') and I burst out laughing. Rino and I were destined to become good friends.

Anyway, we were all looking forward to the start of the season and got our Serie A campaign off to a great start by beating Sampdoria, who had the great Roberto Mancini and Juan Sebastian Veron in their side. The opportunity to once again play in front of our fans had turned agitation, tension and emotion into excitement and exaltation. I was calm, because I was both mentally and technically ready for the big kick-off. I played like a veteran, and midway through the first half I threw myself at a cross coming in from the right – I can't remember if they still speak of a beautiful cross from Carmine Gautieri or an accidental, lop-sided shot, but with a committed lunge, I managed to slip the ball past the Sampdoria goalkeeper.

I had scored just under the curva occupied by our red-and-white ultras. Still on the ground, I looked immediately towards the linesman to ensure I had remained onside, and even when the referee's whistle sounded for the goal, the initial feeling was one of disbelief and then, driven by adrenaline and unbridled joy, I walked towards the corner flag, where this incredible feeling of really having achieved something came over me. I had just scored my first goal in Serie A, the moment every young Italian fan dreams of. I tried to absorb as much of the atmosphere as possible. It was amazing and watching that goal back still gives me goosebumps even to this day. The best thing to bring me back to the land of the living was the feeling of my team-mates piling on top of me. It was only then I realised I wasn't dreaming.

I couldn't wait to get home to my parents to tell them all about my first Serie A goal, but a rude awakening awaited in Monfalcone. I walked into the house like an excited schoolboy, clutching my number 18 Perugia shirt. I couldn't wait to hand it over to my father, but he made me sit down. He had something to tell me – and my heart sunk. My mother had fallen into a state of deep depression a few weeks previous, and my father hadn't told me because it was such a delicate moment in my career. I tried hard to take it all in, but I was going from the highest high to the lowest of lows. I slowly opened her bedroom door and saw her lying in the dark and curled up in the foetal position. I greeted her with the usual hug and kiss, and asked how she was. It was a stupid question, of course, but I had been completely unprepared, and she said she wanted to be alone. Not even my arrival had perked her up enough to want to sit up. She said she might come through in a few hours.

I was devastated. I passed my two days off with a huge lump in my throat. I had arrived with the desire to yell to everyone my satisfaction and, instead, my happiness had been strangled. The same feeling when a striker misses an open goal. It took a few years and, most importantly, the understanding, patience and love of my father to heal my mother's emotional situation, but the image of her lying in bed that day disturbed me a lot and naturally I will never forget it. If anything, her helplessness and fragility bound me to her in an even deeper way.

After our opening-day victory, football presenters and pundits, as well as journalists, started to talk of Perugia in glowing terms, not just for the result but the manner in which we had won the game – playing football the 'correct way', they said. Our captain, Federico Giunti, was even called up to Arrigo Sacchi's national team. Suddenly, however, something broke. Or, more accurately, 'someone' broke that winning toy. The wins dried up, the coach was under pressure, and I managed just three goals in nine matches. It wasn't fun anymore. It was so different from the euphoria I had experienced at the start of the season. I wasn't getting involved as much and that worried me. In short, I felt my potential was not being exploited correctly.

Throughout my career, the one constant had been a season-on-season improvement, but I didn't feel that was happening. I felt I was standing still and my initial cockiness had given way to a more withdrawn attitude. I started to question whether or not I was good enough for Serie A. Then the first transfer window of the season, in November back then, opened, and I was wanted by Espanyol, a team from Barcelona. My dream had always been to play abroad, but I didn't think the opportunity would arrive so soon. But while the prospect of playing in Spain thrilled me, I could hear the taunts in the back of my head. Behind my back, they were saying, 'Serie A is too tough for Marco Negri, Serie B is his limit.'

What I needed at that moment was the advice of someone who wasn't family, a friend, or a team-mate. Up until that point, I had sorted out all financial deals and contracts myself, but I now needed a good agent to play a leading part in my career. I knew a man called Cavalleri from my time with Ternana in Serie B. He had been introduced to me by a friend. When I signed my first important deal, I had arrived at a hotel on Lake Como accompanied only by my brother who, in reality, knew very little about football contracts, despite his undoubted competence in business. I was lucky then, though, as I was dealing with two wonderful people – the coach Clagluna, who was, to me, like a second father, and club president Gelfusa – the grandfather everyone would like to have. I knew dealing with football clubs would not always be so simplistic, and beneficial. After all, every football player had an agent.

Cavalleri helped me gain good sponsorship deals, and we worked well together, but we had never established a deep friendship, nor a confidence that transformed him into my true confidant, and someone with whom I would share deep secrets. There were a lot of things going round in my head at that time, and I knew I had a decision to make. Stay at Perugia and try to get my mojo back, or move to Spain and begin a new adventure. I decided to call Clagluna for advice and it was the best thing I could've done. He didn't push me in any particular direction because he had nothing to gain personally from any advice he might offer. He told me if I stayed in Perugia, I would score at least 15 goals, and even bet me an expensive dinner that I would.

The Clag also said that ordinary people would pay to live in Barcelona, and that it was a great opportunity. Reassured by the conversation and accompanied by my lawyer, I met president Gaucci at one of his offices in Rome, along with representatives of Espanyol. The negotiations started well, but with each passing hour, problems arose and then, everything stalled. It was getting late and I was told to go back to Perugia. They would continue to talk and Cavalleri would let me know the outcome. I stayed in Rome and waited for the phone to ring, but it didn't. I decided that a good night out would help banish the disappointment. The next day, probably irritated by the fact he had just watched a financially beneficial deal slip though his fingers, and armed with the knowledge that I didn't exactly break sweat the morning after my night out in Rome, Gaucci fined me and put me out of the team.

I would have to train twice a day for two hours – seven days a week – on my own, and even recall plugging away on the training field while the first team were playing, within earshot, and there was I working out with coach Mauro Amenta.

As a 'treat' I would listen to the commentary on a little radio, and thankfully no one ever saw me in such a strange situation. But I took it all in a positive way and used it as a period of deep reflection, thinking about everything that was happening to me, my career, and the reasons why things were going wrong – and my mistakes.

I came to the conclusion that a bath of humility was the best way to get back to playing football again. I took advantage of a month's purgatory to get into the best shape I had ever been in, and also to strengthen my ankles, which were thin and fragile, and had definitely limited my performances. We had just heralded the beginning of 1997 and my motto was 'new year, new start' and I eventually got back into the team and even surprised myself by how quickly I was able to hit the ground running. I started scoring goals, and with that came happiness off the field, which clearly showed how much football was a fundamental part of my life, and that without professional satisfaction, it was hard for me to live a satisfied life.

A feature of the exterior of the Perugia stadium was a clutch of white poplars, which grew like wildfire on the tarmac of one of the parking lots at the stadium. One spring day, my partner Carmine Gautieri and I decided to burn a cluster of the pollen. However, the fire immediately took hold, as if soaked in petrol, and in a flash we lost control of the situation and it began to burn down the hedge that was really close to a nearby restaurant. Only the arrival of a fire crew salvaged the situation and Carmine and I had to act as innocent bystanders.

On another occasion the players were sent directly to the hotel after a disappointing game and we were forbidden to leave the premises until the next day. I waited for the stroke of midnight, took the car and left, as for me it was technically 'the next day' but I had the misfortune to meet – and overtake – the coach's car. Nevio Scala, the architect of such a successful Italian national team, as well as the great Parma side, was a fantastic man, but he had recognised my Mercedes SL, which was far more flashy than the modest A112 LX of my beginnings. Noting the licence plate, he spoke to me next day at training, and I immediately defended myself, saying – none too convincingly – that I had loaned the car to a friend and that, absolutely, it hadn't been me driving. He didn't believe a word, but in the end offered some fatherly advice by inviting me to tell my 'friend' not to drive at such high speeds again, especially when it wasn't his car!

I would have played with a broken leg for a man like Nevio, and knew he forgave me because I gave him everything in training, a fact he acknowledged publicly in the newspapers. He was also smart enough to realise he couldn't punish me when he had also left earlier than the time laid down by the president. I made the most of my second chance and went toe-to-toe with some special players in the second part of the season. Zinedine Zidane, Gabriel Batistuta, Hernan Crespo and George Weah were all in Serie A, and when checking the top scorers on Teletext, I would regularly see my name alongside the likes of Beppe Signori, Pippo Inzaghi, Baggio, Alex Del Piero and Francesco Totti, despite being marked by some of the best defenders in the world, such as Ciro Ferrara, Fabio Cannavaro and Alessandro Nesta. It was a clear signal that I could hack it in Italy's top flight, and my joy was compounded when we re-signed my good mate, Marco Materazzi. He returned in a new role, that of central defender, and the position that would see him find unprecedented success with Inter Milan and the national side.

While I continued to score goals, the fortunes of the team nosedived, and it wasn't long before we were involved in a battle to avoid relegation. It was around this time I met Monica, who is still my partner and mother of my beautiful son. We met in Bologna at my birthday party and, after a few months without any contact, started seeing each other regularly.

But back to the football, and our last match of the season, in Piacenza, suddenly became a straight shoot-out for survival. Sadly, we lost the match 2-1, and were relegated back to Serie B. Gaucci was furious and informed us that, as punishment, we would train until the last day of June, while every other player from Serie A was lying on a sun-kissed beach.

It was a sad end to a season in which I, personally, had achieved so much. The childish antics of the club, added to the anger of the fans, sickened me if I'm being honest. When we returned to Perugia after the defeat in Piacenza, we were on a real downer. We were so disappointed at getting beat and, ultimately, being relegated, but required police assistance to get our cars out of the stadium as the supporters had laid siege to the ground. It had been a long, hard season and there was a great deal of physical fatigue among the players. Everything added up to a mix of complex emotions and we certainly didn't need Gaucci's silly behaviour.

Personally, my season hadn't been too bad. I had scored 15 goals (just like Clagluna had said) in 27 matches and, moreover, so many of them had been important goals. I had scored the winner against teams like Roma, Sampdoria, Atalanta and a double against Reggiana. Above all, though, I had enjoyed vital goals against Juventus, Milan and Piacenza. There was also a beautiful hat-trick against

Bologna, the acrobatic turn at Udinese, the memorable goal against Cagliari and another against Sampdoria in the return at the Marassi Stadium. I had reacted positively to a negative period, proving I could play at the highest level in my country – and also very well. But it was time for another chapter in my life to begin, and this one would be very interesting indeed.

X

HELLO GLASGOW!

DEALING with a bitter relegation was tough, as was slipping back down to Serie B. After years of continuously improving, I was forced to stand still, or even take a step back, although, if the truth be told, I did expect my agent to call and tell me that a Serie A club had made enquiries about me. Playing in Serie B offered little stimulation, but the phone remained silent, despite me now being considered by the 'experts' as 'a good striker with goals in him'. But moves back 'upstairs' came only to my team-mates. At that point, I began to think they had people in their corner who were more capable than I had in mine.

All I had to occupy my mind were the lengthy training sessions until June, the ones that Gaucci had forced upon us in the wake of relegation, although we found an unlikely ally in the local newspapers, who showed a hint of solidarity towards us. It was no fun, but then, straight out of the blue, came a chink of light. Glasgow Rangers showed an interest. It was timely because I was becoming a little fed up looking on as other young Italians moved to teams in the likes of England and Spain.

It was an interesting proposition because Rangers had just signed Rino Gattuso, and Gaucci was fuming mad. He jumped up and down and shouted loudly about developing Rino and then this foreign club comes along and takes him, so there was a protracted compensation battle going on in the background. But Rino had decided to move, and perhaps I would be next. It was perhaps the perfect scenario for both clubs. Rangers knew Perugia were unhappy with the manner in which Rino had moved to Glasgow and perhaps saw an opportunity to sign me and build in a compensation payment for Rino at the same time. This might have calmed down the warlike intentions of chairman Gaucci, who had threatened to take Rangers all the way to UEFA.

That summer, Rangers had been spending big on new players and were obviously keen to try and make an impact on the Champions League, and their signings had a distinctly Italian flavour. Roma midfielder Jonas Thern, a Swede, signed up, as did defenders Lorenzo Amoruso and Sergio Porrini from Fiorentina and Juventus.

I called Rino to ask him about Glasgow, Scotland, Rangers and even the Old Firm, and soon realised that if all the talk was true, I had a unique opportunity to play for one of the oldest and most famous clubs in the world – who, in 2005, would win their 51st national title, and earn a badge with five stars – who were adored by a set of fans capable of creating an electrifying and fantastic atmosphere. My old friend explained to me about the spirit of Scottish football, which was far removed from the excessive tactics of ours, and told me of the great players at the ambitious club: from Paul Gascoigne to the Danish 'brother of Art' Brian Laudrup and the Ibrox idol, Ally McCoist. He told me of wealthy chairman David Murray, who had invested heavily in a bid to make Rangers a force in European football.

Up until the interest shown by Rangers, I had never even considered the possibility of playing Champions League football, but suddenly the bar was raised, and by quite a considerable height. If, however, professionally speaking, I had already decided to try my luck across the English Channel, it was my relationship with Monica that might have led to me staying in Italy. We were getting on so well, and the partnership was blossoming. We saw each other only when my schedule, and her work patterns allowed, which was usually a couple of days a week. I was worried that any transfer abroad would have an adverse effect on our relationship, especially as I realised she could be 'the one'. My doubts, however, were swept away when Monica, courageously and without hesitation, said she would come with me to Scotland if the move went through – if that was what I wanted. Of course it was!

My agent confirmed that Rangers were definitely interested and I instructed him to get the ball rolling. I had little trouble in convincing *him* it was the right move (thanks to his hefty cut). I followed the instinct that had always helped me make the right decisions, even if this was the most risky to date. That instinct had led me to wander around a lot and change teams regularly, but it had always been for the benefit of my career. I was always up for deepening my knowledge of the game and the best way to do that was with different clubs and traditions, even more so as this potential new experience would be played out abroad. I planned a trip to Glasgow to see for myself if this really was the move to open a new chapter in my life.

Cavalleri and I agreed to go to Glasgow, and he was waiting for me in the lobby of a hotel on the outskirts of Rome and, knowing me well, asked if I had remembered my passport. Less than a minute after arriving at the hotel, I was back behind the wheel and speeding towards Perugia to pick it up. I had left it in a drawer at home, and I eventually reached Fiumicino Airport just in time to take off for Glasgow. It wasn't the best start, and goodness knows what Perugia director Ermanno Pieroni, who was accompanying us on the journey, thought. That evening, I met Rangers coach Walter Smith for the first time during dinner in a nice Italian restaurant and I spoke English like the classic tourist, but was able to understand something of the conversations thanks to Vincenzo Morabito, another FIFA agent involved in the transaction.

Mr Smith spoke with a real passion for his team. He talked about his desire for success in Europe, the importance of winning a tenth successive championship and how he wanted to set out his team on the field. He even told me that with my record I would score more than 30 goals a season. He was so positive and I was sat facing an affable, balanced, elegant man, with a great sense of humour and someone who knew me as a player, and appreciated my qualities. We said our goodbyes and agreed to meet up in a couple of days to deliver our answer. That night, we stayed at the very elegant Cameron House Hotel, a fairy-tale castle in the countryside, overlooking Loch Lomond and surrounded by a beautiful golf course.

The day had turned out to be long and stressful, and it was late when we got to the hotel. At midnight, I decided to take a stroll down to the edge of the loch just as the sun was setting. I stood transfixed, staring at the beauty in front of me. Moments later, a thin and light rain had taken the place of the sun. Rather than falling, those drops literally 'sailed' in the air which, I believe, the Scottish call 'drizzle!'

While playing in Serie A, I had adorned some of the biggest and most intimidating stadiums around. I had played in the likes of the Meazza, Olimpico, Dall'Ara and San Paolo. But while all these stadiums have their history and a certain fear factor for visiting players, I had never once felt the need to buckle under the strain. On the contrary, in fact, I would say I enjoyed them, and thrived in red-hot atmospheres. When I played against Inter Milan, in the San Siro, the thought of facing players such as Paul Ince, Ivan Zamorano and Xavier Zanetti aroused in me emotions never felt before. There were more than 60,000 inside the stadium, and while the two captains, Federico Giunti and Gianluca Pagliuca, carried out the tradition of exchanging pennants and handshakes near the centre circle, I looked up and saw this massive 'human wall', easily capable of drowning out the players on the field. It was an imposing sight, and one had to bend the neck in an almost unnatural way just to see a small part of the blue sky above. I thought to myself, 'Marco, you had better get going today.' It was the reason I had wanted to become a professional footballer, to play in famous grounds in front of big crowds.

And when I returned to Glasgow for further talks with Rangers, I knew it was a love affair I would be able to continue. The sight of Ibrox — a real, authentic jewel — left me open-mouthed and speechless, due mostly to its perfect mix of old world charm and modern innovation. It was an amazing arena, and I hadn't even seen it full yet. Supporters even had the privilege of being able to have their own seat in the stands with a plaque adorned by first and last name.

I told Rangers I wanted to play for them and it remained for club and legal teams to attend to the finer points of the contract. Meanwhile, I was taken along the famous old corridor to the trophy room, and it's no lie to say an entire afternoon wouldn't be enough to look round it. What an incredible room, full of cups and trophies but with history oozing from every brick. And then it was time to sign the contract, and once again I felt enormous pride in signing my name on that sheet of paper. I was a Glasgow Rangers player and boy did that sound good. I had one last look at the ground before saying my goodbyes and leaving for the airport. I knew something good was happening and I had positive vibes about the club I had just signed for.

The main Scottish newspapers had published a photograph of me and it seemed everyone recognised me. They said hello and asked politely for autographs. This was also a natural occurrence in Italy, of course, but in this case just four hours had passed since I signed my contract, and I hadn't yet pulled on the Rangers jersey. It was a great feeling and I didn't want to hide it. In fact, I didn't want to return to Italy – I wanted to get started with Rangers straight away!

XI

MARCO GOAL-O

THE last day of our absurd Perugian 'imprisonment' was up and it was time to head to Glasgow – I was a free man. It was important to get to Scotland as soon as possible as Rangers had started back early due to their involvement in the preliminary rounds of the Champions League. I certainly didn't mind spending my summer holidays at Ibrox. It was only a few minutes' drive from Glasgow Airport to the Moat House Hotel, the traditional temporary home for newcomers, and the first face I saw was a welcome one – Rino Gattuso. He was the first of my fellow Italians to arrive in the country and we hugged like long-lost cousins. Sergio Porrini and Lorenzo Amoruso would come over the following week but for now, Rino and I had a bit of catching up to do.

I was amazed at how much he had matured, both physically and mentally and he told me of how enjoyable and positive his new experience had been. It was also quite hard given the distance from home and the fact he had been unable to sign a proper contract due to the legal wrangling between Rangers and Perugia. He had only been able to train with the team so it had been tough, although I didn't realise just how tough. He said he had been tempted to walk away from Rangers several times. He started to think that maybe he had been a bit hasty in signing for a club so far away, and I think the protracted negotiations had taken their toll. And let's not forget Rino was only 19 when he signed for Rangers. He told me if I hadn't have arrived in Glasgow when I did, he would've headed home for some peace of mind. Fortunately for the future of Mr Gattuso, and the whole of Italian football, things would go in a very different way.

From the moment I started training with Rangers, I realised football in Scotland was very different from that in my homeland. At first it was like I was a star in a very surreal film.

After getting changed in the dressing room, we would get on a little white bus, which took us to our training base for the day. Sometimes it was a cricket ground, other times a rugby pitch. There were no white lines to mark the penalty area but only a slew of yellow cones to show where I should be. To be honest, it wasn't a big problem. While in Italy, I would break away from the others twice a week, move to another part of the training ground with a goalkeeper, and concentrate solely on shooting and goalscoring techniques. Things were different in Scotland, though, and after a signal from the coach, we would jump on the bus – muddy and sweaty – and head back to Ibrox for a shower. It might have been July, but I think someone had forgotten to tell the weather man!

However, we worked closely with the ball at our feet, concentrating on 'pressure' games on a reduced field. It was very tiring, but good fun. The times when my football week was divided between a good dose of athletic work, without ever even seeing a ball, and tactical exercises aimed at greater attention of the opponent, were over. And I didn't miss the days preceding the Sunday match, during which we would test – in a crazy way – hundreds of potential dead-ball and free-kick situations. They might have been important to penetrate the 'enemy' but they were really boring for a striker.

My only concerns were the lack of specific training, the fact I didn't know my new team-mates and some finer details, such as timing to avoid the offside trap, which was always a secret weapon of mine. Oh, and then there was the food. The Italian professional footballer routinely follows a strict diet of strong doses of carbohydrates and proteins. He is certainly not free to swallow whatever he chooses, only the things that are more suitable for the body of an athlete. In Glasgow, before the game, while I was struggling with a fresh oil and parmesan plain pasta, I stared incredulously at the other players scooping fried eggs, beans, toast soaked in butter, chicken, and a couple of forkfuls of spaghetti into their mouths. And they were all together on the same plate! Initially I was almost convinced I had been following the wrong diet throughout my career. To be honest, though, it was all a question of habit.

What counted was performance. The main problem arose when we played an away game and the chef wasn't used to preparing certain-sized portions of pasta with tomato sauce. I remember even having to repeatedly put aside the spaghetti in front of me because, at the first forkful, I lifted the entire content off the plate as if it were frozen. Often, I would take to the field with just a few slices of bread and jam in my stomach.

I remember on one occasion, I convinced Rino that we should eat like the Scots before a match – 'just once', I said. A few hours later, when the match began, he wasn't his aggressive and dynamic self. After 20 minutes we conceded a corner, and I asked him with a smile, 'Can you not burp?' He gave me 'that' look, put his hand on his stomach and promised to drink a litre of Coca-Cola after the game. He said, 'A great belch is the only way we will be able to digest the rock inside our stomachs!' We didn't do it again.

Another thing that differed from the game in Italy was the behaviour of referees during matches. That was when I began to understand the definition of 'arbitrage'. The entertainment and pathos of the challenge should never be interrupted. Physical duels, tough but fair, were part of the game and only unsportsmanlike conduct (never spit, simulate or elbow) were punished with severity. Without exaggeration, I played matches during which I heard the referee intervene less than ten times. There was the initial whistle, interval, start of the second half, a few goals and the final whistle. That was it.

The aspect that impressed me most was the spirit of Scottish football, along with the wonderful atmosphere created at all stadiums – especially Ibrox – and the need to play attacking football whenever possible. Our stated mission was always to score one goal more than the opposition, having fun and giving everything we could to win. Put on a show for the paying public. When you came off at the end of the game you knew you had given everything you had – and you had a clear conscience. And when that game was at home, it was a sweet feeling playing in front of our fans, and we invariably won.

There were certain things I didn't miss about the Italian game. Like the controversy surrounding the most innocent of mistakes from the referee. If an offside or goal kick isn't given in Italy, everyone is up in arms. The coaches are going crazy at the side of the park and everything is a drama. In Scotland, they didn't let it bother them too much and everyone just got on with the game. It was like a breath of fresh air. I always found many goalscoring opportunities in the dying minutes in Scotland, as opposing sides, inevitably losing the game, went in search of an equaliser. That meant supporters got their money's worth as we all battled until after the 90th minute. And after the game was over, and we were all back in the dressing room, there wasn't as much finger-pointing and blaming people for mistakes as there was in Italy.

One month was enough for me to get to know my new team-mates and the staff working at the stadium. The summer friendlies saw me play regularly, and as Monica was still in Italy, there was little else to do than check out the city centre with Rino, and he was very generous in introducing all the Italian restaurateurs he had met in his previous months of loneliness. And given they were the only ones who could understand him, as his English was still in its infancy, at least he was being fed! Many of them had emigrated with little money but a pocketful of dreams. They had come to Scotland in search of fortune, exploiting their innate culinary skills and taking with them the tasty secrets of pizza. They were soon well placed in society.

And I made many new friends, and people in which I could confide. For example, Toni from O' Sole Mio, Mario (future father-in-law of Rino and proprietor of La Rotonda), Renato, who ran the restaurant Ariosto, and Guerrino, Marco and Mariangela, who owned and worked at Il Pavone, were always available. And even though they were all Celtic supporters, I could see the pride in their eyes at this large colony of players coming over to Glasgow from Italy. It was a piece of their land that was missing from their hearts. As well as Gattuso, Negri, Porrini and Amoruso, we also had the Celtic pair Paolo Di Canio and Enrico 'Tarzan' Annoni, so the link was strong.

As a city, Glasgow turned out to be a pleasant surprise. The third largest in the UK, it was very lively downtown and featured many fine pubs and restaurants, historical sites, major universities, huge pedestrian precincts, main streets full of shops and a variety of eye-catching shopping centres. There were also many fantastic parks and, how can I forget, some great pubs, all with their own unique style. Until signing for Rangers, I had only heard about Glasgow, so it was a real eye-opener.

The only significant obstacle was the language barrier, but after training, Rangers provided Rino and I with English lessons, although inevitably the presence of Gattuso meant it usually resembled the plot of the Woody Allen film *Zelig*, and a sea of laughter from us both. Rangers gave me a car, which was a nice gesture, although I almost caused a few accidents due to driving on the 'wrong side' of the road, and I soon got used to the main beams of other drivers heading straight for me! It also meant a few broken wing mirrors and a punctured tyre, following a clumsy collision with a pavement.

My brother was involved in a serious accident in the north of Scotland, although thankfully no one was hurt. But my heart went out to Monica one day when she was leaving our house in Bearsden, a nice residential area composed of individual villas set on a hill. She left the house early in the morning, started the engine and, just as she was about to drive off, realised she had left her phone in the kitchen. She jumped out and ran back up to the house, but when she returned, just a few seconds later, she saw the car driving off on its own and making straight for a neighbour's fence. The car had an automatic gearbox and she had forgotten to engage the handbrake. She called me, very shaken, and said, 'Do I have to call at the neighbour's door?' 'No, dear,' I said. 'Let's pretend nothing happened, maybe he won't notice that you have parked practically inside his house!'

When the driver of the tow truck came to retrieve the vehicle, he was stunned, and the owner of the adjacent villa was very good about it and insisted the insurance would cover the damage. Perhaps he was a Rangers fan. Meanwhile, I was looking for a comfortable home as I wanted my family to visit and, more importantly, somewhere for Monica and I.

For me, everything was a welcome change. We Italians were even invited to Troon, in Ayrshire, for the final day of the British Open golf championship. It was a must-see event for thousands of Scots, but not for Gattuso and I, thanks to spending the previous evening at a disco. We soon found ourselves asleep on the grass near the last hole, happy under a rare and beautiful sun, and to the amazement of those present.

To be honest, I had little interest in golf, but would appreciate it with the passing of time. I started to play a little at Bearsden Golf Club, but never quite got the hang of it. I once surprised myself, and my playing partners, by securing a par three – but I'm afraid that was as good as it got.

On one occasion, I was about to play a shot when I noticed a man on a large lawnmower. It was the greenkeeper, so I stopped, but he motioned for me to play my shot and I lined up to hit the perfect tee shot. The grip was great, perfect posture and I had a good feeling about this one, even if I was a little nervous due to the extended audience. The little man got out to check if the blades of his mower were clean and efficient, but also to stare at me curiously. I started with the swing, hit the ball confidently, and the impact sounded good. I raised my eyes to follow the trajectory of the ball, and like all good golfers, started to talk to the ball. 'Go on, yeah, come on….no, not there, no.' Bang! It hit the lawnmower and when I looked over, he was crouching down and protecting his head with his hands.

I raised my arm and waved to apologise with my white glove. He responded with a right hand, using his index and middle fingers to form a 'V'. But not a sign of victory. It was simply the genteel British way of sending you to hell, while screaming, 'Fuck off! Hopeless c***!' I picked up my clubs hurriedly, and wisely decided to quit the game while still a novice. I left immediately and didn't show my face there again.

It didn't take long to realise the extent of the rivalry between Rangers and Celtic. It was like no other I knew of in the game, and the Scottish Protestants used a different handshake from others. It was less vigorous than normal – almost just like rubbing skin. The moment I realised just what the Old Firm meant to some was when I was awoken the night before a match. I was staying at the Moat House when the fire alarm started ringing 'accidentally' at 2am. It was triggered by a Celtic fan's cigarette at a dinner organised by the hotel. Of course I was concerned and covered myself with a blanket and headed down to reception. I was eventually allowed back into my room but it was impossible to get back to sleep, and this seemed to happen most Fridays.

Meanwhile, my friendship with Rino continued to grow and it was nice when the other Italians, Porrini and Amoruso, arrived. Sergio was the most experienced of us, and had won many cups and leagues with Juventus. He was married and seemed like a quiet guy off the field. On the field, though, it was a different matter, and I knew him very well. He was a very good and aggressive defender, and I knew this first hand, having felt his tackles during the previous season. I also knew Amoruso well from Serie A, and had played against him just a few months earlier in a crunch game for Perugia. He was the most expensive of the four Italians and I'm sure Rangers pinned a lot of their hopes on him.

To say he was a confident guy would be an understatement, but I thought he was funny and generous. He was also confident that his English was as good as it got, although I laughed when he translated the 'corner flag' with 'the bandier'. When he didn't know the right translation, he simply took away some letters from the Italian word, in this case 'bandierina'. In fact, on one occasion when he headed back to Italy, he left me the keys to his apartment so that some of Monica's relatives could come over for Christmas. I was also very sorry when he suffered an injury to the tendon, which led to him missing the first part of the season. He needed surgery, and I would soon discover the many negative aspects of the 'real' Amoruso – much to my expense.

But the new season was just about to start – while players in Italy were still enjoying their holidays. The action got under way earlier in Scotland so, after a short acclimatisation, it was soon time for the preliminary round of the Champions League. We were up against a little-known team from the Faroe Islands called Gotu. It was an unforgettable tie, thanks to the sight of flocks of nibbling sheep on the grassed roofs of houses, and the second leg at Ibrox being played with a red ball on a snow-covered field – when it was still July.

I will never forget running out on to the pitch at Ibrox for the first time. Gotu were already out there, while our skipper Ally McCoist had us waiting in the tunnel. As we started to move off, you could hear the noise of our metal studs clanking on the floor, and the shouts of the players in the tunnel. We meant business, and were like gladiators entering the arena to do battle. It was so different from Italy. We were pumped up and the noise of the crowd was feeding our thirst. Every time we ran out on to that field there were 50,000 supporters willing us on to victory – and Tina Turner sang 'Simply the Best'. It was the greatest feeling in the world. I had only played in front of such a crowd three or four times in my career, but it was a regular occurrence at Ibrox, regardless of the opposition. It didn't take long to realise I had made the right decision to come to Scotland.

However, the start of my Rangers career was marred by a dreadful result in Gothenburg. It was the third and final preliminary round of the Champions League and we went there with very little preparation. I was desperate to make the knockout stages but we lost 3-0 to a team that should have been well within our reach. It was unforgivable. The day before we left – just 48 hours before the tie – there was no practice. Instead we went to a huge gym for a bizarre session based on sauna, Turkish bath and Jacuzzi. We were to leave at dawn the next morning and stayed in a hotel near Glasgow Airport. We were up at 4.30am and faced a long and arduous journey.

At the same time, the technical-tactical preparation left much to be desired. We were told very little about our opponents, and knew nothing about their current form, how they would play or their star men. It was such a shock to me, as just a couple of months beforehand the complete opposite had been the norm. In the build-up to games in Italy, you were given every last detail on the opponent.

It was a two-legged affair, and we knew we could count on our supporters to help us at Ibrox if we kept it tight in Sweden. We didn't do that and had an unrealistic mountain to climb back home. We were punished, especially on the counter-attack, and it was all so unnecessary. In the dressing room after the match, our assistant manager Archie Knox exploded with rage. It was ten minutes of hell as the attack was aimed especially at me. He was gruff and rude. Often, while he spoke, he would burp loudly before grinning from ear to ear. On other occasions, it was much worse as he would spit on the floor when we were getting changed. He was the exact opposite of Smith, who was always the epitome of elegance.

Knox took training and had a huge passion for Rangers. In the previous nine years, the team had been more than good enough to win most times in the Premier League but I had serious doubts about his technical preparation. I was never able to ascertain the level he had played at but he could not have been in his youth an elegant playmaker with velvety feet like Laudrup. He treated players like horses. If you were playing well, you got a 'carrot' and were praised and pampered. If you weren't up to scratch, he would come out with the whip and scream and shout at you, with more than the odd 'fuck off' in there for good measure. I had witnessed something similar in Italy when I was at Cosenza and the furious sporting director Gianni Di Marzio had only been prevented from breaking a chair against the wall by the coach. On another occasion, after a series of disappointing results, the same Di Marzio showed up to give us a lecture. Our style of play had been compared by some journalists to that of Bruges, a brilliant Belgian team of a few decades earlier. Well, Di Marzio began to shout 'Bruges here, Bruges there… forget about all this shit!' Then, he pulled down his pants to bare his buttocks and added, 'If we continue like this, the only thing that burns will be my ass.' In Italian, Bruges sounds quite similar to 'brucia', which means 'burns'. It was designed to give the team a boost, but instead, only produced a lot of laughter in the dressing room. In Scotland, on the other hand, the older guys in the team were well aware of Knox and accepted him for what he was, admiring him as a tireless worker.

Personally, I have always considered myself reasonably intelligent. I knew straight away that I had to change the way I played to suit the country I was in. I knew all that but, like everyone else moving teams and countries, I needed a little time to adapt – not someone screaming and shouting and telling me to 'fuck off'. How was that supposed to help? Football Archie Knox-style was so different. It was all passion, determination, physical exuberance and generosity, which really weren't characteristics associated with me, but I would change. After just a couple of training sessions, I heard him mutter that I wasn't the player of his dreams, while it was clear that he didn't like some of my behaviour. Most of the time I couldn't understand a word he said, but would try and gauge what he wanted, like more commitment, by the volume of his voice. One thing I did know was that he wouldn't be cutting me any slack any time soon.

Knox's rant in Gothenburg wasn't at all constructive. I was always a self-critical player and knew myself I didn't play well that day. To be screamed at by Knox hadn't been so much humiliating as embarrassing. I was even frustrated at not having sufficient English to reply immediately. I didn't care that the coaching staff preferred players who could demonstrate their commitment through unnecessary things like running fast to retrieve the ball or returning to the dressing room covered in blood. Surely it was all about the result. I had always been of the mind that I should preserve as much energy as possible so that I was ready if and when an opportunity to score arose. Surely if there was someone to blame, then it was the coaches for not preparing us properly.

I wasn't in a particularly great frame of mind for the next game, a league match against Dundee United at Ibrox – and little did I know that it would be the greatest game of my life. My family couldn't have picked a better time to come and watch – although Knox was at it again after just 15 minutes. Before the match I had spoken to my brother, Alessandro, and told him I would be better prepared, and that I wanted everyone to see the REAL Marco Negri, but the start didn't go according to plan and there was Knox standing on the touchline yelling at me. He was telling me to press the defenders more, make them work harder, and of course it was all peppered with expletives. I didn't expect any less or any more from him, but it was time to let him know exactly how I was feeling. Using my best English, I relayed the following message to him. 'If you don't like the way I'm playing, replace me with someone else. If not, just sit down and shut up!' Some of my team-mates noticed the altercation, while others pretended not to hear. I must admit I was shocked, though, when Gascoigne started shouting at me, and taking the coach's side.

But within a sensational five-minute spell, I had hit a glorious hat-trick, and after a really beautiful third, a fantastic lob from 25 yards, over a goalkeeper well in excess of six feet, I sent Knox literally to hell. I looked him straight in the eyes, just to leave no doubt about who was the recipient of my reaction, and even to this day I'm proud of that outburst, which has been captured for posterity on YouTube.

By the end of the match I had scored five. The match ball was mine, and each player scribbled a little personal message on it. In addition, I equalled the Scottish record of five Premier League goals in the same match to join Paul Sturrock, ironically a former United player, in the record books. However, instead of celebrating such a tremendous feat, I first of all felt the need to clarify a couple of things with Gazza. I told him in private that I didn't care who he was. On the field, a player couldn't afford to behave superior to another, so I advised him to mind his own business. He didn't answer. I spoke in Italian, a language he understood perfectly, but it was important to me to take the pebbles out of my shoe that were making me uncomfortable. I then went to collect my award for player of the match (a glass beer mug with the date of the game and my name engraved above), grabbed the signed ball and joined my family as I wanted to share that special day with just them.

It had been the perfect afternoon for Rangers and I. We won the game, which was the most important thing, and I had played the game of my life. From the altercation with Knox to my verbal and technical reaction, I had demonstrated that my attitude on the pitch was part of who I was. It was natural and, most importantly, very, very profitable for all. It was a big turning point for me, as after that I went on the most incredible goalscoring run. I scored every type of goal, and from every position. The Italian phenomenon had been unlocked, and I teased and tormented defences on a regular basis. I was unstoppable and scored in ten successive matches, a new Scottish record.

The night before we played down at Kilmarnock, I didn't even manage an hour's sleep because of the most annoying toothache. I arrived at Ibrox in the morning and hadn't even changed clothes. The players were already at a hotel in Troon but I was on my way to the dentist, who pulled out a decaying wisdom tooth. All I can remember from the dentist is lying there on the chair, looking up at a ceiling adorned with a gorgeous poster of a Caribbean beach. It was a stroke of genius, and immediately cheered me up and took my mind off the guy standing over me with a big pair of pliers! For the evening kick-off, I started the game with my mouth still dripping blood and the anaesthetic coursing through my veins. Just imagine the joy felt by Knox. My head was spinning but I scored another two goals, and we won. I enjoyed hearing our fans chant 'there's only one Marco Negri'.

At that time, things were also going very well for me off the field. My English was improving and my relationship with Monica was good and we were enjoying learning all about a new city and, whenever I had a few days off, we would head for London or Paris on a mini break. Back in Glasgow, though, I heard that an Italian boy had been pretending to be my young brother, and had been getting the best seats in busy restaurants, or skipping the queues at city-centre nightclubs. It was all a bit crazy, especially as I had only been in the city a couple of months.

I have special memories of a variety of players during that season. Playing with the likes of Brian Laudrup was such a joy. He had enormous natural talent and was such a balanced individual off the park. Many of the goals I scored were as a result of some wonderful wing play by the younger of the Laudrup brothers. I also admired Jorg Albertz, a German with a precise and powerful left foot, which earned him the appropriate nickname of 'The Hammer'. He was funny and loyal. Jorg loved Eros Ramazzotti and would sing his songs with an unmistakable Teutonic accent, although he worked extremely hard at putting across the romantic mood of the Roman artist's words. He was the perfect team-mate and friend. On the day of my birthday he surprised me by showing up at my house. We had a great time and, as a 'gift', he shoved a custard pie in my face!

Our goalkeeper was Andy Goram. Nicknamed 'The Flying Pig', he might not have been blessed with the body of an athlete but you would struggle to find someone with better reflexes. He was also one of the most agile goalkeepers I have ever played with and there was no one better in a one-on-one situation with a forward bearing down on him.

Andy was a top-class keeper. In addition to this, he was also the first person I ever saw take his false teeth out before a match. It might not have given him much of a winning smile, but he was the perfect guy to have between the sticks. He was quick with a joke, although one day after training, as we were heading back to Ibrox in our minibus, he read the headline on a billboard outside a newsagents, and said, 'The secret lover of Marco Negri, that should be interesting,' and looked directly at me. 'That sounds like a juicy story Marco.'

Thanks to him, it was the worst 15 minutes of my life, and he started to tease me by saying I had been caught like a chicken and that I would be kicked out of the house by Monica. He then offered to take me into his house and finished off by saying he could teach me so many things. The whole team was laughing loudly, and I couldn't wait to get back to Ibrox. I went down to the dressing room to read the offending article and discovered that my 'secret lover' was indeed Monica, who had taken part in an interview with a journalist without my knowledge – nor hers!

Goram was, however, the only player that ever asked me the meaning of the white cuff I wore in every match. Of course, I told him it was a tribute to my old friend and colleague Giuseppe Campione, who had died tragically in a road accident. The Goalie was genuinely moved and wanted to know every little detail.

My perfect striking partner was definitely Gordon Durie, who was a hard-working and tenacious forward. I loved playing alongside 'Jukebox', as he was fearless and even after receiving a horrific head injury during a game at Kilmarnock, which brought on concussion, he was back in place for our next game – despite being hospitalised for a few days. His indomitable character epitomised the depth of spirit that flowed through our team. It was the Scottish mentality never to give up and Gordon epitomised that quality.

However, the heartbeat of the team was Stuart McCall, a tireless midfielder and easily recognisable due to a thick mop of red hair. He was a great professional and even though he was recovering from a serious knee injury, and the issues that brought, he was always available with words of encouragement for those who needed it. I remember we were in Puerto Banus for a few days in the Scottish winter and the players had gone out for dinner to relax. At the restaurant I saw him take up an odd challenge from an

On my first set of wheels

Mum with Alessandro and I

With big brother Alessandro in Milan

Learning to ski at the Sappada training school near the Austrian border

Dad shows off his silky ball skills

Sandro Gregori was my first basketball coach

The Italcantieri basketball side, with me at the front with the ball

*My first trophy...
player of the
tournament for
A. R. Italcantieri,
organised by the
Monfalcone naval
base*

*With the Udinese
youth team...I'm
in the back row,
fourth from the
right*

Dressed to kill with Udinese…I'm in the front row, second from the right

Moving up…with the Udinese senior team

Starring for Ternana

The glory goal! Scoring against Verona – and Perugia are in Serie A

In pensive mood for Perugia

Brothers in arms…I served in the army with Silvio Casonato, and teamed up with him later at Cosenza FC

Ready to defend my country

With old Bologna mates. My dear friend Giuseppe Campione is in the middle. On my left is Andrea Tarozzi, while on my right, Martino Traversa

With my good friend Andrea Pasian

My first day at Ibrox – it was magical!

My boss at Rangers, Walter Smith. He is a gentleman

One of the magical five against Dundee United – number 4!

I think United goalie Sieb Dykstra is getting fed up with me

I always did enjoy scoring goals

I received the Player of the Month trophy

Time to pop the champagne!

I enjoyed my goal against Celtic at Parkhead

Gordon Durie was my ideal partner in attack

Gazza is right up there with the best of them

With Rino Gattuso and Jonas Thern at the Scottish Motor Show

Rino, Sergio Porrini and I enjoyed the Oasis concert

I wonder if champagne tastes nice from a football boot!

With my Danish 'brother of art' Brian Laudrup

Rod Wallace, Michael Mols and I, with
Italian chef Peppino, enjoy a night out

I was proud to wear the tartan on a photoshoot

We Italians were in demand to pose for the camera!

With fellow Italian Lorenzo
Amoruso

Training ground fun with
Fernando Ricksen, Tony Vidmar
and Barry Ferguson

Moody Marco? Not me!

*Scoring
against Hibs…
notice the
white cuff!*

*And a goal
against
the other
Edinburgh
side…*

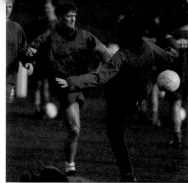

Relaxing in the sauna…

With Rangers legend Richard Gough

I was extremely proud to represent Glasgow Rangers

Old Firm battle, jousting with Alan Stubbs

Celebrating with two talented team-mates… Jorg Albertz and Stuart McCall

Explaining 'something' to Arthur Numan

My Chilean team-mate Sebastian Rozental

Training with the reserves

I was a 'victim' on the Scottish satire show Only an Excuse

Virtually unrecognisable with 'Jim Morrison' beard!

Feeling the heat at our training camp in Florida

I loved exploring Scotland as a 'tourist'

I struck up a great relationship at Ibrox with Daniel Prodan

Feeling the benefits of Dr Vranceanu's magic laser

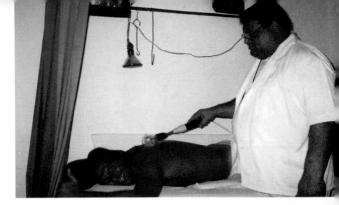

Gazza and I had a great day out with the birds of prey at Gleneagles

With the Romanian 'magician' and Petre

I felt proud wearing Scotland's national dress

With Gazza and Jimmy 'Five Bellies'... but what about that yellow shirt?

Jorg Albertz gave me a custard pie for my birthday!

Mum and I having a laugh

With Alessandro at Edinburgh Castle

Byron is definitely man's best friend

Is this what I looked like when I played for Cosenza?

With my mum and dad…I'm very proud of my parents

I have enjoyed 'looking back' over my career

With Monica and Christian, who is growing up so fast

English guy who was sitting at a table close to ours. The challenge was to drink a pint of beer upside down, but with his body perfectly upright and leaning against the wall. Some of us helped the two contenders by holding their legs, although it ended in a draw when the last sip of the second beer started coming out of both of their noses. It was crystal clear that Stuart was no quitter and would never refuse a challenge.

Midfield player Ian Durrant was equipped with the purest talent around. He could have played at the highest level in Italy, such was his technique and ability on the ball. His capacity to read the game was second to none but his rise, unfortunately, had been stunted by a serious knee injury that, even to the naked eye, meant the knee appeared twice the size of the healthy one. This deprived him of a successful international career, but during training, even with just one leg, he was able to run and play brilliantly and his speciality was the nutmeg, the ability to stick the ball through an opponent's legs. Still, an extremely bad injury hadn't robbed Ian of a fantastic sense of humour – and infectious smile.

Another midfield ace, Jonas Thern, might have been born in Sweden, but spells at Napoli and Roma had left him with near-perfect Italian, which was fantastic for me. He was such an outgoing guy and did a fantastic impression of television character Mr Bean, by walking around with his pants pulled up as high as they would go!

Ally McCoist was the darling of the Scots and it was he and I who were normally going head-to-head for the number nine jersey. He had a terrific scoring record, bettered by no one at Rangers, and the thing I regret most from my time at Ibrox was that my lack of English stopped me understanding the endless stream of jokes and anecdotes he told in the dressing room and on nights out.

Mind you, on one occasion he walked into the dressing room and his trademark smile was missing. Instead, he seemed furious and was muttering 'fuck' every second word. He made Knox sound like a choirboy! It was really strange to see him like that, and while everyone comforted him, I asked Jonas what had happened. In perfect Italian, he told me Ally had been left out of the Scotland squad for the World Cup in France, which was a major surprise to us all. Ally might have been my rival for the striker jersey but I wanted to say something, although I didn't, and I don't know why, but I'll say it now, even though it happened many years ago. I'm not a manager, but Ally should have been in that squad. He was playing really well at the time and scoring important goals for the team. He also had the enthusiasm of a kid. Imagine how much of a boost it would have given to the nation with McCoist coming off the bench, but sadly it wasn't to be. Super Ally later had a spell as Rangers manager and I bet he still played friendly matches with his players, even though he was a little heavier. He was a razor-sharp striker and I liked him a lot.

I reckon the only team-mate I didn't hit it off with at first was Ian Ferguson. I don't think he was a drinker and perhaps this made him angry but on the field we would regularly rib each other and I often heard him call me 'fucking Italian', or some other derogatory term that I didn't understand, especially when I fell on the ground (too easily, according to him) after a challenge from an opponent, or when I didn't track back to help out the defence. I would answer him in my native language – something he couldn't stand because he didn't understand it. I would refer to him by the nickname I had chosen, 'piedi di padella' – which meant pan-feet, or iron feet, as I didn't consider him a player of great class, talent or technique. As far as I was concerned, he was a very tough player, and his game was all about covering every inch of the pitch. There wasn't a lot of mutual appreciation between us, but everything we did was for the good of the team and, most importantly, remained on the pitch.

But the real soul of Rangers was, and always will be, Ibrox Stadium itself. At the reception desk was Peter, always there to welcome you with an affectionate smile, even after a defeat. He was particularly meticulous in preparing the mail delivered to the players, and his attitude always made me start the day with a smile. Laura, meanwhile, was the secretary and organised everything to perfection, including travel and our commitments as players, and was always able to make it seem like she only worked for me. And there was Tiny and Irene, the sweetest sisters in the lounge, where the food was excellent, although they were always under fire from Ian Durrant's jokes. Finance was the baby of Douglas Odam, and he was always 'on the money!' Mind you, I showed up at his office one day and pointed out a little mistake in my pay cheque. The rent had been deducted twice in the same month and to look at Douglas you would have thought he had just fallen off the Kingston Bridge. His pained expression was that of a man who had made a mistake for the first time in his life. And perhaps it was.

And last, but certainly not least, was Jimmy Bell – the jack-of-all-trades and club kitman. He also helped organise the youth players, as it was their responsibility to ensure the dressing rooms were spick and span and that fresh training gear was laid out for the first-team squad. They even looked after hot tea and vitamins, and cleaned muddy boots. At first, I thought it strange, but it soon became clear that it was a fantastic idea. It was the perfect way to integrate the youngsters into the ways of the top-team players and because it was a gradual process, it would soon become a way of life. It taught the young guys a lot, about things such as humility and respect, as I never once saw anyone treat the boys with contempt or superiority.

Indeed, a fantastic and genuine relationship soon developed between the boys and first-team players. Of course, they might from time to time be the butt of innocent jokes, but they would also be the recipients of invaluable nuggets of advice, and gifts such as new boots or t-shirts. Those kids who progressed to the first team already knew the dynamics and rules of the dressing room. It was an ingenious idea, and even those who didn't make the grade would have many great memories, and even more so if they had grown up a Rangers supporter.

Jimmy also drove our minibus to training every day, and also drove the 'big bus' to games. He was a massive Rangers fan, proud to work for the club, and because I still have such fond memories of him, I can't reveal what he put in the hampers when we visited Celtic Park! He was as straightforward as the day was long and if he didn't like you, he told you. For this reason, he was respected by all the players. At times, partly because of my lack of English, I found it difficult to understand his fast and at times indecipherable Glaswegian brogue. Naively, I once made a joke with a reporter, pointing out that I had settled in well, and that my only problem was understanding our kitman. It was only a joke and Jimmy understood this, but it didn't stop him coming up to me and saying, 'So, you don't understand me. Maybe you will understand this a bit better,' and he held up his fist. We both burst out laughing, and at least I had realised it was a joke. In fact, I was delighted to discover he had hung a photograph of my goal against Celtic at Parkhead in his office. It was only his favourites who would find space in there, and woe betide anyone who touched his pics of Ian Durrant!

But while things might have been going well on the domestic front, there was still a real sense of frustration as far as Europe was concerned. We had also been eliminated from the UEFA Cup by Strasbourg which prompted another outburst from Knox, although this time he wasn't able to pick on me, as I had been replaced by Gordon Durie. It was explained to me that the management team had plumped for the strong-running qualities of Durie, although I didn't think that was a valid explanation. To be honest, it might have been wiser not to even try to justify the decision.

After the disappointment of Europe, we had to concentrate on the league, and everything was going well. I was on the winning side in my first Old Firm match, and it was an occasion that I enjoyed immensely. It is a special challenge for everyone involved, so much so that if someone tells you it is just another three points, they don't know what they're talking about. An entire city is literally split in half as a football match takes on far deeper meaning. It isn't just any old game. Running out for that match was one of the most incredible feelings of my life. Everything gives way to feelings and emotions that are kept hidden for the best part of a year, and unleashed only when Rangers face Celtic. The decisive goal that day was scored by club hero Richard Gough, captain par excellence, and the player who had returned to Ibrox to answer a personal

SOS. He ended up the hero of many, many thousands of people that afternoon.

I didn't score, but wouldn't have long to wait for my debut Old Firm goal. The next instalment of one of the oldest and most fascinating matches in world football would provide me with a large dollop of personal satisfaction. I don't think I'll ever forget it: 19 November 1997, Celtic Park – the almost impregnable lair of our great rivals – and without doubt the most important and prestigious goal of my career. The match had initially been postponed due to the tragic death of Princess Diana, and when it was eventually played, the atmosphere was incredible. You could almost reach out and touch it. Before the match we went out for a warm-up and even then the adrenaline was pumping. I looked up to the stands and every time I caught the stare of someone decked out in green and white, I would hear the shout, 'C'mon Marco, give me the cross!' Within a few seconds I had been verbally assaulted by everybody in that section of the stand calling for the sign of the cross, the symbol of Catholicism. And so it went on throughout the warm-up.

I looked over to where our own supporters were housed, and although they were very much in the minority, they were making lots of noise, and were certainly positive, which I tried to take on board to give me an edge when the match started for real. And it definitely helped, as I latched on to a pass from Gordon Durie and lashed a shot into the net, past the keeper at his near post. It was the greatest feeling I had ever experienced and I went, well, crazy. I was in a trance and ran to the nearest corner flag to let out the joy I was feeling, but the referee arrived there at the same time, and started telling me not to overdo it. But I was celebrating the greatest goal of my career with my own fans. 'No you're not,' he said, 'these are the Celtic fans you're embracing!' I looked up and he was 100 per cent right. And they all looked pissed off, screaming, 'Fuck off, you bastard!' Fortunately, my team-mates arrived to protect me, and we continued to celebrate – although just a little bit further from the furious Celtic supporters.

The three points gained in the match would more or less guarantee the championship, while maybe not in mathematical terms, certainly psychologically, as we had shown we could go to their place and win. But unfortunately, with almost the last kick of the ball, Celtic equalised, which highlighted gaps in our young defence. I was deflated but still received lots of praise from my team-mates after the match in the dressing room, which was appreciated, although when Knox joined in and offered his congratulations, and a warm embrace, I immediately became suspicious. Mind you, I felt appreciated. One goal had made me special, and I was now part of the Rangers family.

We were top of the table at Christmas, which allowed us to enjoy the traditional annual party by letting our hair down. It was a day devoted entirely to fun, and we started off with a morning on the go-karts, and Sergio Porrini once again showed his competitive streak by winning in style. We then hopped on the bus – adorned, wall-to-wall, with cases of McEwan's Lager (our sponsor) – and travelled to a nice restaurant where food (and more beer) was served. En route to the restaurant, the sound of the CD was almost drowned out by the noise of clanking beer cans every time we turned a corner! After that, it was back to Ibrox to get changed for the fancy dress party. I had convinced Rino Gattuso to go to the party as an ape, and suggested he wouldn't need a mask. He took it in good fun, and we headed off into Glasgow city centre on a legendary pub crawl. We laughed, joked and, of course, drank hard.

It was a unique atmosphere and certainly something I hadn't experienced before. My evening ended at the disco, and while I was much the worse for wear, I was still happy to have had the privilege of participating in such a fascinating tradition of Scottish football. And, no, I haven't forgotten to tell you what I dressed up as – I just left it to last, to give it the show it deserves. I had the honour of playing Dr Jekyll, while Gazza was Mr Hyde. We were an unlikely partnership but, as you will read in the next chapter, we soon became firm friends.

I celebrated Christmas 1997 in Glasgow with my family, the culmination of a period of calm and happiness. I loved the Scottish atmosphere during the holidays, when the city was full of lights and the downtown streets were thronged with people buying up last-minute gifts. There is a story that goes around which suggests the Scots are mean. In truth, it is a complete myth, and I consider them big spenders who have as their motto 'Live for the day', similar to a motto in Trieste that says 'Live life and then you'll see'. Sharing that state of grace with the people I loved was the best thing I could have asked for, and I felt blessed with my life in Glasgow.

XII

MY FAVOURITE GEORDIE

AFTER having words with him during the match against Dundee United, Gazza and I developed a good relationship and became friends. His mid-match outburst was forgotten and he invited Monica and I up to Gleneagles, a fantastic place about an hour's drive from Glasgow, and with three golf courses considered among the best in the UK. It had all the luxuries you could imagine and seemed to have been plucked straight from a fairy tale. It was perhaps the most fascinating place I visited during my time in Scotland. The journey to and from Perth allowed Gazza and I to open up more with each other, and he told me a lot about his time at Lazio, and of a mutual friend, Luigi Corino, the victim of his Roman jokes and with whom I had played at Cosenza.

Once at Gleneagles, I discovered we were there for the falconry – and there started one of the most enjoyable afternoons of my life. We jumped into the guide's 4X4 car and drove off in the direction of the woods. When we came to a closed gate, our guide jumped out to open it. Gazza pulled on the handbrake as hard as he could, and the result was it took the guide around five minutes – and both hands – to release it. With a puzzled expression, he drove on. It was a great day out and while the falconry was good – Gazza was unbelievable. We went hunting in the woods with the volatile creatures and the jokes were coming thick and fast. It was tough to keep up but I tried my best. Gazza then produced a thermos flask, out of which I believed I was drinking hot tea or coffee. Wrong, Marco, it contained only the finest whisky and I didn't want to refuse, so I necked a little. Perhaps Gazza saw in my pained expression that I wasn't used to such a drink, although I tried to hide it as best I could.

And then it was time for these amazing birds of prey to do their job. Our guide went over to the car and brought out two crates. He handed us a bird each and showed us how to release them properly into the sky, but when we tried to help them on their way, they just slumped straight to the ground. The guide was both confused and embarrassed. Were his birds angling for a day off? He called for backup birds, and while we awaited their arrival, I noticed Gazza's cheeky grin, and he let me into a little secret. When we were travelling down to the woods in the car, Gazza had been sitting next to the hawks, and had been feeding them chips and sandwiches, which was supposed to be our lunch. The poor birds must have felt like they had just eaten a three-course meal, so of course they weren't in the mood to perform.

During the return trip to Glasgow, Paul slept like a baby, and no wonder, as he had been busy making sure Monica and I had never laughed so much in our lives. But that certainly wasn't the last time we would be in Paul's company. When we had a short break in the season, he invited us to New York and we decided to make the trip aboard Concorde. It was just the most fantastic experience. Concorde flew at a height of 57,000 feet, where the air temperature reached -56 degrees, and it took us just three and a half hours to reach the Big Apple, thanks to maximum speeds of up to 2,200kph – faster than the speed of sound. It's strange, but one of the things I still remember is the partial disappointment derived from the grey leather seats. They were extremely elegant, but not the most comfortable.

However, the rivers of champagne started to flow at 11am, while the rate of acceleration during take-off – it touched 360kph in just 30 seconds – literally crushed me against the seat. In fact, while Concorde was smashing the sound barrier, it increased a few centimetres in length due to the heat causing the aluminium to expand.

The rest of the flight was quite normal and without incident – probably because Gazza was already in New York! He sent a limo to pick us up at JFK Airport, and we were soon dining with him in a rather nice restaurant. He told us of how on his way to a restaurant the previous day, he had come across a young homeless woman with dreadlocks and had invited her in for a meal. Gazza had a heart of gold, and he certainly didn't do it for the publicity, although it was in the New York papers the next day. He told us that before entering the restaurant, the homeless lady had covered her hand in saliva, and ran it through her hair, like a natural gel.

After we'd enjoyed a meal at the restaurant it was off to a New York Jets game for the evening. I recall a stream of people walking towards the entrance of the now demolished Giants Stadium and Paul stealing a cigar from the mouth of an unknown supporter, and continuing to walk as if nothing had happened. The guy looked at me in disbelief and I, wisely, pretended not to understand what was going on. 'Good start,' I remember thinking to myself. During the NFL match, the talented midfielder managed to convince me there was a fantastic prize for anyone who could get their face up on one of the giant screens. I wasn't the only one he had convinced, and there were all sorts of people doing silly things in an attempt to grab the gold. Moments later, Paul nicked some children's popcorn, and I simply couldn't look anymore.

During the break, there was a fun game in the concourse, where supporters could try out some shots. Gazza took part and almost stole the show – and all with a ball that wouldn't have bounced properly on the football pitch! When the game re-started, the result wasn't important, as the real show was taking place in the seat next to me. After the final whistle, we were making our way out of the ground when we noticed some fans having a barbecue. Gazza wanted a piece of the action and decided to eat a few sausages and hot dogs. Boy, he could eat, although as he dropped sausage after sausage down his throat, a large man, well over six feet tall, turned to me and suggested that Gazza was mad. In reality, he wasn't. As far as I was concerned, he was a genius.

Naturally, that evening ended in the hotel bar and while Monica and I, and Gazza's friend, Jimmy 'Five Bellies' Gardner, enjoyed a drink, Gazza did push-ups in the middle of the floor. After each push-up, he emitted a thunderous burp, and even Jimmy Five Bellies suggested it was perhaps time for bed, and asked Monica and I if we wouldn't mind heading off to our room. I pretended to be really tired, and we walked off, but we slipped out of the hotel and went for something to eat. It had been a great night and we returned to our room exhausted. It was straight to bed, but the phone rang thunderously at 4am. It was Gazza. 'Hi Marco, it's Paul, I enjoyed yesterday but that's me awake and I'm going down for a sauna. I wondered what you were up to.' I didn't even have time to mumble something, but the phone was down. What a character!

Gazza was something else but I like to think that I got to know someone much deeper than his public persona – the real Gazza, if you like. The Gazza that left a fine bottle of whisky at my place in the dressing room because he knew Monica liked it. He always behaved like a total gentleman around her and would open the car door for her – something even I didn't think of doing. I'll never forget the time we handed over a gift for his son's birthday and how he cried.

Then there was the occasion when he spotted a Rangers supporter sitting in the front row during a game at Ibrox. The guy had long white hair and a white beard and Gazza took me over to meet 'Santa Claus'! The last time I had the pleasure of spending an evening with him was for the feast of St Valentine. We were joined by a couple of Italian friends as Monica had arranged a romantic dinner for four at Cameron House, in Loch Lomond, where by chance we met Paul. He was wearing a terrible yellow and black shirt and I was proudly wearing, for the first time, an elegant kilt and, just as tradition dictates, no underwear!

By then I knew exactly the meaning of Jimmy Gardner's nickname, Five Bellies, which suited him perfectly. It described the shape of his stomach, which had become so big and swollen from eating chips and drinking beer. It stood out even more because he wasn't the tallest guy in the world. They had known each other since childhood and Jimmy soon became Paul's driver, secretary and handyman, who dealt with his 'boss' 24/7. It must have been the most difficult, challenging and unpredictable job in the world, but it didn't take me long to realise that Jimmy was also his best friend and confidant. Gazza could trust him all day long, even if he had always been the target for his jokes. These included the 'naked butt challenge', where Gazza would use Jimmy's butt as a target for his airgun, with Five Bellies being handsomely rewarded. I remember Jimmy waking up from a nap one afternoon to discover Gazza had shaved off half of his hair and both eyebrows.

On one occasion, when Paul and I were seated at a table chatting, he told me about his latest idea to wind Jimmy up. Paul explained to me in Italian that he had sent Jimmy to hunt for a particular tobacco sachet, like a teabag, only much smaller, which he would put between his lips and gums. Now this stuff was apparently all the rage in Scandinavia, but not in Glasgow. Jimmy was away for three days, trawling through most of Europe's capital cities in a hunt for this elusive tobacco – but he eventually hit the target and returned triumphant. To make things just a little bit more difficult, Gazza had booked Jimmy's flights, but not a direct flight to Scandinavia, which would have been too easy, but a flight with four connections before he was able to land in the deep north! Just recently, I was delighted to hear Jimmy had fallen in love with a personal trainer, which is an added bonus. She has already made him lose many pounds and apparently Paul is searching for a new nickname.

But the night we met at Cameron House was just like the old days, as Gazza decided he would encourage me to get up and sing the old Italian classic song – and former Eurovision Song Contest entry – 'Nel blu dipinto di blu'. Finally, he began to dance on a table, and obviously lost his balance and fell, tumbling spectacularly to the ground – but without suffering an injury. He simply jumped to his feet and invited the wife of Walter Smith, who was also there for a romantic dinner, to accompany him in a slow dance.

Paul was always very generous and one of his gifts, which I still value greatly, was left on my hanger inside a nondescript black bag one day. It contained the England jersey he had worn against Cameroon at Wembley, which was one of the last appearances he made for his country. And, most importantly, he had signed it, 'To my friend Marco'.

Gazza was often misunderstood. For example, he had a special way of dealing with sick or unlucky children. He would tell them lots of jokes, or how to draw moustaches on their emaciated faces with the same pen he was supposed to use for an autograph. At first I thought it disrespectful but then, seeing the smiles it brought to their faces, because of the attention he was giving them, I soon realised it was the right way to approach the situation. They were normal children and he treated them just as he would anyone else. There were other times, of course, when he perhaps crossed the line. Like when, during stretching exercises, he peed on the leg of a stunned Erik Bo Andersen, who'd had the misfortune to be next to him. Or when you found yourself minus a pair of socks because Gazza had decided to wear them home, or when he used your toothbrush to brush his teeth.

One afternoon we went to a gym in Glasgow city centre for a workout. We borrowed the Rangers physio's car, and stopped at a fish market on the way back to Ibrox. 'Just a second,' he said, jumping out of the car. Moments later he returned with a nice-looking piece of fish. We had no money, but in Glasgow he was a hero, and I asked him, 'Is that for your lunch?' He looked at me, almost offended by the question. Before reaching Ibrox, and returning the vehicle to the kind owner, we stopped again and he began to tinker with the rear seats. He was hiding the fish, the catch of the day. The poor physio apparently spent days searching for the source of such a foul smell, and then many more weeks trying to get rid of it. It was just another of Gazza's legendary pranks and perhaps the physio will finally discover the perpetrator through the pages of this book. Sorry Gazza!

One incident that wasn't in the slightest bit funny was something I discovered by accident. During a night out with his friends, which certainly wasn't recommended (one of them had the nickname Anaconda, earned by virtue of the size of his 'baby'), I saw him writing a few numbers down in the palm of his hand, continuing with these notes for many hours. In essence, he knew how the night would pan out and wanted to remember in the morning where his money had gone, because he would inevitably be 'burned'.

He was the guy in the squad I bonded with most, although it's a regret I only saw him at around 70 per cent of his enormous potential. He had so many strings to his bow and was a phenomenal mix of talent, personality, technique, strength, aggressiveness, vision, passion, imagination and generosity. He was the real deal. As a person, I also considered him intelligent, funny, brilliant, sensitive, exaggerated and never boring. We never discussed football but golf, hunting, Italy, Newcastle, family and children, and he promised to take me salmon fishing.

I am extremely proud of the fact he considered me a friend, and not just a colleague. Gazza will always have a special place in my heart, especially for all the wonderful memories that were drawn from those few, but intense, months. And, in general, I will always defend to the hilt Paul Gascoigne the person. I think nature chooses special subjects from time to time, who can perform special roles within a team. He was undoubtedly one of them. It's crazy how many things I remember about him, and in such detail, even though they took place a few decades ago, but maybe that's because Gazza made such a lasting impression on me, and those memories have become indelible.

Sometimes it's as though I still see movie trailers with myself and Gazza as the stars, a strong background characterised by 'Live Forever', a beautifully written song by Noel Gallagher of Oasis. The following March, Gazza moved to Middlesbrough and I'm still convinced that cost us ten in a row, because while he had at times been uncontrollable, he was also irreplaceable. Maybe I'm being selfish, but it also deprived me of a unique friend and companion. José Mourinho might not be happy about this but for Marco Negri, the 'Special One' will always be Paul Gascoigne.

Sadly we lost touch after he moved to Middlesbrough. A few years later, while browsing in a bookshop at London's Heathrow Airport, I spotted his biography *My Story* – awarded, among other things, the Sports Book of the Year title. I bought it and was pleased it included a photo of Paul and I. It was taken during our trip to Gleneagles, and brought back a lot of nice memories. I managed to get a hold of his mobile number through a lawyer, and sent him a heartfelt message and thanked him for remembering me in his book. He included the photo in a small private snaps section, and said it was one of the photos that reminded him of happy times. You can imagine my excitement when he texted back 'Fuck off!' which I took to mean 'Oh, hello Marco, great to hear from you. How's it going?'

I saw him more recently, although unfortunately not in person, when he was on TV during a match between two of his former teams, Lazio and Tottenham. He had aged, like all of us, but he is a character that always warms the heart; one you never forget, especially if you've had the good fortune to share a piece of life with him. There is only one born like Gazza every century and I won't be around to meet the next one. So, I don't even want to consider the possibility that he won't recover once and for all from his problems. It is my hope that his well-documented fall from grace won't be the end of an incredible character.

XIII

MY LIGHT BLUE NEMESIS

THE arrival at Ibrox of fellow Italians Sergio Porrini and Lorenzo Amoruso should have helped transform a little corner of the stadium into our Italian heaven, but instead, and for vastly different reasons, it had the opposite effect. Sergio and I got on just fine, although there was that unfortunate squash incident. With Amoruso and I, though, things had started okay – but went downhill in a relatively short space of time, and it didn't take me long to work out there was far more to Lorenzo than met the eye.

Actually, in a roundabout way I owed my move to Glasgow to Amoruso or, more specifically, the Fiorentina team with whom he played in the season before we both arrived at Ibrox in the summer of 1997. Perugia had to beat *La Viola*, as they were known, in the final match of the season to stay up. It was goalless when he kicked me in the penalty box, and Fausto Pizzi scored from the spot to put us 1-0 in front. However, our luck was out. Fiorentina equalised in injury time with a goal that was clearly offside and the loss of those two points proved crucial. That late, late equaliser was bad enough but Amoruso also elbowed me in the face during the game with such venom that for two days it was impossible to eat.

Amoruso is one of life's alpha males, but rather than use the strength of his personality to entice people to follow him because they wanted to, he preferred to try and lead by pushing his opinions on everyone else. He is the type of person who would travel around the world so that it could see him. His initials are LA and I sometimes wonder if even the city that houses Hollywood would be large enough to take his big head. Let's just say self-belief will never be a problem for Lorenzo.

The three of us quickly formed a friendship based around our shared nationality and the fact we had all arrived at the club at the same time. Rino Gattuso was a welcome fourth member of the 'team'. In those first two months we all lived at the Moat House Hotel on the banks of the Clyde and hung out together, sharing cars into the city or out to the stadium for training and match-days. Amoruso was desperate to be leader of the pack and when he wasn't deciding which restaurants we should visit each night, or whether we should eat inside or out, he would be busy telling us how he could have signed for Manchester United instead of Dutch defender Jaap Stam. Sure Lorenzo, sure.

My heart actually went out to him in those early days because he had developed a serious Achilles injury and all footballers understand the mental and physical anguish that comes with time spent on the sidelines, as I would come to know only too well. He wasn't out of the game for weeks, he was out for months and it clearly hurt him in many ways. One evening, for example, we were all dining in the fabulous L'Ariosto restaurant, in Mitchell Street, the oldest Italian in Glasgow, when a Rangers fan approached our table to ask for autographs. He offered his pen and paper to Sergio, then Rino, then me, and we all signed happily. Lorenzo sat and waited for his turn to scribble his signature, but the fan moved to walk away from the table, clearly not recognising him as a Rangers player, which was no great surprise as he had still to feature for the club. 'Hey, why don't you want my autograph?' he asked the supporter, quite seriously. He was also very upset with us for not letting on that he was also a Rangers player. He always wanted to be the leader, the centre of attention. It was an attitude that was strange to me; funny peculiar, not funny ha ha.

In those early months my opinion was very much 'each to his own' and he didn't impact too much on my life because he had gone back to Italy after surgery to rehab his injury and I was in my element, scoring goals left, right and centre. Mind you, even then his presence was still felt around the club when one day an Italian guy showed up at the front door of Ibrox asking to see Walter Smith. He was there for a trial and to say Walter was perplexed was an understatement. The guy wasn't even a professional player but an associate of Amoruso's, who had told him to turn up at Ibrox, mention his name and he would be taken on trial. I can still hear Walter laughing now. I think the guy was taken in for one session out of courtesy before being politely but firmly pushed in the direction of the exit door and back on to Edmiston Drive.

It was on the return of Amoruso to Glasgow came to the conclusion his behaviour was less blustering boaster and more that of a cold, calculating and potentially poisonous personality. Alarm bells started to chime when he moved in with Rino because the nature of his Achilles injury meant his apartment was out of bounds as it required him to walk up and down some flights of stairs. One Saturday evening after a game Amoruso was at home and Rino was in Glasgow city centre when the youngster's father called to speak to his son. Amoruso told him his boy was out on the town, something he was doing often, he added. Rino's father was so concerned about the undercurrent of the conversation, suggesting all was not well with his son, that he took the next plane to Scotland to have it out with his boy. Let me state for the record that Rino was never anything other than an absolute professional. He was 20 years old, for goodness sake, and Sunday was a recognised day off. Was he not entitled to spend some time with his friends on a Saturday night in the city centre and come home at 2am?

Naively now, I recognise, Amoruso remained a confidant of sorts but if alarm bells were beginning to chime over that episode with Rino, they should have been clanging when he sat me down one evening over dinner and told me there were going to be big, big changes at the club the following season. He hadn't even played a game for Rangers and yet he was confident enough to tell me I was looking at Rangers' next captain. For sure, we knew Walter was in his last season and the arrival of Dick Advocaat had been predicted in the press, but how could Amoruso know so much? More than that, he told me there were going to be some big-name players arriving. He knew he would be skipper, he said, because that position would not be chosen by the coach but by the chairman of the club. I knew then he was speaking to more influential people at

Rangers than his team-mates and that he was seeking to extend his own political power base beyond the first-team squad at Ibrox.

However, there were two episodes in particular that ended for good the friendship between Amoruso and me. One of the incidents almost cost me the most important person in my life and one of them irreparably damaged the relationship between me and Walter Smith. Firstly, my relationship with my girlfriend Monica, now mother to our beautiful son, Christian, entered a rocky period. We had started going out together the previous season and I knew straight away she was The One but there is a big difference between being together once or twice a week, as we were in Italy, and almost every hour of every day in Scotland. For the first few months everything went brilliantly, on and off the park, but circumstances changed when I picked up my eye injury and struggled to re-establish myself in the team. To many Scottish people I was 'the moody Italian'. I didn't always agree with that assessment, especially when I was scoring goals, but at that time in my life, when I was out of the team, I deserved the tag. Monica bore the brunt of my sadness and disappointment. I was wallowing in my own misfortune and stopped listening to the mundane and everyday aspects that make up most relationships as I closed my ears to what she had done that day and was planning to do the next. We were still young, these were ups and downs every serious relationship faces and must confront and, in a short space of time, our love was back on track, the bump in the road thankfully manoeuvred.

Stupidly, however, I had spoken to Amoruso about my relationship with Monica, trusting with my personal life someone I never should have trusted in the first place. By the way, I had the same conversation with other friends such as Rino and Sergio, but they knew their role in these discussions, which I have played myself to other pals in similar circumstances since then. Their job was to provide a kind ear and soothing words of comfort and support for a friend going through some difficulties. Amoruso? The day after our conversation he turned up unannounced at the home I shared with Monica to tell her it would be best if she packed her bags for a few weeks and returned to Italy, because I was struggling in the relationship and it was doing me no good. She was incandescent with rage, almost as angry as me when I found out shortly afterwards. Monica is no puppet, I think she told him to fuck off and mind his own business.

To tell the truth, she never did take to him. He once told her she should do something more constructive with her time, such as university study. 'Why don't you take a degree?' he asked. 'I've already got one,' she replied. She called me once, absolutely aghast, from the supermarket, where she had gone shopping with him and his girlfriend of the time, Cristina. Amoruso insisted on paying only for the items in the trolley he would use. Other goods, Cristina's feminine products and low fat yoghurts and the likes, she had to pay for herself – and all this from a guy earning a substantial salary.

Amoruso made some unkind comments in his own autobiography that led me to consider legal action, particularly when he alleged I was spending too much time in Edinburgh drinking at that dark moment in my career, early in 1998. His book was released at a time when I was trying to re-establish myself in British football and I believed his allegations could have unfairly damaged my reputation in the eyes of a potential employer or manager, but in the end I let it go. Alcohol has never been a crutch for me, emotionally or otherwise. My name isn't Amoruso. Mind you, let's just say I raised my eyebrows when I read in his book that he had turned to drink to get him through his bad injury spell. Bailey's Irish Cream, wasn't it? Hmmm. Any time I was with him, he barely had a glass of wine. Did I enjoy a beer after a game on Saturday night if we had the next day off? Absolutely, it was not a problem – and if I look back I don't ever recall seeing many of my Scottish team-mates sitting at the bar with glasses of sparkling water.

But, really, when it came to the drinking at Rangers I was the equivalent of that boy Amoruso told to turn up for a trial: an amateur, well out of his depth. Soon after arriving in Scotland I accepted an invitation to go with Rino to meet my new team-mates at TGI Friday's on Buchanan Street. Gazza was there, along with Ally McCoist, Ian Durrant, Andy Goram and others. My God, these boys would have given my Roman forebears a run for their money when it came to organising alcoholic orgies. Never have I had such a funny and enjoyable afternoon, but never have I hoped a day out would end so soon. At one point I lifted my head off the table and asked Gazza, 'Can't we at least order some food?' He looked over and laughed, 'Don't bother eating, Marco, it will only make you vomit.'

Amoruso did make me sick, however, with a sneaky backstab too far after I had stupidly poured my heart out to him again, this time about my unhappiness at being out of the picture at Rangers. Why did I trust him? I guess it's impossible to keep all your feelings locked inside and I was having similar conversations with Rino, Sergio and other friends. The difference is they weren't running behind my back to tell tales to the manager or chairman. It was a betrayal of trust. I opened up to him, and told him one evening I was feeling low because I wasn't in the team. Ally McCoist was playing well, my enjoyment in the game was waning and the Scottish rain was getting me down. My chance of playing a part in ten in a row was disappearing by the day and I was losing my opportunity to win the Golden Boot, never mind play for Italy. The eye injury had changed everything. Foolishly, I told Amoruso I wished the season was over.

A couple of days later I was summoned to Walter Smith's office, which was strange in itself because I'd had only two in-depth discussions with him before then, which may surprise some people. The first was early in the season when we met to speak about my ongoing problems with his assistant, Archie Knox. The second was in Puerto Banus in the February when he spoke to Sergio, Rino and me about how pleased he was with his Italian signings. Now it was the end of April and much had happened in those two months, almost all of it negative. He told me something had clearly altered in my mind, and that I wasn't training as well as I had done previously. He knew I didn't like the weather but that the season wasn't finished and I had to give him 100 per cent. It clicked with me immediately where he had received his information and I resented the fact he appeared to be showing greater trust in someone who was telling him stories, rather than someone who had scored 36 goals for him to that point.

Didn't Walter understand I'd suffered a serious injury? Didn't he realise I had lost so much fitness and had been rushed back into the team? Didn't he understand my unhappiness at being left on the bench or sat in the stand while Ally McCoist led the forward line? Didn't he realise I had been so unhappy and yet he was only coming to me now, to tell me off, because Amoruso had spoken to him? If he was so interested in my situation, why hadn't he spoken to me before?

A snowball had been rolling since the second that squash ball smacked me in the eye and now it had gathered such momentum it was in danger of flattening me completely. Walter Smith has a fantastic reputation for man-management, which I had seen with my own eyes in the way he had nurtured Gazza, like a father to a son, through some of my team-mate's most troubling periods, on and off the field. However, at the time, when I needed him most, Walter tried to play the wrong type of mind games. He could have given me the boost that might have helped lead us to ten in a row, but instead I felt undermined that he had listened to Amoruso and our relationship would never recover. The last time I met Walter was a few months after he had left the club and was manager of Everton. I was with Monica in Il Pavone restaurant in Princes Square one evening and Walter was there with his wife, Ethel. We shook hands and said hello, but that was all.

The aftermath of that conversation in his Ibrox office led me to rebel like a teenager and, sadly, I started to do things that were not so professional, although not exactly crazy. I still trained every day and did what was expected of me as part of the team, but I turned against one of the traditions of the club simply because I knew Walter wouldn't like it. It was selfish and stupid. When I arrived at the club, he expressed a preference that players wore ties to training and, if possible, were clean shaven. The shaving bit was always going to be a problem as I liked to go seven days at a time before picking up the razor again, but as the season drew to a close I stopped lifting it altogether. Soon, my picture appeared in *Rangers News* in a 'lookalike' feature and, true enough, I did bear an uncanny resemblance to Jim Morrison from The Doors. Walter didn't say a word, but my body language also screamed of my unhappiness and in the end it cost me a place in the squad for the Scottish Cup Final against Hearts.

Had things worked out differently, could I have scored the goals towards the end of the season that would have led Rangers to that fabled title? If things had gone the other way, I could have helped Rangers win ten in a row, I'm sure. I have regrets about that and should have done things differently, but life cannot be paused, rewound and re-recorded. Advising myself now, I would have gone to Walter and knocked on his door and asked, 'What's happening?' I would have told him I had scored goals for him, but that injury had left me struggling for fitness. I would have pleaded with him to reach out to me, to give me something. I would have asked for his patience, his support and not just to be left in the corner. We could have been good for each other. It was not easy for me to find balance in that first season in Scotland. It was another level from anything I had been used to before in Italy. Never had I experienced ten or 20 people following me in the street and shouting my name and treating me like a rock star.

You know, my mentality could have been better but I was younger then. I was a penalty box predator who relied on his sharpness and instinct to score goals. I played on the edge, highly strung like a thoroughbred horse, and that type of character can never be perfect. I'm also Italian. I'm proud, we're always looking for respect. That's the way I was and the way I still am, to some degree, even now. You cannot be what you are not. Sure, I was too macho, I should have been more intelligent and cleverer and approached Walter in an environment that allowed us to speak together more positively about the issues we had to address. You would have to ask Walter if he would treat me differently today in the same situation than he did back then. However, I also acknowledge he was working under the suffocating pressure of trying to deliver ten in a row, which put a much greater strain on the Scots at Ibrox than the others. We Italians had been in the country only a matter of months, while the likes of Walter and Ally McCoist had lived for many years with the nine-in-a-row record first set by Celtic. They had matched it the season before and they, more than anyone, knew what it would mean to Rangers fans to go on and beat that record.

Looking back, I was waiting on Walter to reach out to me, without the interference of Amoruso, of course. At the same time, Walter was probably waiting for me to approach him but maybe I was too young, too headstrong. Maybe I was wrong, but maybe he could also have handled the situation differently. In the end, I knew he was stepping down at the end of the season and pretty soon, I told myself, I'd be following him out the door. 'Another two or three weeks,' I remember telling myself, 'and I'll be leaving all this shit behind.' I knew Amoruso was destined to become the new skipper and that he couldn't possibly change. I was counting the days until I could follow Monica's example by telling him to fuck off. As it turned out, I'd be waiting quite some time until we said goodbye.

XIV

FALL FROM GRACE

FILM director Woody Allen once said, 'I'd rather be lucky than talented.' People are often afraid to admit how much luck counts in life, but it counts for a lot. In the context of football it's always there. The ball takes a lucky deflection and ends up in the net, or a net-bound shot touches a defender and trickles agonisingly past the post. It's the same in life. If only you had turned a different corner…

Wednesday 7 January 1998, at 5pm: the great Marco Negri, idol of one half of Glasgow, and plucked from Perugia at a cost of £3.75m, and worth perhaps ten times that since scoring 23 times in the first ten matches of the Scottish Premier League; the best strike rate not only in Scotland, but in Europe. I had a stream of man of the match and player of the month awards and was the undoubted front runner for Europe's prestigious Golden Boot award, but isn't it amazing how quickly things can change? If you'll pardon the pun, in the blink of an eye!

It was at 5pm that I ran in to Rottenrow Hospital with a bag of ice pressed over my right eye. I was in the wrong place and was sent to Stobhill, an accident and emergency hospital in north Glasgow, and a few miles from Rottenrow. I was seen quickly but, in my mind, the doctor failed to properly assess my situation. The squash match we had just played was still fresh in my mind. In order not to lose eye contact with Sergio, I had turned my head towards him, but at that very moment, with every bit of strength he had, he hit the ball in my direction, even though there seemed to be a lot of wall available. It hit me square in the eye at a speed exceeding 100kph. Our supporters would sing, 'Nine in a row, one more to go,' but perhaps not for me, if this injury was as serious as it seemed.

Everything was fantastic up to that point. I was living the life of a rock star, and thanks to Gazza, Monica and I got to meet a couple. We went to see Oasis in concert and were invited backstage after the gig. Noel and Liam Gallagher were big pals with Gazza – but we didn't get off to the best of starts. I was introduced to Noel, but shook hands a little too vigorously and he let out a squeal. His hand was obviously sore after plucking guitar strings for a couple of hours, while even Liam and I managed to get involved in a misunderstanding. We were chatting away but perhaps it was because of the thick fog of 'aromatic' smoke that hung in the air – an atmosphere much more 'Jamaican' than Glasgow winter – that I managed to put my foot in my mouth. In trying to compliment his pretty cool shades, I said, 'Nice pair!' The future Beady Eye frontman said something, which I didn't quite catch, took off his glasses and handed them over. I took them, had a look, noticed the brand and gave them back. He looked quite angry and bewildered, muttered, 'Okay, okay,' and put them back on. Monica immediately attracted my attention with an elbow worthy of a Scottish full-back, and started to mouth, 'Take them. They were a gift.' So, instead of returning home with a great souvenir of a great night, I was empty-handed apart from a sharp pain in the ribs thanks to my razor-sharp other half!

Just before the New Year, the popular Scottish comedian Jonathan Watson decided he would take the mickey out of me on the annual satire show *Only an Excuse*. I didn't see it but was told it was very funny. I suppose the mere fact that I was part of such a cult show proved my name was on everyone's lips. I was then the star of an advertisement which appeared on billboards around Ibrox to promote a beer which was apparently 'the most delicious in the world'. Next to the bottle were listed the major advantages of the drink and I was apparently the head, while Brian Laudrup and Paul Gascoigne were also considered to be vital ingredients in this special brew. I was proud to be associated with two such fantastic players.

Meanwhile, the most important thing on my mind was the problem with my eye. After an initial prognosis by a junior doctor, I was sent back up to Stobhill to see a specialist, Dr Saba. He told me that part of my retina was like a sail, flapping in the wind. A week later, I was back at hospital as I had been experiencing sudden attacks of flashing light. I saw Dr Murdoch, a specialist in ophthalmology, and underwent an emergency operation with the Argon laser. The intention was to get the retina back flat and adherent to the eyeball. The treatment was extremely invasive and more than once I felt like vomiting. Surgery went well, though, and the intra-ocular pressure decreased progressively. However I've been warned that, from my mid-40s, I could begin to experience serious vision problems and he strongly advised me to monitor and control the pressure of the eye and condition of the retina.

I was really worried for my future, but also the here and now, because I knew how much it meant to Rangers fans – and everyone at the club – to win ten in a row, so that weighed heavy on my mind. Celtic and Hearts were genuine contenders and we couldn't afford to concede any ground in the title race, but my contribution was zero. 'No physical exertion' was my instructions. No training, no gym, no driving, no flying, on and on went the list of things to avoid.

When I was eventually fit to return to the team, I managed just three goals in three and a half months. That just wasn't me. In fact, apparently it was four goals, as I was later credited with a touch on a Jonas Thern shot from outside the box! I genuinely did get a touch on it, and Jonas and I spoke about it and he had no problem with me taking the credit, although Archie Knox apparently scoffed at the suggestion. But when a striker is suffering a goal drought, he will take them any way he can, a fact I'm sure Jonas understood.

Our next match was away to Dunfermline and I drew a blank in front of goal. We still won, mind you, and Jonas scored a smashing third goal. After the game, while we were getting changed in the dressing room, Knox approached me, face contorted with that sarcastic smile of his, and said, 'I suppose you will say you got a touch to that shot as well.'

At that time, my life was a mixture of visits to hospital and football for Rangers. But despite the Scottish doctor doing a great job with the laser, I wanted a second opinion, and went to see a specialist in Italy, just to be sure that everything was as good as it could be. I wanted every possible advantage in the penalty box and, of course, I had the rest of my life to think about. I still had problems with floodlights, though, which was particularly significant, given the number of midweek matches we played on dark winter evenings.

The injury affected me psychologically, as well as physically. When I was out of the side, even when I thought I should be playing, my attitude reflected this. To a certain extent I rebelled. I grew my hair, cultivated a beard and wore a pirate earring, all things that sound a bit silly now but at the time it was my way of dealing with what was happening to me. My body language had always been very expressive throughout my career and especially when I went looking for controversy. It expressed dissatisfaction.

In April, I was told to be at a player of the year awards ceremony at a top Glasgow hotel, also because I was one of the candidates for a prize. It was a real gala occasion with the cream of Scottish football in attendance. The evening started off with a few speakers, and up flashed a selection of football highlights from the season just gone, and I was in among them. To be honest, until that damned squash game, I was the number one candidate; a sure winner in everyone's eyes. Then the lights came on again, and everyone was ready to acclaim the winner of the prestigious prize, and I got up and walked out. Rangers had forced me to attend, but no one told me how long I would have to stay. I was out of there, and you know why? I was jealous! Perhaps I was hoping that my behaviour would annoy someone, because I was just so frustrated.

By this point I was training just because I was contracted to do so. No passion, no thrills, nothing. Just a contract dictating that I had to go through the motions. This attitude cost me a place in the team even for the final of the Scottish Cup against Hearts, which ended in disappointment for the club. On the week of the match, the manager asked me to play with the reserve team to prove my fitness, as he planned to recall me to the squad. I told him bluntly it was out of the question. I was fit and ready to play and that was the end of it. I demanded some respect and insisted I had nothing to prove to anyone. Certainly not among a group of kids.

I looked on from the stand as we lost the last trophy of the season. It wasn't a nice feeling but even I was amazed at the attitude of our fans after that game. They had watched their team lose out on the European front and, even worse, watched ten in a row slip through their fingers, yet they still gave such an incredible standing ovation to the players, many of whom had just worn the famous blue shirt for the last time. It was a poignant sign of gratitude for all the trophies won during the previous years.

But my head was all over the place. It was a season that had started beyond my wildest dreams, but one that couldn't have ended any worse. I was determined never again to set foot inside Ibrox, as it had been driving me crazy for months. With time, however, I realised it would be a long time – some would say 'too long' – before I would be able to wave goodbye to Rangers.

XV

THE TUNNEL
OF MISFORTUNE

THANK God for the summer holidays. It might not have been a time to celebrate but at least it gave me an opportunity to get my head together and, to be honest, there probably weren't many players who had just endured the type of season I'd had. It was the ultimate in highs and lows, but the one thing that kept me sane throughout was Monica. We'd also had some ups and downs but our relationship was once again heading in the right direction, which was great news. We had taken ourselves off to the United States and visited anything worth seeing between Los Angeles and San Diego, as well as beautiful Hawaii.

One hot afternoon we were walking along a sun-kissed southern Californian street, and had stopped to admire the daring stunts of a group of young 'Evel Knievels' when my attention strayed across the road – to a tattoo studio. I've always been terrified of needles, and have fainted at the thought of giving blood, therefore getting a tattoo had never crossed my mind – ever. Monica? Now that was different. She had always loved them, especially small, tribal and colourful ones. I had an idea, and that was to seal the newfound stability in our relationship with something everlasting. I suggested we get each other's names tattooed on our arms. She looked at me, in amazement, but loved the idea and in we went, both to different cubicles. My artist asked if I was ready. 'As much as I'll ever be,' came the reply.

I rolled up my sleeve, he lifted the needle, and was just about to pierce the virgin skin, when it all came flooding back to me. I jumped out of the seat, made my apologies and ran out of the shop. From 0-40mph in five seconds! I stood outside for 20 minutes trying, in vain, to come up with the words to explain my cowardice. Soon, a jubilant Monica came bounding out of the shop, waving her tattooed arm in the air. 'Show me yours,' she was shouting excitedly. I tried really hard to explain my dramatic U-turn, and said, 'You know Monica, Marco is such a common name that if we ever broke up, chances are you wouldn't have to get rid of it.' Maybe it was the gag, or the fact that she knew only too well my fear of needles, but the moment ended in laughs – and I still haven't found the courage to keep up my end of the bargain. I have, mind you, had tattoos of tigers, scorpions and eagles done, although these are temporary ones that my son uses!

I enjoyed the close season, but all the time, I was subconsciously waiting for the phone to ring, to tell me that a new club had come in for me, and that I would be leaving Rangers. It remained silent. I returned to Italy, and just before the start of pre-season training in Scotland, the phone did ring. Real Betis had just been promoted to the Primera Liga, and the Seville club were interested in taking me to the south of Spain. Their president, the wealthy Manuel Ruiz de Lopera, was close to agreeing a deal with Rangers and my bags were packed. I was to be their 'marquee' signing, although my cases would remain packed for a month. I liked the idea of playing in Spain, as I considered Iberian football the most technical in Europe, and also a game suited to my style of play.

For the next 24 hours I answered every call within half a ring, but the decisive day passed without any news, and although I tried to keep calm and remain optimistic, I had a bad feeling. I called my agent the next day and he told me negotiations had stalled and there were serious issues between both clubs. He suggested I return to Glasgow where pre-season had already begun. Once in Scotland, I was told I could speak freely with the new coach, Dick Advocaat, and also with the chairman, with a view to trying to resolve the situation that had forced Rangers to try and sell me to the highest bidder. I was still convinced a parting of the ways was best for everyone concerned. Still, I was well aware that Rangers had paid a lot of money for me and that they hadn't had value for such a huge outlay. It was only right they would want to recoup as much of their cash as possible, although I didn't think Real Betis were the right club to offer that.

I was back home in Italy when my aunt Franceschina passed away, and I stayed on for the funeral. When I got back to Ibrox, I realised that the new manager was just like an army drill sergeant, which would certainly result in a high level of fitness and, just as important, an avalanche of trophies. I went straight to Ibrox to meet Advocaat, although if truth be told I didn't hold out much hope of reaching a settlement with the club. He seemed curious to know the truth about my situation, and asked about my relationship with Amoruso. He outlined his plans for the team, but never really asked me to return to play under him, while at the same time prompting me to leave behind the disappointments of the recent past. Mind you, I still found him frank and sincere, and felt that he valued my qualities.

Ally McCoist had left the club and I was really the only penalty box player, but unfortunately no one is so deaf as the one who doesn't want to hear, and I had already made up my mind to leave. I was willing to risk everything to convince the club to let me go. Returning to the stadium, the city, my team-mates and, most importantly, Amoruso, had reopened old wounds, which had really only been set aside during the summer months, and if Real Betis were interested – and I knew they were – I would have taken advantage of this opportunity with all my strength.

It's strange, but looking back, I believe that the tough and uncompromising Advocaat would have been my ideal coach. It was he who dictated the rules, the players only had to follow them. He was the leader, responsible for the team and its performance. Due to his highly technical and meticulous knowledge of the game, Rangers won everything there was to win in the ensuing years, and even achieved some terrific results in Europe. Had my situation been different, I could have achieved great things under Advocaat, scored a ton of goals and, more importantly, lifted some silverware too.

Next up was a meeting with the chairman, David Murray, who had made his fortunes in steel. As a young man, he had been a promising rugby player but a serious car crash had led to both of his legs being amputated. It was a cruel twist of fate but rather than let his situation get him down, he had used it to drive him on, and had become a powerful and shrewd businessman. He was an intelligent, interesting and polite man who had suffered much, but he never stopped fighting. In my first year at the club, I hadn't spoken much to him as he didn't visit the dressing room all that often. I still rated him highly, though. During our meeting, we both held firm. I insisted I wanted to leave, and pulled out the old story about the Scottish weather; cold and continuous rain. Without exaggerating, I said that during my first season I had enjoyed just 20 sunny days, which made me unhappy, sad and unable to give my best on the field. In addition, I promised never to play under the new captain Amoruso and said Mr Murray would have to choose between me and him.

He looked at me for a moment before asking me to rewind to that 'good, rainy day' when I signed my contract. Yeah, it was drizzling, and an excellent memory, and I had known that Glasgow wasn't exactly the Caribbean. He looked me straight in the eye and urged me to find better arguments than mere childish excuses. He said Real Betis hadn't come up with the cash and until they, or any other would-be suitor, did exactly that I was going nowhere. I now knew exactly where I stood.

A few weeks later, I was summoned to another meeting with Mr Murray, although this time the talks were scheduled for his Edinburgh office, which gave me time to have a good look at his bespoke Ferrari, one of the few in the world, if not the only one, with all the controls on the steering wheel. The meeting was far friendlier than previously and he spoke with real passion of his hopes for Rangers. He spoke of victory in Europe before scribbling on a piece of paper a new-look Rangers line-up which, to my surprise, included me. He spoke of new players before advising me to put my skills as a striker to good use for the team. Then, he insisted, that once the team had achieved great success on the park, it wouldn't be too difficult to sell me on, if that was what I still wanted. He also spoke of the overwhelming pressure on Walter Smith to win ten in a row.

At that moment, a strange feeling came over me. For just a few seconds I was envious of the special relationship Amoruso had established with such a person, but every time I tried to drink in what Mr Murray was saying and, more importantly, accept it, that damned pride forced me to stand my ground. The reality was I was dealing with internal conflict and was a victim of my own ego – and was angling more and more for a move to Spain. All of this had clouded my mind in a negative way and it was as though I didn't want to hear any more flattering words. As a means of justifying my thoughts, and to avoid playing for the club, I invented new eye problems!

Of course, these claims were instantly refuted by an eye specialist so I would turn up at Ibrox every morning and get changed in the dressing room before going off to train with the youth team.

The message I was sending out was loud and clear, 'Sell me now and recoup some of your cash, because you will *never* see me line up alongside Amoruso.' The dynamics of the dressing room changed towards me. Some of the new players warmed to me, and even urged me to re-join them in the first team, but my problems were with Amoruso. I didn't even look at him, never mind speak to him.

The thing that surprised me most, though, was my relationship with Porrini. He started to display a certain coldness towards me, and showed no sign of easing the tension, perhaps with an approach like, 'How's the eye that

I hit, just when you had the world in your hands?' Things became awkward between us, and he eventually stopped speaking to me altogether. Several months later, he sat beside me on the club minibus and, for the first time in a long time, he asked me how I was. I told him I was both amazed and annoyed by his behaviour which, frankly, I didn't understand. He tried to justify it by saying that part of his character led to him breaking off friendships for trivial reasons, and that he had once fallen out with a team-mate at Atalanta in the same way. I wasn't buying it and from that point onwards our relationship cooled further.

But there was always Gattuso, although by now, Rino had started going out with a girl, Monica, who would become his wife. She was the daughter of restaurant owner Mario Romano, a man I had known since first arriving in Scotland. My Monica and I spent a few evenings with Rino and his Monica, although they usually ended in disaster.

Everything would be going well when, without warning, something unexpected would unleash this young woman's jealousy, and she would kick off and cause uproar. Rino would take her bags, and she would be screaming and swearing. However, the anger would soon vanish and the two young lovebirds would hug, kiss and promise themselves eternal love. They were really cute and funny.

But even if the time Rino and I spent together was becoming less and less, I always held him in high esteem. I considered him a true friend and despite my continuing problems with Amoruso, I never once asked him to side with me, nor did I try to influence him in any way. I was aware of his determination and boundless desire to go as far in the game as possible and knew that any distractions would have stunted his progress. He didn't need any negative outside influences in his career. In saying that, I was slightly disappointed that, despite remaining close, he didn't show even a hint of solidarity with me in my hour of need. It wouldn't have taken much, perhaps just a phone call or a few words in the dressing room. In short, a bit of the personality he showed so much on the field. I know he was only 19 at the time, but I considered him more than just a mere team-mate.

Maybe I thought I was due something back, after acting like his big brother, first in Italy and then at the start in Scotland. At Perugia, for example, I went against all my team-mates to get him his bonuses following our promotion to Serie A. He had only made two brief appearances during the season but he was also allowed to participate in our celebrations. For me, it was all about fairness, and it seemed right to reward the commitment and sacrifice of everyone in the first-team squad. I also knew Rino could have done with some extra money in his pocket. Many years later, I realised I had probably been demanding too much from Rino, who was certainly more mature than his peers, but still a boy, far from home and family, and dealing with very complex dynamics in a strange country. On my part, I could have done more to help him understand what I was going through, although if I'm being 100 per cent honest, I myself would probably have kept my distance from Marco Negri at that time.

There were moments when I tried to visualise how different my Scottish experience could have been without the other Italians; countrymen that, instead of giving mutual support to overcome any difficulties, had proved anything but a help. In all my years playing football, I had never encountered any problems getting on with players from all corners of the globe. I played alongside Finns, Aussies, Danes, Swedes, Chileans, Serbs and, of course,

Scots, but the only problems I had were with Italians. Had I been on my own at Ibrox, there would have been nothing else for it but to embrace everything the country had to offer and get a better grasp of the language. But my situation was now crystal clear in as much as it was spiralling hopelessly out of control.

No team was interested in me, and no wonder. Both my mental and physical shape had become totally unacceptable, even for a back-up player, and it had been six months since my last match. My moods were becoming darker and darker, and watching Amoruso – who I now openly hated – lead out the team each week, and see the adoration he received by our fans, led me deeper and deeper into an abyss of confusion and anger. I even sacked my agent, Cavalleri, without a second thought. I hadn't forgiven him for pushing me to take risks in order to be sold. I reasoned that it was easy to be firm and courageous when you were 2,000 miles away, before advising me to once again become part of the team because it was my only option. That was unforgivable in my book. For God's sake, I had scored 40 goals that calendar year (including 12 in Serie A) and now found myself in such an unenviable position. How was this allowed to happen? Where was my proper guidance when I needed it most? But all these goals had somehow been allowed to slip into footballing obscurity. I was alone. A prisoner in a country I didn't want to play in any more, and I couldn't see any way out. I was tired of waiting for something that would never come – and my nerves began to give up.

At that time, Rangers had been decimated by injury, when one day the phone rang at my home. It was David Murray, and I screamed at him, 'Don't you dare call me at this time of day and disturb me at home. Maybe you haven't figured out who I am yet and, if you must get in touch, call me only when you have decided to sell me, although you could have done that some time ago.' These are the words I used to answer a friendly and professional call from the chairman, who was simply asking me to return to help out the team in its hour of need.

Mr Murray believed the time had come to draw a line under my situation. He believed there had been faults on both sides. He had offered an olive branch, and what did I do? I threw it back in his face – and then slapped him with it. I was completely out of order. Mr Murray, of all people, certainly didn't deserve that reaction. I mean, it wasn't as if he had called at 3am – it was only 9pm. I didn't stop to think for a moment about the words coming out of my mouth. There was no sugar-coating this conversation. I had behaved like an immature brat, and shown not an ounce of respect to a man who had faced so many challenges in his life; certainly far more challenging than a brash, arrogant Italian player who, by now, was specialising in just one thing – bad moods!

Looking back, it amazes me how a player who was known for patiently waiting to select the right moment to release the ball wasn't able to show the same quality in his personal life. The outburst had left me in a lot of trouble. Mr Murray slammed the door shut on any return to the team – and who could blame him? The ball was no longer in my court. It wasn't up to Marco Negri to decline an invitation to train or play with the first team. It was Mr Murray who didn't want to see me anymore – not even with binoculars!

But the biggest bombshell was still to come. The club stopped my wages. I was still welcome to train with the reserves, but I wouldn't be paid. It was the strongest possible message from Mr Murray. I knew what I needed, and it was a wise and mature football person who could help me: someone to advise me on how to handle a situation that was quite simply too big for me. I contacted dozens of FIFA agents and each time the answer was the same, 'Sorry, but can't help you.' Some even suggested the damage was irreparable and it might take a UN peacekeeper to broker a deal favourable to BOTH parties. My frustration was growing by the day and I felt like the central character in the movie *Groundhog Day*, in which Bill Murray is trapped in a vicious circle of time and every morning, at the same time, is awoken by the same piece of music on the radio, while the rest of the day pans out the same as the day before, and the one before that.

I waited for a miracle, but it never came. I tried to take comfort in the well-known motto 'Health is enough', so I celebrated the worst birthday of my life in a Spanish club in Edinburgh where people danced the Flamenco, perhaps to remind me of the doomed deal with Real Betis. I was with friends, including the owners of the restaurant Pavone, Guerrino and his wife Mariangela, as well as Enrico Annoni and his family. The former Torino and Roma star was nicknamed 'Tarzan' for his athletic build. He was a footballing contradiction: a tough and uncompromising guy on the pitch, and a pleasant and delightful person away from football. We had a great night, although unwrapping birthday presents on a freezing cold night in the car park, and trying on a couple of jumpers probably wasn't one of my better ideas.

The next morning I was running a fever and while in bed reading comics and having tea and toast, I had a visit from Dr Duffy, the Rangers doctor who, it turned out, also loved comics. He confirmed I had the flu and ordered me to rest. A couple of days later, however, my situation hadn't improved and I was admitted to Ross Hall Hospital, where x-rays found a white spot the size of a lemon on my right lung. I had bronchopneumonia and was put into a room where smoking was permitted, which perhaps wasn't the best way to treat my condition. I was prescribed a course of antibiotics, but that wasn't the only medication I required. I needed something to help with my moods, which had slipped dangerously towards depression.

I was in Ross Hall for ten days, and was only released when doctors were happy that my lung was clear. It was incredibly cold, though, and not conducive to a quick recovery. Ideally I would've taken off to sunnier climes, back to Italy perhaps, but I was still contracted at Rangers and would have to wait for the first ever winter shutdown – which was a couple of weeks away – before I could get away. I never did get that sunshine break, though, as the shutdown coincided with the opening of the January transfer window, both in the UK and at home in Italy, and that meant a chance to get a move to another team.

I had a new agent, Vincenzo Rispoli, and he was working hard on my behalf. Midway through the month, I was invited to train with West Ham, who were managed by Harry Redknapp. Rangers gave me the green light to head down to Upton Park and I caught the first available flight. The Hammers had good players, like Frank Lampard and Rio Ferdinand, but it had been almost a year since I had kicked a ball in anger and I had also spent the last month on the couch and in hospital. I played more like a pensioner than a poacher, and despite my commitment and determination to make the most of a wonderful opportunity, it simply didn't work out.

I showed some undoubted potential but, to be honest, at other times those looking on saw only the work of my slow twin brother, clumsy and predictable.

Mr Redknapp needed a player who was ready to play immediately, not someone who would take time to get up to speed, and after three days, I was called in for a chat. He told me I wasn't ready and he was right. While it was disappointing to hear, he was spot on and dealt with the situation professionally. But he also told me he could see why I had scored so many goals in Glasgow, which was nice to hear from a manager of his standing. From that moment on, I had a lot of respect for Harry Redknapp.

But the days remaining in January were dwindling and I was desperate to find a club. While in London, my agent told me that Vicenza, who played in Serie A, were keen. It was an interesting proposition as the British finance company ENIC had just bought a share in the club, and they also owned 25 per cent of Rangers, which could have had a bearing on the move. On the final day of the transfer window, a meeting was arranged in London, in the shadow of Big Ben, but set in the luxurious surroundings of an office just above the Warner Brothers store in Oxford Street, in the bustling centre of the city. Rangers were represented by Douglas Odam, a very competent man, while Vicenza, the first Italian club to end up in foreign hands, had manager Sergio Gasparin looking after their interests. I had spoken with him the previous evening and liked him.

My agent was also present and would prove a formidable opponent for any club chairman. He had brokered a deal to take Attilio Lombardo from Sampdoria to Crystal Palace, so I believed he was the right man to be by my side. That wouldn't turn out to be the case, though.

Douglas Odam opened by saying that Rangers had no problem with me going out on loan to Vicenza, but only if I gave up my claim to five monthly pay cheques that I insisted I was still owed. I soon realised I was on my own, and was getting little help with the negotiations. I was the only one who understood English, as Rispoli had forgotten to book an interpreter and, moreover, was constantly talking on his mobile phone to Lombardo, who was also eager to return to Italy. We were getting dangerously close to the 7pm cut-off point for registrations and I was becoming increasingly concerned. Fortunately, Gasparin understood my embarrassment and offered valuable support and advice. His timing was impeccable.

Negotiations lasted an entire afternoon between proposals, faxes and phone calls, and had been an exhausting experience, but now we were deep into stoppage time and I needed a result. At that point I agreed to give up the money I was owed, but only because the alternative would have been to go back to Glasgow, and once there, I knew I would become miserable again. I signed a contract that tied me to Vicenza for the next five months and only at the end of the season would I find out if that contract would be extended. I was happy and confident that I had made the right move. I was finally free of my problems in Glasgow, but I had paid dearly for my behaviour. I was ready to write a new chapter in my career, armed with enthusiasm and the knowledge that I would never have to return to Scotland.

XVI

OFF TO VICENZA

THE brief spell at West Ham had proved I wasn't 100 per cent fit, but I was desperate to show Vicenza I still had an eye for goal. It was a case of working harder than my new team-mates in order to be competitive in such a tough league. I was never an 'impact' player; I needed to build an understanding with those around me and I was determined to do just that. This was the opportunity I had been craving and I didn't want to let it slip through my fingers.

Vicenza were in a relegation battle, and I had been signed to get the goals that would maintain their top-flight status, but after just ten days at the club, coach Franco Colomba was sacked. I knew his replacement, Edy Reja, from my time at Bologna, and I liked him. He had been brought in to save the club from the drop, so we were in it together.

He was an old-fashioned coach, pragmatic and practical, and I had enjoyed working with him previously. I knew he would bring a calming effect to a troubled team.

He liked me and I viewed him as the ideal coach to witness the rebirth of Marco Negri.

With the benefit of hindsight, though, the best thing for me would have been to sacrifice my first three weeks at Vicenza purely to get match fit, and ready for the challenges ahead. No centre-forward ever forgets how to score goals, but only if he is at the top of his game, both mentally and physically. Instead, I threw myself head-first into the fray, putting myself on a par with my team-mates through heavy sessions which were completely different from those in Scotland. And it showed. We played a couple of challenge matches and I was way off the pace. I didn't play well and failed to find the net. I was a shadow of myself and Reja even asked if someone had tied a washing machine to my back, as I was slow and clumsy. Gennaro Scarlato took over as the main striker, and he was a player who would eventually make a name for himself – at centre-half!

Despite my commitment and determination, it simply didn't happen for me on the field. I had placed far too much pressure on myself and had too little time to prove I was the goalscorer of before. I did very little to convince Vicenza to keep me, and my fresh beginning was rapidly turning in to one big frustrating nightmare. I wanted it so much, but my mind had already fast-forwarded to June. Instead of concentrating on one match at a time, regardless of how boring that sounds, or simply thinking about the team, my mind was always racing ahead. Patience has never been a virtue of mine, thus the frustration felt in seeing things take such a turn for the worse once again made me react in the wrong way.

We played at home against Perugia and were 3-0 ahead before the interval. The match was all but over and

I was keen to do well against my old club, and get the goal that would hopefully set me on the road to redemption. With half an hour remaining the coach took me off and I reacted in the worst way possible. Apart from winning the team a penalty, I hadn't offered much else, but had always hoped. I kicked off and headed straight down the tunnel to the dressing room. I was angry because I desperately wanted that elusive goal and was thinking only of myself. As far as I was concerned, Reja quite clearly didn't understand how desperate I was. It was as if I was wearing a clock and the chimes were a constant reminder of the hours ticking away – and my future was anything but settled.

For my childish outburst, I was fined and suspended for two weeks. I deserved it, there was no denying that, but I was also accused of harassing the coach through some late-night phone calls, and on that charge, I was definitely not guilty!

During my two-week hiatus, a far more serious problem threatened to once again ruin the Negri career. I'd had some issues with my back but it was really starting to play up. I had been working non-stop in a bid to get up to speed with Vicenza and thought that all the physical exertion was to blame. That training, which I had undertaken in a bid to save my career, was now in danger of ruining everything. For my fortnight in the doghouse I was working with trainer Angelo Fulvio Sguazzero, and Gustavo Mendez, who was also in Purgatory for disciplinary reasons. We immediately developed a warm friendship, one which continued for a few years. He liked my personality, to the point of asking if I had Uruguayan ancestors!

As well as demonstrating infinite patience towards us, Sguazzero was also very intelligent and advised me to take advantage of this spell to work hard and get fit. I liked him and he would later call to wish me good luck just before I went under the knife in a bid to have my back problem sorted once and for all. In fact, he was the only member of the coaching staff at Vicenza to do so. My time working under him had been put to good use. I felt fitter and, more importantly, was ready to do what I could for the team. Something inside me changed while working with Sguazzero. I stopped looking to my future and started living for the present. What would be would be at the end of the season, and for once I was content with the here and now. I was welcomed back into the team by Reja, who proved the bigger man by holding no grudges, and my performances definitely improved. I was almost like a new player, and finally in a good state of mental and physical shape. I started to have fun without the sword of Damocles constantly hovering above my head.

I regained my place in the team and partly repaid Reja by scoring an important goal at home to Empoli in a valuable 2-0 win. We were fighting for our lives and the three points gave us a chance. Sadly my back worsened and I missed a week's training, only being able to play against Inter Milan with the help of painkillers. It was a fantastic match, and probably the best I had played at Vicenza. It was also eventful and I hit the bar before missing a penalty. I didn't give the Inter defence a moment's rest – especially Taribo West – and when I was eventually replaced, I didn't question the decision. We got a valuable draw and I really felt as if I was starting to get back to my best.

We were back in on the Tuesday morning for training and I had a bad feeling in my back, but the first thing I noticed was a slight pain in my right foot. I wasn't too bothered though, as I had always suffered from a fragile ankle and it was nothing, I believed, a nice bandage wouldn't solve. In the changing room, though, I stumbled several times which caused my team-mates to laugh and then, once the session began, I found myself without even the strength to kick the ball. I couldn't even raise my foot fully and Reja was annoyed, thinking that after a good performance, I had already relaxed. I was to discover that the major problem was coming directly from my back and an MRI scan showed the leakage of the intervertebral disc at levels L-4 and L-5, and a lot of crushing and damage to the sciatic nerve. That was why I had been feeling such intense pain and the function of the foot appeared compromised to such an extent.

I underwent a course of injections of nitrogen in the back and then a week of cortisones that swelled me up like a balloon. I tried everything in my power to recover, but was soon forced to face up to reality. Surgery was the only solution, and for a sportsman it was a very delicate procedure. But it was necessary, and I needed it straight away. My season was over. I went under the knife at Bologna's private Villa Alba clinic and was in the capable hands of Italian-American surgeon Anthony Fabrizi.

Post-surgery, I spent my convalescence period walking in the green hills of Imola, in Dozza Toscanella, which is considered one of the most characteristic medieval villages in the region. It was a beautiful place to recuperate, and the rugged landscape gave me my first proper physical test. During one walk, in the shade of a bright sun, a large and scary black snake appeared from under a rock, which made me jolt and jump back. I got a fright, but suddenly realised there were no twinges in my back, which was great news. It was the evidence I needed to assure me that the operation had been a great success.

I walked back to the Hotel del Re, an ex-convent, alone as a frightened Monica had long departed the scene. Mind you, it was a bittersweet moment, as arriving back at reception I was told that Vicenza had been relegated to Serie B. But after realising the op had been a success, I discovered a real desire to get fighting fit for the following season. I wanted to be in the best possible shape and was ready to play for any club in any country of the world. I was desperate to recapture the form that had seen me bang in goals at Perugia and Rangers.

Looking back, perhaps I had achieved too much too quickly at Rangers. They were a massive club with legions of fans all over the world. The first half of my first season at Ibrox had been incredible and the world was my oyster. I had the balance just right. I spoke just a little with the press and my attitude on the field was always first class. I had a job to do and wanted to do it to the best of my ability. But then I decided to 'sell' my image to the highest bidder. I even posed semi-nude for a calendar, The Italian Collection, in exchange for a large sum of money; I left my sponsor, Nike, and accepted a far bigger offer from Pantofola d'Oro, who were keen to market me as a contender for the Golden Boot, which gave me a huge advantage over my rivals. Soon I realised I hadn't actually achieved an awful lot. Pantofola d'Ora, based in Ascoli Piceno, went bust at the end of the season and I didn't see a penny of my money, which was a real blow.

But a new season was looming, and after the disappointment of Vicenza, I realised I needed a long soak in a bath of humility. I wanted to look back at my career and see where I had gone wrong, and try and learn from my mistakes. I still had time to salvage my career and make something of myself, but there wasn't much time to lose.

I was still tied to Rangers, so my destiny wasn't exactly in my own hands, but I did have a say in it.

I looked at certain aspects of my character, such as the conceit, arrogance, intransigence and stubbornness. These, if not exaggerated, can be potentially positive factors in a sportsman's career, but woe betide should the dose be wrong. Then, these traits can be extremely detrimental. My job required me to be part of a large group, but there was also the need for a single-mindedness, because when you went out on to that park, you had to battle with people twice your size and still find the time and space to stick a ball or two in the back of the net. You also need the mental toughness to battle back from injuries – and I had more than my fair share – as well as the anger and tension towards referees, opponents and coaches. The last thing you want to show to a hulking six-foot-six defender is weakness.

Rightly or wrongly, I grew up with a winning mentality. That had been thrust upon me from early on, but while I did very well in my first season at Rangers, I soon realised I was just a good striker, and not a world beater. It was the ability to realise my standing in the game that allowed me to return after injury with my feet firmly on the ground. I took advantage of every single moment of that summer in Bologna to cure my back problems at the Isokinetic Centre for Rehabilitation. I wanted – and had – to go back to Glasgow to face my immediate future in the best physical condition possible, but above all, I had promised myself to walk quietly, on tip-toes if necessary, through the front door at Ibrox to prove I had changed, and that Rangers could finally count on me. I had two years of my contract to run and I wanted to make it up to the people I had let down. That much, at least, was in my hands.

XVII

A 'SPORTING'
OPPORTUNITY

THE talented surgeons in Bologna, and their detailed rehabilitation programme, ensured I arrived in Glasgow with my back feeling as strong as ever. It was only a month since surgery, and the last thing I wanted, or needed, was a setback, but I was definitely moving in the right direction. I started off with some light running and exercises, nothing too strenuous. I had to be 100 per cent to have any chance of getting into Dick Advocaat's team. The Dutchman had assembled an incredibly strong squad – and they had just won the treble of Premier League, Scottish Cup and League Cup. They also had an amazing togetherness, and appeared to have the perfect manager. Advocaat had the ability to set his teams up perfectly, and had operated shrewdly in the transfer market.

Rangers had also become increasingly ambitious, and seemed determined to impose themselves more than ever on the European stage, and especially the Champions League. The positive vibes around Ibrox had also rubbed off on me and my attitude at training was first class. What also pleased me was the ease with which I integrated back into the squad. I was very grateful for that. Finally, I could sense that both parties – the club but, more importantly, myself – had left behind the grievances of the past in an intelligent and constructive way. The only blot on my reintroduction to Rangers, but one I chose to simply ignore, remained Amoruso.

Anyway, I had other matters to think about, like where Monica and I would live. After a thorough search of the Glasgow area we found a beautiful penthouse in front of the Moat House Hotel, and along the banks of the River Clyde. The other thing I had to occupy my time was my rehabilitation programme. The staff at Bologna had given me a table of dos and don'ts, although the don'ts, marked in red, were the most prominent. A relapse would have proved disastrous, so I followed it to the letter. I had already suffered more injuries and endured a greater number of operations than most, but had always dealt with them in the correct way, armed with patience and positivity – and always with the mindset that I would return the player I was, if not stronger. That's why I had taken care of even the smallest details on time and phases of recovery. I felt good and improved day after day, always showing commitment and availability.

I worked hard and just two months after surgery, I picked up a newspaper and was surprised to read the manager talking about me to the press. He had publicly praised me, saying I was a 'first class player', which was nice to read. I continued to push towards a first-team return, although perhaps I had been pushing too hard. We were taking part in running exercises one day when I pulled up with a strange sort of pain. It was as if a series of air bubbles had crept into the muscle leading up to the right buttock, and someone was massaging deep into that part of my body. It wasn't a stabbing pain, but more a kind of low-voltage shock. I wasn't too concerned at first, and believed it to be a simple muscular problem or a slight fatigue. It wasn't too uncommon in someone returning after a long injury. Indeed, it was almost necessary for the body to gradually adapt.

Nevertheless, in the days that followed, my back stiffened up again. Although I was worried, I thought a little rest would help, since it was now three months since the op. Apart from this small setback, things were going well at Rangers although I was taken aback when a call arrived completely out of the blue one day. It was from Marco Materazzi Snr., a coach at Portuguese side Sporting Lisbon, and he was looking for a striker to strengthen his front line. I still wasn't 100 per cent fit but wanted to know more and took the first available flight to Lisbon. Monica and I were met at the airport by a rather interesting individual. He was a thin little man in his 70s, with white hair and a bushy goatee, just like Robert De Niro in the film *The Deer Hunter*. He was the kitman at Sporting and throughout my stay, he was also my driver. I'll call him Mr Nao, as even though I don't remember his name, I was very impressed by the way he said the word 'no' in Portuguese, Nnàààààààààào, while vigorously shaking his head, as if you didn't understand how he felt.

Despite the language barrier, we were able to communicate perfectly, especially the following morning when I noticed a number of journalists and cameramen in the hotel lobby. I called him immediately, as I knew the Sporting chairman wanted to keep the deal quiet until my signature was on a contract. 'What do I do, shall I say a couple of things just to keep them quiet?' 'Nnàààààààààoo,' was his reply before telling me he would organise my escape through a back door. He told me which emergency exit to take. Try and imagine a quiet little grandpa who suddenly turns into a cunning bodyguard. When we got to the rear of the hotel, the car was waiting with open doors and we were whisked away at high speed. Monica and I had a great time in Lisbon, and that afternoon I had an appointment with the eye doctor as the Sporting medical staff wanted to make sure that particular problem was solved before any deals were finalised.

The effects of the drops, used in the past to help dilate the pupils, were particularly troublesome, and brought on dizziness and vomiting. After the tests, I asked Mr Nao to take me back to the hotel to rest a bit. 'Nnààààààààààoo!' was his answer. He had other plans for us. I tried to explain my symptoms, and put on a pair of sunglasses, but he was determined to show us the beauty of his city. Guiding us like the Roman politician Cicero, he took us to see many entrancing sights, from the cathedral to the Belem tower, the castle De Sao Jorge up to the Igreja de Sao Roque and the old town. We walked down the long bridge 25 de Abril over the Tagus River, and finally found ourselves near the sea to eat the best fish I ever tasted in a local beach bar. Who needed a nap?

Meanwhile, I started training with my new team-mates, including former Manchester United goalkeeper Peter Schmeichel, and I took it easy. Between one session and the next I also underwent an MRI scan on my back – Rangers had warned Sporting about my physical situation

– and it showed up some intervertebral discs which weren't particularly healthy. Later, when we started negotiating a contract, it became clear that the will of the coach was not fully supported by his board. In fact, Materazzi was removed just a few days later, although that was nothing to do with me.

The Portuguese press already had the story and suggested my signature was imminent. Sadly, I now knew different and they booked me a quick return to the UK. One thing that struck me was the look of disappointment on the face of Mr Nao, as he set off with Monica and I in his car for the airport. He barely said two words and perhaps thought I was the reason for talks stalling, or that he hadn't done his job of selling the city well enough to us. He had no fears on that count and we were very fond of him. When we arrived at the airport, I embraced him with sincerity and said, 'Muito obrigado.'

There was still only one small problem to solve, and that was to persuade Monica to get on the plane to Glasgow because she adored Lisbon and in just a couple of days had seen me at my happiest for a long time. Sadly, it was back to reality. But I had just one thing on my mind during the return trip to Glasgow, and that was to get back playing as soon as possible. However, the pain had become acceptable only with the help of anti-inflammatories. Otherwise, I had regular stabbing pains in my back and also a strange numb sensation in my right foot. I quickly lost the sensitivity of three fingers, while the sciatic nerve started to cause unpleasant tingling in the leg and calf. I was also dragging the limb badly because the tibial muscles, which should allow the toe to rise, had a deficit of 70 per cent. I found it difficult to perform even the most mundane daily movements and slept no more than three or four hours a night. Getting comfortable in my bed became an unmanageable task. There was no escape, and no matter what position I tried, sitting, standing or lying down, it was accompanied by the most excruciating pain.

Had it just been discomfort in the foot and leg, I could've put up with it, but my situation was deteriorating rapidly and I had to do something about it. Getting in or out of the car was a real struggle and Monica had to accompany me to Ibrox. Like my carer, she helped me to walk, climb stairs, take a shower or just sit down. The only way to find a bit of relief was when I lay down on the carpet in the living room and leaned my legs on a chair in order to form a 90 degree angle with my head resting on a soft pillow.

I spent an infinite number of nights in this position but the main difficulty was always trying to get up again. Alone, I just couldn't do it. The worst of it was, I was a professional footballer, not an elderly gentleman in the twilight of his life. The pain never left me: it was devastating and consuming me slowly and inexorably. I'm reluctant to abuse the term 'depression', as I've seen with my own eyes the damage it can cause, but let's say, pain aside, I was sad, disappointed, discouraged and suffering. If before I had been the guilty party in the destruction of my professional career, then this time it was the turn of fate that made me suffer the torments of hell and forced me to sit on the sidelines as a spectator. I was still being paid, but without the pleasure of playing. I wasn't on the field to share the joy of victory or despair of defeat. No more could I live the atmosphere and excitement of the game with my team-mates. In short, I couldn't even enjoy the best job in the world.

I had, however, developed a way of surviving as best I could, which included doing only the things I needed to. In the morning, thanks to medication, I was able to make it to a mandatory meeting at Ibrox with the doctors. Then, as soon as possible, I would return to rest on the carpet, hunting for the least painful position. An MRI scan confirmed suspicions that what remained of the leaked intervertebral disc had started to press again on the damaged sciatic nerve. A phone call from surgeon Anthony Fabrizi, the specialist from Bologna, informed me that they were willing to operate. At this point, the most serious risk for me had nothing to do with football. That was farthest from my mind. I was interested only in the full restoration of the nerve function and sensitivity of my foot. I had a heavy limp and no longer wanted to leave home, even for a simple walk. My mood worsened and when my worried parents came to visit, I gave my mother both barrels over nothing really. It was a shameful outburst, but I had become so irritable, inconsolable and helpless. I couldn't do anything for myself and I was frightened.

I was so thankful for having Monica and my family around me as goodness only knows what I would have done to help alleviate the pain. Monica understood my enormous difficulties and also the frequent mood changes, enduring with patience and devotion a person who had become so aggressive and unbearable because of the cortisone. The constant pain made me think only of myself. I saw everything through negative eyes and was definitely at the end of my tether.

I consider Daniel Prodan by far the strongest defender that Rangers ever purchased. The problem is, no one was ever able to see him in action due to a serious injury to his right knee. It had prevented him from training at 100 per cent, but he had already proved himself as a giant with Atletico Madrid and Steaua Bucharest, while he boasted more than 50 caps for Romania, and was captain at the US World Cup of 1994 and Euro 96 in England. We struck up an instant relationship. Of course we had something in common – our injuries, but he was very nice and outgoing, and while we had to communicate through broken Spanish, we definitely understood one another. He couldn't speak English and I became his translator. When you know the anguish someone is going through, and there are the additional problems a language barrier can bring, you do what you can to help. We comforted one another, and helped with things like morale.

Daniel was a well-built defender of at least six feet and could have lived by bullying strikers but suffered from 'Peter Pan syndrome'. He has always been a remarkable professional and very intelligent person who loved life in the dressing room, and the problems with different languages never prevented him from joining in the fun. Let's just say the day they delivered shyness, Daniel arrived late. He was able to create a gag from next to nothing, and peerless was his impression of a sumo wrestler wrapped only in toilet paper! It speaks volumes for the man that he did this while facing such difficulties in his career.

I was honoured by the invitation to join the Orthodox baptism of his son Razvan, held in Glasgow with a beautiful ceremony during which the infant was immersed in a marble basin filled with holy water – and given the desperate cries of the baby, I think it must have been quite chilly. At the party that followed, Daniel had invited, as well as many relatives, a Romanian orchestra that played Balkan folk songs for hours. Everyone was singing and dancing and we dined with bottles of whisky, as there was no water and it was bad manners to refuse a toast! He turned to me and asked with a smile, 'Are you angry with us?' and I replied, 'Not at all.' Even poor Monica missed her chair at one point and ended up on the ground, as everyone around us joined in with the laughter.

After workouts in the gym each day, Daniel returned to his wife and two children at his beautiful home in a location halfway between Glasgow and Edinburgh. So, in his spare time we couldn't see much of each other, but in the morning, at Ibrox, we became inseparable. We knew each other only for a short period of time but I discovered a warm and genuine person, and someone so highly respected in his own country. I am not surprised that, as a result of the esteem in which he is held, he was offered a role of great prestige by the Romanian Football Federation.

I looked forward to hearing what he had been up to as he was always good for a laugh. He had a terrific sense of humour and a vivid imagination. One day he had a surprise for me, and it took the form of a special Oscar-type presentation. I had often laughed at the underpants he wore, and one day he presented me with my own special pair, which I later had framed! Serious injury had been our shared problem. We had both been down the road of surgery, but sadly that had solved nothing and the problems had recurred tenfold and even more worryingly. We were looking for answers and, at the same time, someone who could perhaps help get us back playing.

The new Rangers team doctor was a lanky Dutchman in his forties and, if I'm not mistaken, he had been a good, young volleyball player in his day. He was a leading light in sports medicine and had already worked with several professional teams. Even though he was Dutch, he spoke with a broken English accent, although he had a poor sense of humour. He hardly ever laughed, and you could forget the odd joke or two. He was always in a hurry, and showed a sense of superiority in front of his colleagues. What really did get on my nerves, though, was that Daniel and I were treated superficially and whenever we asked for something, there always seemed to be someone more important or something more pressing. Perhaps it showed in our eyes, but I sensed from the doctor that he felt we should be doing more to recover from our respective injuries which, of course, was nonsense. They were far too serious to depend only on our willingness and dedication.

A new rule meant that injured players would have to report to Ibrox an hour before training so as not to hinder the preparation of the team. We were also ordered to remain at the ground until mid-afternoon. It was crazy, because if I was recovering from a slight muscle injury, or if I had to work harder to regain my place in the team, I would have been the first player to commit myself to eight hours a day, but given my condition, there wasn't much I could do, and I soon found myself suffering and wandering the corridors of Ibrox, waiting for the clock to strike a certain number.

The attitude towards me by club and coach was understandable. I wasn't playing, was costing the club money and my value was rapidly depreciating. Also, I was injured during a loan period that, instead of raising my price, had ended up scuppering the deal altogether. But I still think the behaviour of the club doctor was quite strange. In Italy, in the event of a serious accident, I would start my rehabilitation followed by specific medical guidelines depending on the individual case. When unfortunately a recovery was complicated, the doctor would have an important role to play. He would offer, above all, important personal support, focusing on human relationships and paying great attention to the psychological facets of the player concerned. And Italian medical staff often put aside unnecessary charts and predictions on the date of a probable return, focusing only on recovery. It cost what it cost in terms of time, attempts, patience and effort. My case exactly, and that of Daniel.

Most likely, the Dutch doctor had been put under pressure by Advocaat and perhaps also by the chairman but, in the end, instead of helping aid my recovery, he put my health at serious risk. He seemed rather irritated by the fact there had been little improvement and came to the conclusion, rather hastily, and in my opinion, too riskily, to opt for further surgery.

I wasn't happy about it and, more importantly, I worried about my after-care. What I needed was someone who had experience of proper recovery and rehabilitation. Unfortunately, this 'someone' didn't exist within Rangers' medical team and even less in the technical one. It was unacceptable that a player undergoing an operation on the hernial disc could be forced to take part in all training sessions just two months after surgery, when back experts all over the world insisted that the timing of the return depended purely on the physical structure of the individual. I have never been a warrior but, roughly, those periods are on average between six and eight months like the most recent cases of Gigi Buffon and Alessandro Nesta, which were similar to mine.

I was often forced to train alone because we could only work when therapists were free from other commitments. On rare occasions, I found myself dribbling and passing the ball to our Dutch doctor, although certainly not with the quality of his compatriot Marco Van Basten. I also found it pointless accompanying my team-mates on a ten-day pre-season tour of Scandinavia, looking on as they played friendlies. What made it worse was the lack of specific therapy or exercises to aid my recovery. On top of that, I was known as a spoiled brat and coward, even, who was afraid to go under the knife when, in Vicenza, I had chosen the operating room without a second thought.

Meanwhile, despite a positive and cheerful disposition, I noticed that Daniel wore the appearance of a frustrated man. I saw him one afternoon in the Ibrox gym, pedalling away on the exercise bike as usual, but not with his usual funny commentary of an imaginary competitor in the Tour de France. Instead, he looked deep in thought, down and, above all, seemed close to surrender. I suggested he visit the Isokinetic Centre in Bologna, where he could meet with esteemed medics such as Dr Gianni Nanni – one of the founders – and Dr Stefano Della Villa, and discover the benefits of a specialised centre in knee problems, where players such as Roberto Baggio and Beppe Signori had gone and recovered sufficiently to play many more seasons in Serie A despite serious injury. In 2009, the Isokinetic was recognised by FIFA as the best centre for the prevention and rehabilitation of sports in Italy and among the top 15 in the world.

While I was advising Daniel to visit, I also called and made an appointment. I had started thinking about myself as I couldn't guarantee I was being looked after properly at Rangers. I was almost convinced to risk further surgery, but first wanted to undergo a period of intensive treatment to see if that worked. Rangers permitted me just ten days' leave, and I didn't fully understand the time limit, because another op would've kept me out for the entire season. They were good in Bologna, but they weren't magicians. I agreed to the ten days, just as the Dutch torturer advised, but at the end of the day the back and leg were mine, not the property of Rangers.

I arrived in Bologna without wasting any more time and found that Daniel had gone home to Romania for a few days. When he returned to Italy, he seemed happy to see me and spoke of the improvements he felt had been made. He was more confident than he had ever been, and animated by a light in his eyes that showed renewed hope. I was getting worse, though, and suffering the most acute pain and many sleepless nights. Physiotherapists had little hope of a full recovery. Surgery looked a necessity although suddenly my chances of returning to the football field were given as 60 per cent. That was decent enough in a football sense, but it was the 40 per cent that worried me. There was a real chance that I would never regain the full use of my foot or back – and I was still a young man. But the operating room was booked for the following week in Bologna and Isokinetic informed Rangers. Daniel was aware of my decision, and saw me at my lowest ebb.

One morning, he asked to speak to me in private. By now he was running like a deer and, to everyone's amazement, lifting weights like a champion because he was being treated by a Romanian doctor in Bucharest who had designed and built a special machine, like a laser, the beneficial light of which seemed to have the power to regenerate diseased cells. This was the gist of his speech, delivered in a mixture of Italian, Spanish and Romanian. Daniel seemed to have benefitted immediately: the intense pain was gone, and he felt better day by day. And, of course, his spirit had lifted immensely.

For my part, I had nothing to lose. The surgery date had already been fixed and in the days leading up to it, driven to despair I should say, I tried some alternative treatments. Daniel organised everything and, once in Bucharest, his friend Petre made himself available to me during my stay, along with a translator to communicate properly with the Romanian healer. Monica offered not only fantastic moral support, but also physical help, as I simply couldn't stand up by myself anymore. I took off for Bucharest without informing the Italian doctors nor the 'luminary' Dutch, which, to be honest, I would've found difficult explaining over the phone. During the flight, I tried to imagine what lay in store. This would be my first time in Romania. I thought about the people Daniel had told me about, and tried to imagine this revolutionary laser, but found it impossible to visualise such a magical healing machine.

My head was now like the magic board on which children write and draw with a metal tip and then erase everything by moving the slider sideways. I had a thousand doubts, regularly driven by the despair of back pain, the confident words of Daniel echoing in my brain, and even intoxicated by a little voice telling me to go all the way with this treatment. It was a similar feeling to that I had experienced on the eve of a big match. I spent the journey from the airport to Popesti – on the outskirts of Bucharest, where the healer lived – looking out the window of Petre's car. He was a warm and friendly person who was keen to learn Italian, so much so, in fact, that he would be looking at his little phrasebook and offering random Italian words as we motored along. Sadly I was of little help and was lost in my thoughts.

The tired buildings downtown were a pale reflection of those in the suburbs, and the number of stray dogs wandering around was incredibly high. After hitting every damn pothole on the asphalt road, which caused stabbing pains in my back, we turned into a side street and stopped. I looked at Monica and nodded. I was ready to face the challenge with positivity, but one step at a time; although in reality I knew I needed a miracle. If things didn't go well, I would deal with that once back in Bologna.

I climbed the stairs of the house, which was so different from the luxurious private clinics I had been used to, and the first sight awaiting me was of a waiting room that housed a dozen people, including children. I was immediately taken by their eyes, which were anything but bright and happy, as they should have been at their age, but rather sad and melancholy. I didn't need a translator to tell me they were seriously ill and, at that moment, I almost felt guilty for being there because of a little problem in my back. And, what's more, the doctor invited me to enter straight away.

My instincts told me this guy was no fake. I had a feeling that Iount Vranceanu, a middle-aged man with a plump face that made him immediately likeable, might just be able to help me. He was a funny guy, with braces holding up his trousers, while he wore a strange pendant adorned with a transparent stone, which was probably a quartz. He told me he had graduated from the Faculty of Electronics at the University of Timisoara, before becoming a GP in record time. Finally, he concluded his multi-faceted training by enrolling in the Faculty of Parapsychology, before working as a psychologist in a military hospital. He was fully up to speed with my medical history from my time at Vicenza onwards, and invited me on to his therapy bed. As he carefully studied my movement, he started to prepare the laser. Through his multidisciplinary studies, he had been able to devise a strange machine capable of producing a very warm light that seemed to offer the same benefits as the sun's rays at sunset – when the sky turns so many shades of red – which he called 'Raza Nobila'.

The treatment, carried out in stony silence, lasted around 20 minutes. In the prone position, back turned to the magic machine, I looked at Monica who was analysing every little sensation. I felt a slight heat at the point of the body on which the laser was focused, but the hand of Vranceanu was always on the move, never stopping more than a second in the same position in case he burned me. A strange noise came from the bulb at the tip of the laser while in contact with the skin. I felt small tremors and unusual popping, similar to that in the summer when a mosquito is electrocuted by the 'zapper' machine. Incredibly, I didn't feel at all tense, as Mr Vranceanu's actions were relaxed and peaceful, and he showed great awareness in what he did, which was reassuring.

I was there on the advice of Daniel, and he would never have let me down. 'If you are going through Hell, keep going' was one of Winston Churchill's famous sayings, and it became my motto. At the end of the therapy, before saying goodbye, Mr Vranceanu gave me a follow-up appointment for the next day and suggested I drink lots of water, and avoid pork sausages or carbohydrates because I wouldn't be able to hold liquids. Petre immediately took me back to my hotel in the centre of Bucharest and I felt very, very confused. After dinner I tried to sleep, but it was almost midnight and I couldn't, either because I had become accustomed to sleepless nights, or because I was up and down to the toilet as a result of the amount of water I had drank.

When I awoke the next morning, I was looking forward to seeing the results of the initial treatment, although I still had to perform what had become a daily ritual. I sat on a chair and tried to lift my foot, holding the leg parallel to the floor and trying to form a 90-degree angle with a perfectly straight back. Usually I experienced a stabbing pain high up on the buttock, as well as from the back and along the right leg. It wasn't the perfect way to greet the morning, but necessary. The pain was still there, but definitely felt lighter and more distant.

Over the next three days, I was treated by Mr Vranceanu half a dozen times. In fact, given the benefits, I would've remained under his laser 24 hours. I loved it, and started to ask questions as to how it had all been put together. That place gave me so much positive energy and the improvement was unmistakeable. At that point, I was feeling the benefits, but had taken to asking him every five minutes if what I was feeling was normal – or just a dream. My mood, fuelled by hopes of recovery and, most importantly, without invasive surgery, was now incredibly high. I even accepted an invitation from Petre to visit the beauties of Bucharest, something which would have been unthinkable a few days earlier, when even sitting in a car was veritable torture. Petre was even able to get me into the 'People's House', the former residence of dictator Nicolae Ceausescu.

Before leaving for Italy, Mr Vranceanu assured me most of my back problems had been resolved. At the same time, however, he cautioned me on the need to manage my sporting return intelligently, and to take advantage of my time off. He told me everything would improve gradually but that it was going to take a little patience, as I was dangerously close to injuring the sciatic nerve permanently. The Marco Negri leaving Bucharest was a completely different person from the one who, just three days before, had landed in floods of despair and pain. My back resembled that of a spotty youth's face, peppered with acne, but Mr Vranceanu explained it was a clear sign of body cleaning. Apart from that, though, there was no discomfort, I was mentally regenerated, confident and aware that something positive had finally happened. But above all, I was glad I had met such a special and talented person; one who was able to treat me with a surprising skill and ready to receive me again in his treatment room in the unlikely event of a relapse. Finally, I was able to turn my face towards the sun and drop the residual shadows trailing behind. I was a free man.

XVIII

AN EMOTIONAL ROLLERCOASTER

BACK in Bologna, I was like an expectant schoolkid, refreshed and ready to tell Daniel of my positive experience. I also spoke to Pierluigi Casiraghi, that Italian striker of some note, who had been at the Isokinetic at the same time as me. He had suffered a serious and devastating injury just after joining the likes of Gianluca Vialli, Gianfranco Zola and Roberto Di Matteo at Chelsea. Pierluigi visited Romania after me, and I hope he also had a good experience.

The first thing I did on arrival in Bologna was to speak to doctors Nanni and Della Villa about cancelling my planned surgery. My version of the facts were perhaps not the most credible they had ever heard, and their initial reaction was to question the effectiveness of the treatment. They both gave me the once-over, and after seeing with their own eyes the improvement in my stretching, they were in complete agreement about cancelling the operation in the meantime. At that point, they simply invited me to resume the therapy and try a tentative recovery to see how my back would react. The reality was I was certainly much better and stronger than before. I had dealt with my situation the best way for me, and I would deal with anything that arose with Rangers. I must admit, I was ready to resume my career, and couldn't wait to get back playing again.

I improved day after day without any hitches. I re-started training and the more I challenged myself, the more confident I became, and I eventually overcame the fear of relapse. However, the terror of waking up in the morning and feeling the old pain again refused to go away, but was real only in my nightmares. I promised myself I would deal with the rehabilitation programme properly, and vowed to respect the timetable the doctors had mapped out. There would be no rushing back this time. Rangers' Dutch doctor flew out to Bologna to see where both Daniel and I had been treated and appeared happy with the clinic.

I was delighted to have avoided such a delicate and dangerous operation, and was confident about one day getting back to the player I had been previously. In a nutshell, for the first time in almost two years, I could see a faint light at the end of the tunnel. And all of this, for me, was like touching the sky with a finger. Sadly, I had to deal with the inquisitive eyes and cynicism of a cold individual, who was unable to admit the obvious improvements in both of us.

The cold, hard facts didn't seem to cut any ice with him either, not even the fact that Daniel was able to run, shoot, fight and kick the ball. He also undertook a test of strength and his once-injured leg appeared much stronger than the other. Towards me, the attitude was equally as sceptical, 'Is that it?'

The fact was I didn't feel any more pain, and ran and worked in training like a kid (and, indeed, yet another MRI proved that my back was almost totally healed). That seemed completely irrelevant to someone who should have known better, to the point where he dismissed me with the words, 'Live well in Bologna for another ten days and, I should say, all at my personal expense: visits, travel and accommodation, and then come back to Glasgow and show everyone you can work again with the group.'

Had I postponed the surgery, Rangers would've stopped my wages (not to mention the £90,000 owed from the previous season in Vicenza, which I hadn't yet received). I don't deny I was hurt. The cold and detached attitude, weighed by a ruthless speech that frankly I didn't expect from someone who had taken the oath of Hippocrates, struck me negatively. But after all I had suffered, it would take much more than Rangers' Dutch medical man to sadden and depress me. I took advantage of the rehab time I had been 'magnanimously' granted to learn more exercises, draw up a detailed table to ensure I knew what to avoid, but most importantly I had to accept the idea of being patient because I had been completely inactive for almost five months.

I received regular testing at Ibrox, and perhaps someone even wanted to see pain when they looked into my eyes. Instead, I felt fantastic. I had been working hard on my own and with the physios, but when I asked to take part in a training session to see how I would deal with it, the session took place under the watchful eye of Advocaat's assistant, Bert van Lingen. He was famous among the players for his unique training methods –they consisted of 20-minute bursts, with no rest between runs and extensions. It was tough, and his sessions concluded with stretching exercises that only he, and perhaps Heather Parisi, the famous American dancer, would have been able to perform. And what did that genius make me do? Shots, jumps and somersaults! They simply hadn't grasped the type of recovery work I required, even though it was far from rocket science. Or perhaps they were just sceptical of the methods I had undertaken in order to sort out my back problem.

I was working hard to get back to my old self, doing specific exercises alone in the gym at Ibrox, which can be soul-destroying in itself, and completed the programme by working at home. I was back in full-time training, albeit with the reserves, as per instructions, and was personally controlling what I did and didn't do. I avoided everything I had been banned from doing at Isokinetic, although it wasn't easy at all. Firstly, because even though I had got to know my back like no other, I didn't have a degree in medicine and was only a footballer. I was always afraid of doing something that would hamper my progress, because if I pushed myself just a little more than I should after so much inactivity, I was subject to minor muscle problems, especially at my hamstring due to fatigue, and that forced me to stop everything every two or three days. But overall I continued to improve in every aspect, and the back was holding up well. I could now sleep, I was calm and could even go out for walks.

But it wasn't just me who was getting some much-needed relief from my back pain – Monica also benefitted. And as Christmas approached – and the Scottish season looked forward to a winter shutdown – we made plans to travel back to Italy. I spoke to Dick Advocaat before we left and he told me he was giving me the same amount of time off as those who had been playing regularly. And as a result of working so hard in training, I was to be part of the squad heading off to Fort Lauderdale in Florida for a special training camp. Was Marco Negri about to dip a toe back into the first team at Rangers? The alternative was to return to Glasgow from Italy and resume training with the reserves in the bitingly cold Scottish winter. No thank you!

I was also fortunate enough to visit Romania after Christmas at home in Italy, and it gave me an opportunity to thank Mr Vranceanu, and tell him how beneficial his treatment had been. I squeezed in another session with the great man, but that wasn't all, as I was able to fulfil a childhood dream. While in Bucharest, I met so many hospitable people who made me feel instantly at ease – and I had hardly known them five minutes. Some of them were quite literally willing to share everything they owned with me.

And what comes from the heart, affects the heart. They did everything to make me feel at home, and I had no hesitation in cancelling my booking at a luxury hotel to spend those days at the residence of the Romanian magician. I tasted local specialities such as delicious soups (called ciorbe) and sarmaluzi, meat rolls wrapped in cooked cabbage, which were so appetising. Although I didn't know the language, and they didn't speak Italian (and even less English), the atmosphere was so relaxed that we all understood each other just fine – and that was when my childhood dream came true.

I have always been fascinated by the macabre story of the cruel Vlad Tepes (Vlad the Impaler), better known as Count Dracula from the popular Bram Stoker novels. I was only a few hours' drive from the famous castle in

Transylvania and was desperate to go there. The trip in the Carpathian Mountains turned out longer than expected but was still enjoyable, and when we arrived, it was the most magnificent and exciting spectacle imaginable. It was the middle of winter, snow was everywhere and the scene resembled something equally magical and disturbing. The castle, dimly lit in the dark of night, dominated a village of a few houses and inspired awe, and thanks to Petre's exaggerated tales – he had described the gruesome manner with which the Count punished those who didn't obey him – the majestic manor had a beauty and charm hard to describe in words, to the point that I remained open-mouthed and silent for a few seconds.

During my final meeting with Mr Vranceanu, he told me to be more daring during workouts, and for me that meant 'releasing the handbrake'! It was great news – and now I had Florida to look forward to. As usual, the faithful Petre took me to the airport in Bucharest from where I took off for London, and the short journey to Glasgow would complete the trip. My arrival in Scotland was planned for the evening, the perfect time to join the team ahead of our departure for the USA the next morning. However, what should have been a relatively simple trip from Bucharest to Glasgow soon become the most tormented journey of my life.

We hadn't even got off the ground in Romania when the flight was delayed, and then cancelled, due to dense fog. That was my first moment of panic. I studied all available flights and decided to fly to Paris via Air France. It was late in the day but I managed to get a seat, and I then called Monica in Glasgow and asked her to book me a ticket from Paris Charles De Gaulle to London, which she did. There were still problems in Bucharest and it seemed an eternity before we received clearance to take off. Despite the two-hour time difference between Romania and the UK, I was seriously worried about not making it back in time. Missing the trip to Florida would have been disastrous due to my situation with Rangers.

Eventually, the captain got the go-ahead from the Bucharest control tower, and I let out a mighty sigh of relief. Monica, meanwhile, had booked more than one flight because my landing time in the shadow of the Eiffel Tower was touch-and-go and, once on French soil, I discovered immediately that I could make the connecting flight to London. Bingo! The moment we arrived at Heathrow, I ran like crazy with two heavy bags I had kept with me all the time for fear of losing precious minutes. It was like a comedy film, with me slaloming in and out of people on the run to the final check-in desk, with the occasional bumping, and ensuing insults. I was out of breath when I arrived at the desk, only to be told by an elegant British Airways hostess, 'Sorry, sir, you're too late!' The hydraulic arm for passengers had just been detached from the fuselage of the plane and I couldn't do a damned thing about it – and it was the last flight to Scotland that night.

I called Monica in desperation. We discussed my options and she suggested the train, and started searching the internet for tickets. Meanwhile, I hailed a black cab to Victoria Station. The driver was speeding in the direction of the station when my mobile phone rang. 'About turn driver,' was the cry, as there wasn't a train ticket to be had in the capital. We were heading back to the airport.

Then the phone rang again, and it was my agent calling from Italy, 'You can't afford to miss going to Florida with Rangers. If you do, the consequences will not be so pleasant!' Really? Talk about stating the bloody obvious. But his next piece of advice stopped me in my tracks, and usurped everything 'Monica and Marco's Travel Agency' had been trying to achieve. 'Charter a plane!' Just for me? It was certainly novel, but he wasn't kidding. That's how important making it back to Glasgow in time was to everyone in my camp.

By now, though, the taxi driver was getting a bit fed up, although he helpfully advised that hiring a car at 10pm in London wouldn't guarantee me being in Glasgow by 6.30am the next day. A privately chartered plane was the only way I would be there in time – but it would cost a fortune! At first, we (Monica) couldn't find a plane for love nor money, then my phone, with its ever-depreciating battery, started to ring. It was Monica. 'Okay, in a couple of hours, a small plane from Belgium will land at Heathrow and the pilot is willing to take you immediately to Glasgow.' I will tactically gloss over the price of the flight, but let's just say it was less than the club fine for arriving late in Glasgow. I gave my consent.

It was now 1am and I had spent big bucks and a lot of energy, especially nervous, to get to this point. I was instructed to relax in a private airport waiting room to await further orders. I collapsed on a comfortable sofa and looked at Queen Elizabeth on the wall. I was keeping good company. I was shattered but a television kept me awake and a well-stocked minibar – understandable given the price of the flight – invited me to devour caviar sandwiches and sip champagne at just the right temperature. I'm not a smoker, but I was sorely tempted to pocket one of the Cuban cigars from the elegant wooden case on the coffee table. I looked every inch the seasoned businessman who, satisfied with yet another clinched deal, celebrated with a light supper before the journey. I afforded myself a wry smile, given that a nightmare day was about to end in the best way possible.

Confucius once said, 'When you are in a mess, you might as well enjoy the flavour.' Well, it was 2am and my slumber was interrupted by the roar of aircraft engines, and immediately came the long-awaited call. No need to check in, as I was the only passenger. I just had to climb the ladder of the plane, sit back, fasten my seatbelt, peep in the generous neckline of the hostess and take off. Sorted.

Well, not really. We had started taxiing up the runway when I was approached by the co-pilot, who told me there was a problem at Glasgow. If I heard him correctly, he referred to unspecified asphalting works. As a result of this, we would be landing in Edinburgh! That was the straw that broke the camel's back. I looked for the *Candid Camera* crew but they were nowhere to be seen. But surely the presenter was about to pop up, smile and force a large microphone in my face. Of course, it had all been set up with the help of Monica, the control towers of four European countries, my agent, the Rangers chairman, manager and my team-mates, and even the smiling Dutch doctor.

Perhaps my misfortune could be traced back to Transylvania, where Count Dracula, being unable to impale me, had sought his revenge in other ways. It was only when I reached Edinburgh Airport that I felt confident the Florida trip was no longer in doubt. Apart from the turbulent landing in Scotland's capital, it had been a decent flight, and my taxi was waiting at the pre-arranged spot to whisk me to Glasgow. In fact, I even had time to go home, grab a shower, prepare my bag and reach Glasgow Airport in perfect time, accompanied by Monica, who hadn't slept a wink.

Thanks to a week in the Maldives with Monica, I was pretty tanned and the first person I met at the airport was John Greig, the greatest ever Rangers player but, equally as important, a nice man and a real friend to me. He told me it was great to see me so relaxed. According to Mr Greig, it was clear the days of carefree relaxation had been perfect for me. If only he'd known about the last 24 hours!

But the time I spent in Miami would turn out to be really wonderful. The weather was ideal and the facilities of the university that housed our training sessions were fabulous. I trained at the same pace as my team-mates, and was able to participate in the first practice match without any discomfort. Even the worry of a possible relapse had disappeared and I was finally able to savour the joy of being part of the group, accept the competition on the field and take part in dressing room banter – the things I had missed so much.

One lasting memory is of a night off granted by the coach, and spent with the whole team on Ocean Drive in Miami Beach. Daniel and I were even late back at the hotel, but I don't think anyone noticed. Or, at least, we were never pulled up about it. The one person who refused to give up his bone was the guy in charge of the medical staff. He seemed to be stuck to me like a cat hanging by its fingernails to the living room curtains. Instead of treating me like a miracle, or even just normally, he kept pushing me towards the type of extreme exercises I had been told to avoid. Maybe he just wanted to show that my situation was all a bluff. During one session he went so far as to film my run with the camera before trying to tell me my gait was jerky, and convince me I had a slight limp. A footballer is not a sprinter and the dynamics of my run, because of a certain posture, were never going to be elegant. But we had reached a point of no return, and there was no longer the slightest human relationship, trust or esteem. If truth be told, there never had been.

Thankfully, the attitude of the manager, Dick Advocaat, was different. During a technical meeting he approached me and voiced his appreciation – it was the first time I'd spoken to him face-to-face since our initial chat, which hadn't exactly been the friendliest. It pleased me a lot, so much in fact that I had to look around to be sure he was talking to me. He told me he liked my movement in the penalty area. He was a true football man. I had achieved a good physical condition in Florida and on our return, I was able to train with determination, commitment and continuity, and keep up with my team-mates. Now I had to deal with the chill of a Scottish winter that made pavements slippy and pitches bone hard, which was bad news for my back, as it wouldn't be easy to make the last little step to complete recovery.

I alternated times when I was training well and with excellent results, highlighted by compliments from team-mates, and moments where annoying aches slowed me down. It was as if my body dictated when I could and couldn't train, and told me that perhaps I was pushing too hard on the wings of enthusiasm. February brought my one and only official appearance in the first team that season when we played Morton in a Scottish Cup tie. I started on the bench but came on and played a small part in a 1-0 win. After two long years I was finally back, surprising our fans as much as my direct marker who told reporters he didn't know who I was, but had been intrigued by my tan.

A friend of Monica's suggested I see Dr Jan de Vries, a Dutchman with a degree in Pharmacology, but a strong supporter of alternative medicine. His teacher, Dr Alfred Vogel, was a pioneer in natural medicine, naturopath and nutritionist, and they had worked together in a Swiss clinic for 35 years. When he moved to Scotland, he opened a residential clinic in Troon called Mokoia. There were similar centres in Newcastle, Edinburgh and London, and since 1990 he had undertaken extensive research on the effectiveness of herbal medicines at the invitation of the European Commission, while also working for BBC radio.

I wasn't bad at all, but was fatally attracted to anything that could help complete my healing journey. I became almost maniacal towards my health, a strange attitude for one who had hardly ever even asked for a massage. I remember de Vries as affable and well-balanced, unaware of my job. He treated me the same as any other patient, but immediately realised that, rather than physical help, I wanted emotional support from someone I could trust. After a few sessions, I told him about my career and of the problems with Rangers' Dutch doctor. His candid response left me thrilled. According to a Dutch saying, it was well known that some of his countrymen, to overcome the small size of the mother land on maps, used arrogance and presumption as weapons to make the whole world know of their existence.

His treatment consisted of two monthly sessions of acupuncture combined with a series of light electro-stimulations, before manipulating my back from which regularly came strange clicking noises. It was as though my vertebrae, finally back in line, wanted to thank him. I always ended up with small packs of tablets and bottles of symphytum officinale, a herb I had to drink every day. I had unwittingly created a 'private universal medical team' consisting of the Romanian magician, de Vries, Bologna's professionals, with whom I maintained regular telephone contact, and myself. I became quite knowledgeable on the subject and catalogued every sensation, positive and negative.

Together with my team-mates, I spent a fantastic week in Marbella before the final push for domestic honours. When the league was finally clinched, the presentation ceremony was something else. After the final home game against Hearts, Advocaat invited me down on to the pitch to join in the celebrations. As I stood there proudly in my Rangers blazer, the atmosphere created by our supporters was incredible. Red, white and blue ribbons adorned the trophy, while 50,000 sang at the tops of their voices. It is a moment that will live with me forever. The players wore commemorative hats with the words, 'It's tough being a winner… but someone's got to do it!' Bold, but emblematic.

My team-mates collected the trophy on a small stage in the centre of the field. If truth be told, while I was delighted to have been invited on to the pitch by the manager, I knew I hadn't contributed a single goal to the league win, and would have felt a bit of a fraud collecting that magnificent trophy, so I stood and applauded from the side. Mind you, I still had a burning desire to get up there and kiss the silverware, and it didn't stop me being delighted for my team-mates and our fans. Then we were invited on a customary lap of honour, but I was struggling to keep up with them because of another damned injury, this time a thigh muscle problem.

It had been the most emotional season of my entire career but the story had ended in the best possible way. The only downside was a financial one. From the previous October, I hadn't received the guaranteed bonuses as per my contract, and they represented a big slice of my monthly salary. But this wasn't the time to declare war. Instead, it was time to reflect on how I had ended up where I was. It had been a mentally draining season, and had taken its toll, but along the way I had met some special people, and thanks to them I was living life again and, most importantly, enjoying it.

But it was now the close season and time for a holiday, and Monica and I spent part of it in beautiful French Polynesia. We then headed back to Italy, where we spent time with family and friends, who had remained a constant in our lives. There was rest, but I also trained hard almost daily on the beautiful trails of the island of Bora Bora. The exercises to keep my back flexible and toned had become a constant routine and, now completely healed, I was determined my last year at Rangers would be a positive one. I was finally 100 per cent fit again, both athletically and psychologically, and wanted one more chance to celebrate on the field. Pride pushed me to prove to everyone that I could actually do it, and wasn't finished as a player.

XIX

007, CHAMPIONS LEAGUE AND CIAO, GLASGOW

I APPROACHED the new season with the enthusiasm of a rookie. Every training session was a bonus and I played in almost all of our pre-season friendlies, even scoring a few goals ahead of the preliminary round of the Champions League. I was back and had regained confidence in my ability, even feeling I could earn the esteem and respect of my colleagues. Before a challenge match against Livingston, I was lying on the physio's table when David Murray walked in. I hadn't seen, nor heard from him since our ill-fated phone call, but he wasn't alone. At his side was a gentleman I had seen many times on the silver screen, although this time he didn't have his Aston Martin, Walther PPK or beautiful girl by his side. It was Sean Connery, best known for his portrayal of James Bond. He came straight over to me and said he had followed my incredible start to the now distant 1997/98 season, and asked how it had all eventually panned out. He seemed genuinely interested but I told him it wasn't possible to answer fully in just five minutes – even for 007.

I had struck up some great friendships with the current squad, including Michael Mols, the fabulous Dutch striker whose rise was stunted by a bad injury; Ronald de Boer, one of the most talented players I ever saw on a football field, and someone who could play in any position; Rod Wallace, the great little English forward, and, of course, Daniel Prodan. Harmony reigned supreme and even seeing Amoruso every day had little effect on me. Perhaps it had taken Advocaat and his coaches a little while to discover the 'real' Amoruso. A few weeks later, Advocaat took the bold decision to relieve my fellow Italian of the captaincy and hand it to young Barry Ferguson, who fully deserved it. Barry was a really talented lad who had already proved himself at the highest level. I was part of the extraordinary meeting which was organised in the dressing room to formalise the decision, but was amazed that I felt nothing but indifference. I had never considered Amoruso my captain anyway.

I was content with my lot during this period and would be 30 in October. I had matured so much and the scars had hardened my skin and made me stronger, but also thoughtful and humble. I wanted to return to Rangers to be a good player, but also to finally enjoy my adventure in Scotland. It was vital that I made good memories of my time in an amazing country. I decided to look for a house near Glasgow University and found myself in Byres Road, a street full of cafes, restaurants, bookstores, and even those little vintage shops so fashionable in London. It was the most lively part of the city, populated day and night by students ready to have fun between classes and exams. They had little interest in football, which meant I could go around undisturbed and unnoticed.

With Monica, everything was fine. She hung out with the wives of some players and attended university courses. After training I would go straight home and spend the afternoons in the most peaceful way. It was perfect, and if I wanted the thrill of the city centre, it was just a short taxi ride away. I loved going to the cinema, entertaining dinner guests, or spending the occasional evening at the pub. Equally, I was at home reading a book or organising a trip out of town on days off. I had many friends: Italians living in Scotland, of course, but also Scots people, and not always those with an interest in football. I also kept up to date with the UK and worldwide news, and watched a lot of local programmes on the Scottish channels. After four years, I finally felt at home.

But this apparent idyll was ruined by being forced to chase a large sum of cash owed to me by the club. It was a hefty sum of arrears plus previously-arranged bonuses. I was back at training and with excellent results, to the point that even the Dutch doctor had to face the fact I was once again fully fit. I had also proved I was able to play an entire match without any problems. My agent and I felt the time was right to arrange a meeting with the chairman to make the claim, although just a few hours before the arranged time, Mr Rispoli called to say he had missed his plane. I had to decide quickly whether to cancel or deal with it alone. I looked back to the negotiations for my loan transfer to Vicenza, and how he had forgotten to book a translator. Not knowing any English, I had more or less been forced to deal with that situation myself, and it had given me valuable experience. I was never afraid to face anyone or anything so go it alone I would. Keeping the appointment would also allow me to potentially sort out something that had dragged on far too long.

I arrived at Ibrox with a sheaf of papers – accounts, faxes, translations, and data to help my case – and must have looked more the accountant than penalty-box predator. Behind a huge desk waiting for me was David Murray and his relaxed posture suggested I wasn't in for an easy ride. At his side was a South African friend of his. He kindly invited me to sit down and introduced me to his guest as one of the most prolific strikers in recent years, reminding him of the number of goals I scored. I don't know if it was a psychological move to make me to relax – in fact, I was very tense – or perhaps I missed the sarcasm and irony hidden behind his words. The fact is I was in front of my employer, the one that paid me and to whom I had never apologised for the rude manner in which I had spoken to him two years previous. But I was there, and asking for the money that belonged to me.

We were facing each other, like gunfighters before a duel. It was up to me to make the first move and I tried to be as clear and concise as possible. I showed him the documentation I felt proved my case. My English had improved tenfold and I had prepared for the meeting like a university exam. I don't know if the chairman was anxiously waiting for the moment to make me pay for all my past misdemeanours, although I'm not so presumptuous to suggest he didn't sleep the night before because of the meeting. Nevertheless, a veil of superiority did shine though in his attitude, as well as a touch of detachment and indifference. When I finished presenting my case, he started with a cold monologue that left no room for any form of interruption. He was perfectly aware of the situation and reminded me of the club's version of events.

I had sustained an injury while on loan at Vicenza, and because of this, since my return to Glasgow I had been used only once by the first team – even if documents from the Isokinetic Centre confirmed I was perfectly fit to play. In the second part of the season I had suffered further injuries, perhaps not clearly linked to the back problem but, however, in the same region of the body. During my recovery in Glasgow, from July to October, on several occasions I had closely followed the recommendations of the Scottish medical staff – the famous somersaults, leaps, obstacles and press-ups, exercises strictly prohibited by the Italian doctors. And I had always taken cortisone and medicines without a grumble.

I returned only at the beginning of the 2000/01 season, without even following the whole programme of work. In fact, I trained every single day, even while on my Polynesian holiday. So, he concluded that Rangers had firm reasons for not paying me the money owed, starting from my return from Vicenza, a club against which Rangers had filed a complaint and legal process to recover the unpaid amount while I was in Italy, as well as to claim a capital loss for the injury. In the event that their international action was successful, Mr Murray said I would get my money although, he added, the process could be lengthy. To be clear, Vicenza had paid me everything I was owed. It was Rangers at fault for not paying me according to the terms of my contract. Rangers should have been paying me through Vicenza. Therefore, their legal action to protect (in their view) me would actually constitute an action against themselves. Mr Murray, at the same time, recognised the strong commitment I had shown in training in an attempt to regain a place in the first team, and I realised they'd had to move into the transfer market to compensate for my loss.

It was evident both to my eyes and to those of the coaching staff that the best way to move forward would have been to give me a free transfer. The suggestion of the chairman had been for me to train and play with the reserves for a short period in order to regain the fitness and form that would've made me an attractive proposition to other clubs. In addition, they also offered me a sum of money – much less than half of what I was owed – as an advance on the potential recovery of money from Vicenza – the phantom lawsuit. In this hypothetical duel, I was firing blanks while he had hit me right in the heart. The meeting was concluded with a 'game, set and match' of tennis mould or a violent boxing KO due to a masterful hook. When the pauses between the chairman's speeches began to get a little too frequent, I realised it was time to say goodbye, collect my papers and get out of that room as quickly as possible.

Two days later I was sent to Ireland to play in a youth tournament. Luckily Daniel was also there and his support once again proved invaluable in human terms. By now I was forced to train regularly with boys of 18 and Advocaat had announced, through the sports pages of the newspapers, that my time with Rangers had finally ended. It seemed crazy. Just as I was 100 per cent fit again and ready to give the club value for their money. Although the situation was not exactly rosy, I faced that time in the best way possible. I was training seriously, playing hard and trying to have fun and, in the meantime, I cut out and kept – like all meticulous collectors – all items that spoke of my good performances and goals, potentially useful against the club in case of further arguments.

I ended the relationship with my agent. I forgave him for letting me down just hours before my latest meeting but decided in future to represent myself, and God knows I had learned the hard way. Nevertheless, I just couldn't understand why he had urged me to accept Rangers' offer, 'Just to get out of a bad situation.' In the past, I had given up some decent cash because I thought my agent was right and, I was only too happy to pay my dues, but this time he was wrong and to be honest, not even Luciano Moggi – the undisputed king of the transfer market – would have been able to find me a club. So, while I didn't need to hunt for another agent, I did need a good lawyer to help me take legal action against Rangers. I would have to take my complaint through the Scottish Football Association and FIFA.

Three years previous, I had met a lawyer called Claudio Minghetti, from Bologna, a very capable professional who spoke many different languages including, of course, English. In that period, when many of my Italian colleagues had chosen to leave the country in search of lucrative contracts in the UK, Claudio had turned into a real point of reference for agents relying on his ability to carry out and untangle the technicalities of transfers. He looked after Paolo Di Canio and Enrico Annoni at Celtic, Andrea Silenzi at Nottingham Forest, Gianluca Festa at Middlesbrough and, of course, my move from Perugia to Rangers. Our mutual contact lasted only the period of that particular transfer, but I hired him when I thought I would be the first Italian striker at Real Betis. He was of the mind the deal was 99 per cent concluded. On this occasion, and being only too aware of my situation, thanks to Annoni – whom I often confided in – he had offered to help me again and asked to read all the documents with regards to the case.

By day, I took my role with Rangers very seriously, but in the afternoons I worried about my situation. I also maintained telephone contact with a young lawyer from Manchester, Chris Farnell, a novice in the world of football, but one moving in the right direction. He was a friend of Minghetti. I have always believed a player should just play, have fun and enjoy the privileged life. He should never get involved with external events and even less in financial ones that put him at odds with his club. That should be the job of the agent who, in these cases, must demonstrate they fully deserve the percentage they receive on the salary.

The days after the legal wheels had been set in motion were mixed. Some passed off peacefully, while others brought with them a palpable tension and the heaviness of a stalemate that had gone on far too long. One evening, at the end of yet another day of energy-sapping faxes and phone calls on the matter, I was told I was playing in a reserve match against Celtic. The coach, John 'Bomber' Brown, was in the dressing room reading out the team and giving some last-minute tactics, but I was still on the team bus, gripped by anxiety. While everyone looked everywhere for me, I was sitting there, holding my head in my hands, muttering incomprehensibly and thinking about the way in which my career had gone. I had chosen Scotland to play in the amazing Old Firm games – but not with kids of 18!

Two highly-trained professionals looked at my case and reckoned I had a real chance of winning. In August, the SFA and FIFA were advised to consider my situation. Both ordered Rangers to sort it out by the following September and, in addition to the financial side of matters, challenged the club for excluding me from the first team and banishing me to the youths without any good reason, as medical certificates had confirmed my fitness. It was a clear case of 'mobbing', a term which in Italy would become fashionable in future years. All of this prompted the club to invite me to a meeting at Ibrox in September 2000. Douglas Odam was there, and I was relaxed and confident with Minghetti at my side. He was far too clever to have missed his flight, and he didn't need a translator. David Murray was absent, due to another business engagement. Rangers' approach was not the best, despite the letter from FIFA clearly visible on the desk of the secretary.

The meeting started and I couldn't believe what I would hear. Rangers' proposal was exactly the same as their previous one. The self-same one muttered by Murray just a few months earlier. Minghetti looked at me before staring straight at Odam, and saying, 'At least offer me a cup of coffee before I go!' He looked so confident when he spoke, and he had every right to, even though his words had me thinking inside, 'What now?' But from that moment, the atmosphere in the office changed radically. Perhaps someone had dropped a particular substance into Odam's coffee or, more simply, Minghetti had earned the respect of those present. Maybe it had been a 'tactic' by Rangers, but my lawyer hadn't fallen into the trap.

The results were immediate and, thanks to the level of my recent performances on the field, I was called up by the coach for first-team training. My name was even included in the list of players to take part in the Champions League. I wanted to embrace my lawyer, right there and then, just as though he had scored a winning goal, but I maintained a composed dignity while my insides exploded like Bonfire Night. Minghetti hadn't talked about the actual amount owed, but that didn't bother me. What was owed was getting paid. It was just a question of time. On that day, on that cup of coffee, was born a close friendship that still binds me to Claudio Minghetti, a confidant on which I can rely and with whom we often giggle thinking back to that moment.

My perfect physical state convinced Advocaat to include me in the squad for our Champions League match against Galatasaray. I wish! I would have been extremely flattered if, in reality, that had been the case but the presence of my surname on the squad list, however, was not the fruits of a rewarding assessment on my physical and mental condition, but the script demanded by the club after the meeting with Odam. It was 17 September and ahead of the first-round tie in Istanbul, the papers speculated on my possible inclusion in the starting XI. It wasn't to be, and I sat in the main stand where I was surprised to see an ashtray at each seat – which confirmed that even in the stadium, all Turks enjoyed a smoke. Due to a dearth of attacking options, I found myself on the bench for the return leg at Ibrox and witnessed a draw that gave us real hope of progressing in the competition, if only we could win one of the two remaining group matches.

On 27 September I received a fax from the SFA and, two days later, one from FIFA. Both spoke of finalising the financial settlement and a deadline was set. Sadly, Rangers failed to respect that deadline.

Less than a fortnight later, I was named in the team to face Dundee United at Ibrox. Many fans and journalists reckoned it was born out of superstition, as I had an enviable scoring record against United. The reality, however, was far different, and I knew it. I played because Rangers were still in Europe and had no intention of creating enemies in Switzerland. With my inclusion, they were telling the world they had no problem with Marco Negri and wanted everything settled in an amicable way. I played as though I was the happiest guy in the world and we won 5-0.

Despite a good performance – I had a perfectly good goal ruled out for offside – and the fact I had just proved myself capable of still performing at that level, the following week I was back with the reserves. When a reporter questioned Advocaat's decision, or motive, he curtly replied that it was 'just a normal technical decision'. The squad was down to the bare bones due to injuries etc, yet I was back with the kids. I accepted his decision without arguing, as these were the 'rules of the game'. I must admit, though, that during the 90 minutes against Dundee United, I felt incredible and lapped up every single minute. I was doing all I had ever wanted to do from the start – playing football for Rangers.

Soon 10 October arrived and the club told me they would pay the arrears, although there was a clause. Isn't there always? In exchange for giving me the money they owed me, they demanded written confirmation that I would not contact any other clubs until 28 February the following year. It might have seemed like an innocuous date to most, but it just happened to be the day after the transfer window closed in Italy. Coincidence, or a silly game? I will let others decide. I vowed to take the matter further, as it restricted my chances of getting another club greatly, as Italy was probably the place I would return to.

Meanwhile, I trained hard and played for the reserves when asked to. I was in great shape and was scoring goals, something which drew many compliments, until, unexpectedly, due to injury problems, I was called up by Advocaat for the vital Champions League match against Sturm Graz in Austria. It was 25 October and the best birthday present ever – despite the defeat. I played the last 15 minutes with Rangers already at a numerical disadvantage, and we wouldn't have scored even if the game had lasted three days, but I appreciated such a magical moment in the greatest club competition in the world. Hearing the Champions League anthem inside the Austrian stadium gave me goosebumps and, for a moment, I remembered why I had gone to Scotland in the first place. And it was a call from Rangers I appreciated, as recently the only calls I had received were of the legal kind. Meanwhile, Rangers had prepared my cheque and on the first day of November a six-figure sum was paid into my bank account, and with it closed an unpleasant chapter in my life.

Unfortunately, Rangers were beaten at home by Monaco in the final Champions League match and the subsequent disappointment was palpable, because there was a general feeling around Ibrox that this was the year Rangers would be reborn on the European stage.

Sadly, 13 November was the last time I pulled on the blue jersey of Rangers. The occasion was a reserve league match against Aberdeen. I scored in the first half and then, midway through the second, suffered a crunching challenge on my shinbone. One goal and a serious injury – perhaps the perfect way to sum up my time at the club. It was a shocking challenge and my shinguard completely shattered under the torn sock. The pain was unbearable and blood began to gush out while the bone rose to the surface. I thought it was fractured but, for once, luck was on my side and it turned out to be 'only' a rather deep wound. The studs of a young opponent had removed a rugged section of my skin, and it was a pretty horrific look. My team-mates ran over to see if I was okay but just as quickly turned away with their head in their hands.

It was an evening match and I was rushed to Ross Hall Hospital where I was subjected to a series of x-rays and also a hearty dose of antibiotics. After a night in hospital, I left with the aid of crutches and was then put through a series of sessions in the hyperbaric chamber, which continued for 20 days. Every morning I was forced to spend around 90 minutes in a pressurised structure – much like the cabin of a cable car – which exposed the body to the atmospheric pressure that was increased to two or three times more than normal, allowing me to breathe pure oxygen at 100 per cent (air, as it is in nature, which we absorb normally each day of our life, contains an oxygen percentage between 19 and 21 per cent). The sessions were used to saturate the body cells of oxygen and the result was an increase in control against infection, stimulation of the immune system and also a more rapid healing of the wound.

My only companion was an English crossword magazine and I would sit on an uncomfortable chair, ready to tackle the three sections of the treatment: compression, time of pressurisation and final decompression. Many older people recognised me right away but couldn't understand what a young football player was doing in such a place. When settled, I would look through a tiny window and give the operator the thumbs-up, which made me feel like an astronaut, about to leave on the trip of a lifetime to the moon. Only then could I concentrate on my crossword, but even if the pure oxygen flowing to my brain could have helped, I still failed to finish a single puzzle. I was informed of the need to treat the wound with extreme caution, because it was so wide and deep that, had it not been cleaned several times a day, serious complications, especially a nasty infection, could have arisen. I also had to visit hospital once a week for a check-up. After a month of treatment, swabs taken from the skin failed to highlight any infection and I was free to go. It was approaching Christmas and as a gift I sourced a brightly coloured cuticle to cheer myself up and help close the gaping shinbone.

My family joined me in Scotland and we had a wonderful time together. With the arrival of the New Year, I presented myself at Ibrox to once again train with the reserves. The first team had already left for Florida and I was taking part in regular workouts, with the ball at my feet, when suddenly, bang. I felt this incredible pain in my right knee and leg – the same leg that had been injured in the reserve match against Aberdeen. Initially, I didn't pay too much attention to it as in the past I had faced far greater issues. After a few hours, though, I couldn't even put my foot on the ground to walk. The pain had become intolerable, and I had the pale complexion of a ghost. With the medical staff in Florida, I had to rely on the reserve team physio, who advised me just to rest and use crutches. To get a more thorough examination I would have to wait a few more days until the first team returned from the States. The pain was constant, intense and didn't let up one bit.

When I eventually saw the Dutch doctor, he actually showed compassion and concern for my condition. He immediately booked an MRI and two bone scans with a cocktail of radiopharmaceuticals injected into my veins – a mix of radioactive substances called 'tracers'. I was told to avoid contact with children in the hours after each exam, such was the high levels of toxicity in my body. With a few days off, I travelled over to Bucharest, and I didn't tell a soul. I sat at the boarding gate gazing out from behind the pages of a newspaper, like a spy from a James Bond movie! When I landed in Romania, I was unable to walk without my crutches. After only two days of treatment in the hands of the healer, I started to feel much better. When it was time to return to Glasgow, the crutches were redundant, and I even ran ten or 20 yards at the airport to test the leg. I was overjoyed, but in reality, it was all in my mind because the worst was yet to come. Dr Gert Jan Goudswaard, the Rangers doctor, whom I haven't mentioned by name until now, and you can probably understand why as it's quite a mouthful, told me that the scans had shown up an inflammation of the shinbone. According to him, it was most likely connected to the wound and the clinical diagnosis revealed a likely osteomyelitis (bone infection) at the top of the shinbone. The haematologic response to this infection was minimal with a white blood cell count not higher than 6.9 and other values which were more or less normal. The meticulous investigation carried out on my blood by Dr Hay in the labs of Ross Hall reported a substantial reduction in the number of lymphocytes and also the unbelievable confirmation of a CD 4 Lymphophenia that required urgent attention, and the intervention of an immunologist.

I was immediately hospitalised and visited by a concerned Goudswaard who, yet again, showed his compassionate and friendly side. For the first time I felt like his patient and not just another footballer. In fact, he was genuinely concerned about my health and kept me fully informed about all developments related to the osteomyelitis and warned me I was probably facing invasive surgery, even mentioning that a hole might have to be drilled into the bone to allow the infected fluid to flow out.

But because I was convinced I had solved everything with the trip to Romania, I didn't grasp the seriousness of the situation. The properties of the blood, which had been attacked by a lymphogranuloma or lymphosarcoma, remained similar to those of an AIDS patient, if not someone suffering from Hodgkin's disease. I had witnessed some genuinely cold weather while in Scotland, but nothing like the chill I started to feel inside. It wasn't the fear of having to deal with yet another injury, nor the discomfort of being out of contract and, therefore, the pressure to find a new club, nor even the disappointment of having to end my career in that manner. Rather, it was the terrifying prospect of learning that I could be seriously ill. I hadn't even considered the possibility of being HIV positive but the harsh reality was there in front of me in the medical report, and it was hard to ignore and digest.

I didn't feel able to deal with such a thing alone. I needed my family around me and wanted to undergo further tests in Italy to understand exactly what was going on, the risks and chances of recovery. I had to return to Italy, and not on a temporary basis. I asked my lawyer to speak to Rangers about an early dissolution of my contract. I only wanted to focus on one thing, and it wasn't football. I needn't have worried about Rangers' response because it seemed they too shared my sentiments, and insisted my health was priority. They had no objections to the premature ending of our relationship, which was something I really appreciated, although it also showed me how serious my condition was. As soon as I was discharged from hospital, Monica and I organised a dinner and invited just a few friends. The next morning, I flew from Glasgow to Bologna, where an MRI bone scan had been fixed for 13 February – and where I also feared the most important withdrawal of blood of my entire life.

Luckily, I didn't have to wait long to learn I wasn't suffering from osteomyelitis, but simply a stress fracture of the tibial axis of the knee. This diagnosis was given by doctors in Bologna. In Scotland they hadn't got it right this time, even if the results of three blood tests confirmed some anomalies that couldn't be overlooked.

The immunologist, aware of my recent history, suggested a few days off to relax. After this, we would repeat the sampling. He was reassuring and optimistic, and despite the fact the reality wasn't exactly rosy, he saw some hope. Monica and I visited the Maldives, and followed the advice of the doctor carefully. We relaxed, but were never able to completely forget the problems with my blood. On our return, the results were in and I couldn't have been happier with the outcome. My blood was absolutely fine and there was no need for medication or invasive treatment. My drama had been resolved in the best way possible, and I put behind me the endless days of terror when the worst case scenario was swimming around in my head. On my personal horizon appeared the sunset, the one that closed my adventure in bonny Scotland. But, like all sunsets (especially the ones so rare in Scotland due to the gloomy weather, although incredibly breathtaking in summer around midnight), it was still unique and intriguing: its pastel colours arose in my mind with a touch of melancholy, intimate thoughts and reflections, and a feeling of serenity.

Even after all these years, I can honestly say my time at Rangers was really intense and never boring. Three and a half years on a rollercoaster – crazy for both the speed with which everything seemed to happen, and the constant ups and downs. I was precipitated from a resounding grace period, when everything went the right way, to rock bottom, and I no longer felt like a footballer. And then the emotions…happiness first, then sadness; I shed tears of joy, satisfaction, pain and anger.

I had received many awards for best player in a game, and other 'virtual' ones for the worst possible behaviour. Almost four years was a substantial portion of the life of a 30-year-old man, rich (in my case) of episodes and anecdotes to tell the grandchildren. The sages say that those who return from a trip are never the same as the ones who left. In Glasgow I matured and became a man. I was sincerely fond of Scotland and the Scots, I lived and loved the habits and customs of that fascinating land, rich in tradition and history – but no, I never did see any monster emerge from the water at Loch Ness! I loved living in that cosmopolitan, lively and fun city and, more importantly, had the privilege of meeting many truly special people that I will always carry in my heart.

To answer the classic question, 'If you could go back in time, what would you do differently?' I can only say I have always tried to be honest and fair, both on and off the field, and with everyone but most importantly, with myself. That's why I wanted to cover my time in Scotland in this book with 100 per cent honesty. I have no regrets but some remorse, perhaps. But that's fine. I can't deny that on several occasions I behaved in completely the wrong way, when the aim was to create tension and obtain a strong reaction. Let's just say I assembled the Lego bricks without following the instructions in the manual. I acted on my own and paid attention only to instinct. But I've always dealt with the consequences without feeling sorry for myself and paid dearly for mistakes made. If I could, I would rewrite that damn 'day off' on 7 January 1998, and would have chosen to go shopping with Monica in the centre of Glasgow rather than playing squash with Sergio Porrini. Chasing round after Monica and carrying all her bags would have been just as much of a workout, believe me!

Thanks to the internet, I still follow Rangers with great passion on satellite TV channels. The good thing about time is that it has the ability to erase, or at least to make the more painful memories fade away, so that I only remember the good times. I like keeping abreast of the goings-on at Ibrox, but even that has made for painful viewing these last couple of years. Sadly, Friday 13 July 2012, is a date I will never forget, and not because of any superstitious tendencies. It was the day the Scottish Football Association decided that one of the most famous clubs in the world would indeed have to start in the bottom league of Scottish football. A club with a record number of top league titles, and for whom I was proud to wear the jersey, would play in the Third Division alongside many of the lesser lights of the Scottish game. I followed it step-by-step and it broke my heart. I still hoped the SFA, and its chief executive Stewart Regan, would come up with a plan to allow my old club to remain in the top league, for the benefit of the game, but it wasn't to be.

Of course I worried for Rangers, but also the Scottish game as I wondered what kind of Premier League we would be left with – and no Old Firm league matches for a few years. Unthinkable.

Rangers fans were up in arms, and I felt for them, because they are among the most loyal in the world, and they were hurting. They spoke only with their hearts because their love is unique and unconditional. So, when they insisted they 'didn't want any favours', I wasn't surprised. Most other clubs in the SPL insisted Rangers should start again in the Third Division, and Gers fans agreed. They didn't want to 'buy' their return to a league that didn't want them and, no doubt, many fans were just relieved they still had a team to support. And when they inevitably return to the Premier League, it will be on their terms, and because they have earned that right. But whatever league they play in, Rangers will always be a massive part of me, and I will always follow their fortunes both on and off the field. It has been a bumpy ride, but I'm convinced the good times will return. It has been a long and difficult battle for the club but they will be back. Come on Gers! Come on bluenoses!

XX

TROUBLE IN TERNI

I WASN'T ready to quit the game and was determined that, one way or another, I would make up for lost time. First of all I had to get into shape, and then I would assess my options. In football, you never know when the call might come and you have to be ready to move quickly. I decided the best way to get fit was to head to Cesenatico, a small town on the Adriatic coast, to train with Germano Chierici, a gruff guy Marco Materazzi had introduced to me during our time at Perugia. After failing to build a career as a coach, he had earned a good reputation as a trainer, and specialised in rehabilitation. He himself had suffered serious injury and had single-handedly built up the Green Sports rehabilitation centre, which was both modern and popular.

Many great players passed through his hands, including Materazzi, Ciro Ferrara, Pippo Inzaghi, Alberto Aquilani and Stefano Mauri. His secret weapon was natural and prodigious creams of which he was fiercely protective. In fact, whenever he came up against a sceptic, he would lick the cream to demonstrate how organic his compounds were! His creams acted as a healing agent on the damaged muscle or ligament, significantly shortening the recovery time but, above all, ensuring a positive outcome at the end of the therapy. One quality you had to bring with you was the ability to sweat, because to be accepted by Chierici, you had to demonstrate that you really wanted to recover. Legend states he had no qualms in refusing to treat certain international players because he didn't feel they were committed enough. No one dared visit Chierici just to pass the time.

I was ready for the challenge and on my first morning I woke up just before dawn, as 7am was my 'kick-off' time. First up was a gruelling 90-minute bike ride along a winding path, before an afternoon of various exercises. I can't pretend it wasn't like military training, as all athletes in attendance were forced to do their best to shorten the time of recovery and escape from there as soon as possible. It was a tough day but Chierici's 'miracle' creams were just the tonic for sore and tired muscles at the end of the day. As I showered after the last series of extensions and reps, I felt a quiet delight at what I had achieved. I was hungry to get back playing and had just taken the first steps. In the afternoons that followed I would undergo punishing three-hour sessions in the gym, which was equipped with all the machinery needed to get us up to peak fitness. It was the perfect place to prepare for a new beginning and while I was nervous about more or less starting all over again, I was also excited.

Life at Green Sports was fun and we learned a lot. There were jokes and laughter and the daily improvements helped me forget and overcome the enormous sustained effort, but in February 2010, the government authority

NAS came calling and picked up some of the creams to analyse. Subsequently, Chierici was the subject of a complaint for abuse of the medical profession and physiotherapy, although thankfully he was later acquitted. Regardless, I still have a great respect for him and what he did for me: how he took me in and helped me when I needed it most.

After two months of torture, I began to notice muscles I didn't even know existed. I looked like an 'Ironman' – a rock both athletically and mentally, and ready to respond to offers in the affirmative. In fact, the first club to make enquiries were Ternana, one of my earlier teams. They played in Serie B but were ambitious and had invested a lot of money to fulfil the dreams of an entire city. They wanted a seat at the top table of Italian football, and I agreed to train with them over the summer. They would then decide whether or not to offer me a contract. I was happy enough with that, and knew a lot of question marks still remained over my future. I hadn't played regularly for a long time and, perhaps more significantly, I had been in a foreign league considered 'out of sight' as far as Italian television cameras were concerned.

Many in the game were no doubt wondering what had become of me, and probably didn't know of my contractual and fitness situations but, above all, hadn't the faintest idea if I could or would play again to a good professional standard. It didn't matter much to people that just a few months before I had played Champions League football for Rangers. Reality had forced me to ask for an invitation to train with a club, and this had deprived me of the joy of being genuinely wanted. In addition, if the injuries caused by the many negative incidents that occurred in previous seasons had finally healed, the obvious scars still remained. I had matured and become a man, even though losing much of my carelessness, spontaneity, conceit and arrogance, combined with instinct, had helped make me the player I was. I thought more about things, and was more careful with my words, to the point of analysing things before speaking – and sometimes counting up to 100 before opening my mouth. I would call my lawyer before taking a decision, acting like 'I should' and not as 'I wanted', in short, living with the handbrake on.

I trained hard with Ternana for a month and took Chierici's advice to do so with a touch of gas. My back responded perfectly and I never felt the slightest pain or difficulty during sessions. Training with the ball at my feet was a different matter altogether, although I soon got used to it again and it was nice to establish a good relationship with the coach and other players.

One thing an out-of-contract player needs is a telephone on the bedside table of their hotel room, just in case a coach or agent wants to get in touch. Sadly, the one next to my bed offered nothing but grief. It would ring every night and at the other end would be rude, angry Ternana fans voicing their displeasure at the thought of me re-joining their team. I had to unplug the phone. Some supporters quite clearly hadn't forgiven me for leaving Ternana when I did and signing for their big rivals, Perugia. To be honest, it was a matter of parochial rivalry, and had happened many years before, but some still hadn't deleted it from their memory and obviously considered it a case of high treason. It seems they would have done anything to ward off the possibility of my return. So, after three weeks of hard work, the club decided not to take the relationship any further and although it wasn't what

I wanted to hear, in the end it was probably best as the last thing I needed was more trouble.

With morale pretty low, I sought temporary refuge at my parents' home. Their affection proved vital and the calm I felt allowed me to reflect deeply. I met up with a few childhood friends and visited some old haunts, including the sports ground where I had taken my first steps in the game. I watched a lot of excited and carefree kids cultivating their own dreams of a professional career, and in them I saw myself of years gone by. I recalled the sacrifices I had made as a teenager and enjoyed the time spent in reflective mood. Those reflections were broken by a telephone call, and an unwanted one at that. It was Petre, from Bucharest, and he told me that a terrible tragedy had taken place.

After visiting a remote monastery far from Bucharest, he and Ioan Vranceanu were returning home when the car suddenly left the road. Petre had been protected by the steering wheel, escaping with just a few bruises, but Ioan, my friend and miraculous doctor, had died on the spot. Monica and I took the first available plane to Romania as I wanted to attend his funeral to say an emotional goodbye. During the flight I plunged into a deep silence brought on by a feeling of emptiness. I was thinking about a special person who had taken me into his home even though I was a complete stranger. He had helped me through the darkest moments of my career – and perhaps my life – and been there for me at the drop of a hat. At that moment I could feel only a great sense of loss, the same as I still feel to this day whenever I look at photographs of Ioan and I.

I was angry with fate at the death of such a good person, who was ready to give his time to the study and design of a machine that could help to heal sick and underprivileged children. It seemed a real injustice. What would his little patients do now? What would become of them? They might seem trivial worries of circumstance but these were the kind of thoughts whirling around in my mind. I could smile when thinking of Ioan leaning against the edge of his white Mercedes, an old model he loved and had driven with pride on our way to see Count Dracula's castle. Or how he desperately tried to communicate with his old parrot that, however, sitting on his perch uttered no words, nor even a sound. We had planned projects and I wanted him to come to Italy, but now, it had all vanished like a soap bubble that bursts floating lightly in the air.

Daniel invited me to stay at his place during my time in Romania and I didn't have to say a word when we met up. During the funeral ceremony I met many of Ioan's friends and family, and Petre seemed to be in a rather worrying state of confusion. I paid my final respects in the small church, and it was soon time to head home. I will always be indebted to this great man and I still regret to this day that I never thanked him enough. Now, more than ever, I wanted one last crack at football, just to show Ioan, wherever he was, my thanks and gratitude. I could do that by returning to the game, just as he had assured me from the first moment that I would. This was no time for self-pity.

I wasn't registered with any club, so I had time to hunt for a house I could finally call home, and decided Bologna was the city that, more than any other, I had loved from the beginning of my career. I had always thought that one day I would be back in the Emilia-Romagna region, and would establish my roots. In the meantime, though, we decided to rent an apartment and I trained alone in a large park near the airport, to ensure I was ready for the call. During my spare time, Monica and I searched for the perfect property. In reality, she was doing everything. Six mornings a week, around 9.30am, I parked the car and jogged into the park wearing only shorts, a sweatshirt, running shoes and a towel hanging from my shoulder. I would leave my keys, mini towel and bottle of water next to a tree, before starting the session. I was in the same situation as a musician who tries and tries again but can't find an orchestra to play with. And he doesn't know whether or not he will ever again get to perform in the concert!

I had picked up lots of great fitness tips from many different coaches, and knew exactly what I had to do to get into the best physical shape. The problem, however, was the fact I wasn't working towards a specific time limit and had to make sure I didn't overdo it, which would only make things worse. So I decided to divide the work into small ten-day cycles, during each of which I would pay particular attention to different exercises and training patterns.

As I worked out, I watched the world around me, and realised I could easily have been mistaken for the part-time jogger of between 40 and 50 years old, with the latest training shoes and iPod, complete with motivational music. Kids would poke fun by jogging alongside me, and I used to laugh as I upped the pace to shake them off. I would also watch elderly men and women engage in their daily walk, before they tried to imitate the motion exercises for the neck, shoulders, pelvis, trunk and back that I performed as a warm-up before the run. They would be watching what I was doing, and, rather unfairly, I began to invent some difficult movements they would try to copy, only to fail due to their complex nature. I would smile following with the corners of my eyes the adventures and contortions of these handsome young men of 70.

The most hilarious part arrived with the start of the stretches, when I would lie down on a towel, engage in exercises to relax from the stress just accumulated, and listen to the old men talk as they lay sprawled on the benches. I followed their comments on current events, discovering their personal stories – some dating back even to the Second World War. I discovered the winning moves they would have put in place had they been coach of the national team, and witnessed the heated discussions about politics, and all coloured by the sympathetic rhythm of the Bolognese dialect. So, as I continued to wipe the sweat from my brow, I enjoyed the experiences while awaiting my call to arms.

XXI

EXTRA TIME

I WAS finished with the park as my efforts were rewarded on two fronts just before Christmas. First, Monica and I found the apartment of our dreams, in which we still live today, and immediately afterwards I was invited to train with Serie A side Fiorentina. Sadly, after enjoying ten days with *La Viola*, I was told the club would not be taking their interest any further due to financial difficulties. It was a blow, but the fact my lawyer was beavering away in the background gave me hope.

And it paid off when the phone rang a couple of days later. Bologna were interested; I was delighted and it seems president Giuseppe Gazzoni still thought highly of me. I had developed a good relationship with the club during my time there, although I did manage to let my 'other side' get in the way, especially on one occasion. One Sunday, a few minutes before the start of a Serie C home match, the owner of the club walked into the dressing room to say hello and wish us all the best. Everyone shook his hand politely, apart from me. I refused, and didn't speak to him, even though he was the guy who paid my wages. It was perhaps the wrong thing to do, but I didn't snub him due to a lack of respect, more so because I didn't think he should be coming into the sanctuary of the dressing room at such an important time. I felt it was an intrusion but, as usual, my body language was there for all to see. Of course, it was uncalled for and inappropriate. Once on the field, though, I showed 100 per cent commitment and sacrifice, like always, respecting the club and their prestigious badge.

At the beginning of the new millennium, the coach was Francesco Guidolin, and he was meticulous in everything he did. He was never satisfied but sadly he didn't want me in his team, which meant the contractual situation remained on a knife-edge. I enjoyed some good training sessions with the squad, and was literally flying on the wings of a new-found enthusiasm. I eventually managed to convince the coach I was worthy of a jersey, and showed my commitment by agreeing to play for the minimum wage.

I signed a contract that would tie me to the Serie A side for the remaining months of the season and chose the number 38 shirt, the day and month of the date of birth of the Romanian doctor who had died. I was immediately called up for an Italian Cup match against Atalanta, in Bergamo. I was delighted but suddenly realised I was still taking the pills prescribed by Jan de Vries to keep my back healthy. They consisted only of natural products, but I wanted to be absolutely sure they were legal because all the bad luck I'd had in recent years had taught me to think. The last thing I needed was to be at the centre of a doping scandal.

I spoke to Bologna doctor Gianni Nanni, who, along with the sporting director, invented a problem with my registration to offer to journalists. It was decided I should sit out the match, as a precaution, which would allow time to analyse my urine. As expected, everything turned out fine, which allowed me to start my new adventure. I played a few games, and while they maybe weren't memorable performances, I was just happy I still had the ability to play in Serie A, and above all, to be able to play for a team that had become an important part of my life. I just had to show patience, but the experience gained over the years made me optimistic and confident, while I appreciated the slow, but steady, progress.

Just before the Christmas break, we managed a fantastic draw in Rome against Lazio, thanks to a last-minute goal by Cristian Zaccardo, a future national player. After the final whistle, I was told by team doctor Giovanni Sisca I had been chosen for doping control. I did everything fairly quickly, unlike some of my team-mates, who had to drink gallons of beer in order to carry out the necessary 'duty' in front of the watchful eye of an attendant. Then, once out of the shower, I left the dressing room quickly as I knew the bus driver wanted to leave the stadium as soon as possible to avoid the snow on the Apennines scheduled for that evening.

I met Alberto Zaccheroni, my ex-coach, who was now working at Lazio, and we enjoyed reminiscing. He asked about my physical condition and the Scottish experience, and also gave me some useful advice. It was great to talk to him again, even if I did lose track of time a bit. I really liked Alberto, but bid him farewell and went off to get the bus. The parking lot, however, was completely deserted, apart from a steward, standing in a corner smoking. He said the bus had already left. I knew I wasn't Guidolin's star pupil, but neither was I invisible, and wasn't best pleased so I phoned our captain, Gianluca Pagliuca, and asked if they were still around. Thanks to a police escort, they were already on the motorway and I was on my own. It's quite a distance from Rome to Bologna, around 250 miles, but thankfully someone agreed to come back and pick me up.

We had a few days off after that game and Monica and I decided to travel to Glasgow, where I felt the need to say a proper goodbye to those I knew and who had helped me so much. When I had initially been told I could leave Ibrox, I had upped sticks and left in a hurry, as I had pressing medical issues. It was good to see everyone again and in such a relaxed manner. In fact, I even exchanged a few words with Amoruso, and after a few days I was able to close the Scottish chapter in a positive manner.

In January I resumed training with Bologna. The transfer window – a time of the year I knew only too well – had opened, but I didn't think I had any need for it. Well, not until before a match against Brescia in the Stadio Renato Dall'Ara, our home ground. Guidolin came up with a plan to thwart the two Brescia forwards, who were both six feet plus. At training, he told me to stand on a three-foot high box with a team-mate, forced to impersonate Luca Toni and Igli Tare for over 20 minutes of training, even though I just looked like an ornament, and felt pretty stupid.

I wasn't happy but I didn't make a scene. I started looking at my options, though, because I wanted to play football, and not just be used as a dummy. That evening I called Bruno Carpeggiani, Minghetti's friend and an agent with good connections to clubs in Serie B, and asked for some help. A few days later, just after the market had closed, I received a call from Nedo Sonetti, my first professional coach who had been called in to save

Sardinian club Cagliari, a strong side, but one who were experiencing problems. He remembered me and asked me to give him a hand, so I switched cities, but not colours. Perhaps some players might have thought it better to play one single game in Serie A in the city in which they lived, rather than a dozen in the league below, but I was just desperate to play football, as opposed to being used as an ornament.

When I arrived in Cagliari, I discovered there had been a misunderstanding that I should have rectified straight away. Sonetti remembered me from my Udinese days, when I played for him on the wing, but we were talking a couple of decades later, and I had since scored more than 100 goals as an out-and-out striker. I only discovered this in a match in Siena. We were losing 1-0 and Sonetti told me to go over to the right wing and do some damage. I politely declined the invitation, thinking maybe he had confused me with Maurizio Neri, another player Sonetti had coached, and who didn't look altogether different from me – and our surnames were almost identical! On the bench beside me, we had a player able to fill that role perfectly, so I didn't understand his choice. I went on to the field, straight into the centre-forward position, but spent ten minutes thinking about that embarrassing situation more than helping the team fight for a precious point.

I wanted to be happy playing football. My situation was far better than it had been for a long time. I had the chance to train regularly without physical inhibitions; I had also regained confidence in my abilities and the respect of my team-mates. More than once, some of them had approached me, in confidence, and told me I deserved to play. Knowing my character, and of previous experiences that had become almost legendary among my colleagues, they wondered why I hadn't said anything, but I wanted to be loyal until the end with that coach, as he had given me my debut in Serie B at the age of just 17. Never would I have created problems for him or tensions in his dressing room.

At the end of the season, in fact, my commitment and patience were rewarded when I was called upon to play an important role, and scored in the last two games to earn us a couple of vital draws. On the penultimate day of the season, I netted with the final touch and secured a 2-2 draw in the Marassi Stadium against Genoa. Our last game was against Vicenza, and I came off the bench to head home a second goal, which completed the miraculous salvation of Cagliari. Fortunately, everything ended perfectly for the team. On a personal level, though, I wasn't satisfied. I wanted to go back to Bologna and enjoy my house. It was finally restored, and living with us was a rather cumbersome, but lovable, black Corso dog called Byron.

After spending part of our summer holidays in Spain, where we visited beautiful Seville, I decided to tackle a completely new initiative. I was without a club, but felt training alone in a park wasn't the way forward anymore. I joined a team of unemployed players preparing for the season in the resort of Milano Marittima, in the town of Cervia. It lay on the Adriatic coast and in the summer became a hotbed of entertainment. The team was the brainchild of coach Giancarlo Magrini, and I found it amazing that he could motivate professional players without the lure of a contract. And, most importantly, keep them in line even though they were in a place riddled with dangerous temptations. To become part of the group, you had to demonstrate a strong commitment, as there was no shortage of players asking to join. The coaching staff were first class and the facilities excellent. We trained hard and played challenge matches against sides from Serie A and B. It was a great idea and gave out-of-work players the perfect shop window. If a club showed an interest in me, they could speak to Magrini. I listened to one of his vicious attacks on a journalist who had written a negative piece on some of the players in an article for a national newspaper. He defended his players with a great passion.

My days were filled by training and matches and I was happy when some of the guys found employment because it gave confidence to all, although at other times, my morale sank when I saw opportunities vanish before my eyes. The main problem was that most teams had their full quota of players and it simply wasn't the right time to find a team place. I just had to be patient because I realised at my expense it is always easier to find a job when you already have one. My personal economic situation, moreover, allowed me to deal with the uncertainty of the situation a little easier than others who had perhaps played the majority of their careers in the lower divisions. Some of the guys were struggling to support their families and I hoped they would find something soon.

Magrini and his team had created a special group who worked in an atmosphere of unity, unlike anything I'd ever experienced in my career. There was no envy or jealousy, just solidarity. My summer passed in that way and when September arrived, each of the unemployed would have to start training at home, leaning towards a club in their region. For my part, I owe a debt of gratitude to Centese FC, who offered me training facilities. I maintained my association with the unemployed team and we played midweek matches, always of a high standard, on the fields of northern Italy. My name, like my team-mates, was mentioned regularly in the newspapers and when injuries and suspensions kicked in, teams were soon looking for new blood and I was desperate for the call-up, particularly as strikers are an extremely precious commodity.

XXII

WELCOME, CHRISTIAN!

NO one had to tell me that the clock was ticking on my career, but every player hopes they might be wanted by a club just one last time, so you can imagine the sense of joy and relief I felt when newly-promoted Serie B side Livorno got in touch. The owner of the club, Aldo Spinelli, was an old fox, and not much got past him. He had an exceptional talent for selling players at a profit, but was no slouch as a coach either, and was perfectly capable of noticing anything that might be wrong with his team. Bluffing with him was also impossible, as he was incredibly smart, but I appreciated his frankness. He wanted me right away, but decided that coach Roberto Donadoni should have the final say. Donadoni had been a great player in the legendary Milan side under Fabio Capello, so just playing alongside him in a practice match was an immense pleasure (a little like in the days of Domenghini) and, to be honest, it would have been great for us had he still been registered as a player.

But he wanted me to train with the team for a week, and only after this would he make a decision. Again, I wasn't happy at this, as I felt there had been plenty of opportunities for Donadoni, or his people, to see me in action with the unemployed team, and didn't think it was right to make a decision on someone's future based on a couple of training sessions, so the deal stalled for almost two weeks. Donadoni didn't give up, though, and a friendly call from the president convinced me to give it a go. I trained impeccably and convinced him to sign me, and immediately made my league debut. My performances were very good and I scored five goals in my first four games, including a superb hat-trick in a 4-2 victory over Cosenza at the Armando Picchi Stadium. The points pushed the Tuscans to top position in the league, much to the amazement of pundits.

Our last game before Christmas was a trip to Bari and with just 12 minutes to go, we were 3-0 up, and I had scored twice. Donadoni was a really nice guy, but he often tried to please everyone, perhaps to the detriment of the team. Anyway, he decided to replace me, something I didn't see coming, or deserve. I was anything but happy, and left the San Nicola Stadium fuming. There were no insults, like there might have been in the past, but I walked off with a sarcastic smile on my face that clearly betrayed my feelings.

Donadoni came up, gave me some compliments and told me it was right to give game time to my team-mates. Perhaps he was right, but I just felt I had given enough game time to fellow strikers all over the world and now, when I wanted to play – and I could finally play – he was taking me off. That said, my relationship with the coach remained good.

An unexpected string of draws saw us slip down the table a bit, but we were still safe from the threat of relegation. When the season drew to a close, I was happy with eight goals in half a season and believed I had proved to everyone I still had goals in me. I went on holiday, and on my return expected a call from Livorno – but it didn't come. Many years later I was told, from a reliable source, that the new coach, Walter Mazzarri, had rejected me, saying I was a player who 'scored goals, but not important ones'.

So I was again added to the ranks of the unemployed. Mind you, this time I was finally satisfied I had proved to myself, and everyone else that mattered, that I wasn't finished. I hadn't forgotten how to play or score, and at 32, I still had something to offer. To regain a place in football, I had completed a long and exhausting period, which was why I was tired of always having to prove myself. I was disappointed that I had to start all over again, every damn summer, as if the tape simply rewound automatically. I found it monotonous that there were so many people always ready to give negative opinions about me, even when not required. There was always a 'Yes, but, his age...'

I chose not to return to Magrini's unemployed team and decided to train at the Isokinetic, which meant I was just a few minutes from home and Monica. I wanted to stay close to my family and felt a strong desire to become a dad. During the early stages of my career, I had been completely focused on football. I enjoyed it so much and never considered the merits of fatherhood. It was only after meeting a woman who remained close by even during my darkest periods – an intelligent, loyal and faithful person, the defects of which literally paled in the face of her clear qualities – that I gave it any thought. She had always understood, forgiven, defended, encouraged and also criticised me when it was right to do so. She was there in both good times and bad. She had found the right words at the right time, was supportive and never 'in the way'. I was her first and only thought because she had made sure I never felt alone, even when in fact I really was.

Earlier in my career, I might have enjoyed moving from team to team; city to city, and enjoying the whole experience of moving around, but I was now tired of that. I had put down roots in Bologna and knew it was the correct decision. Anyway, if we were to have a child it would require stability and I wanted to be there for him or her. Similarly, I was hoping my child could grow up recognising his parents and his surroundings, and regularly seeing his grandparents and uncles. All of this was incompatible with the needs of a footballer, especially if I found a team away from Bologna.

I knew I could no longer aspire to play in Serie A. My peak had passed, but pride wouldn't allow me to accept any old contract just to continue to feel like a professional footballer. Also, my intelligence, and bank account, wouldn't allow me to risk further injury. My back was in perfect working order but was always in need of attention and exercise. Eventually I made the decision to try and continue playing, and shelved any thoughts of becoming a dad. Taking my kid to the park, or the football, would have to wait, so the team had to be worth the effort. The days of million-pound contracts were gone, indeed the perfect club for me would've been one in serious financial difficulty, or perhaps one at risk of relegation. I thought about quitting, but still had the fire in my belly. I continued to train regularly, and hard, because there was always hope. I didn't have the support of an agent anymore, so I read the newspapers to keep me up to speed with the Italian game and which team might need a striker like me. When I watched a game on TV, and saw a fellow striker turn in a mediocre performance, it pushed me to get out and train even harder, still convinced I deserved a chance. I had never seriously thought about what to do after I stopped playing, so the longer I put it off, the better!

It's strange how often in life, when you expect and believe you deserve a break, it rarely occurs. You should, however, be satisfied you've done everything right, and have a clear conscience. I had waited for the transfer window to open in January, with more than a little anxiety, but considered it a good time to find a club in need of goals. Instead, the long-awaited call didn't come and the desire to start playing again had reduced to a flicker. I continued to train mainly because it had become habit and I wasn't even driven by what had become a remote desire to prepare for one last dance.

And then, as if by magic, a spark from Minghetti, who was still loudly banging the drum – perhaps even louder than me. I was still delighted, though, when the call came in February, and it was from an unlikely quarter. Derby County, an English First Division side coached by Scotsman George Burley, invited me over to England to train for a few days, which gave me an opportunity to return to the UK and show my Scottish friends I wasn't finished. Equally as important, it gave me the chance to enjoy the charm of football and of British life without the hindrance of an Italian team-mate. To be honest, I initially struggled to accept the invitation from Burley in the city where Rolls-Royce was founded in 1906 because just a few weeks before, I had received the wonderful news that Monica was expecting. But we spoke about it and I headed over to England, where I made a good impression. In fact, a few sessions were enough to convince coach and club I was worth signing.

In the meantime, though, Monica had called to tell me she was expecting twins, but that it wasn't a straightforward pregnancy. Trips and journeys were discouraged and I decided not to take up the offer from Derby. I made the decision quickly as the UK transfer window is only open a short time, and wanted to be fair to Derby. I had to put Monica and our unborn children first. After so many years with football as my only priority, it was time to return the favour. It was a testing time for her and I had to be close by. I also made another very important decision – I hung up my boots.

I needed to do the right thing, and I did – a smart defensive move – although it was perhaps the first of my entire football career. On the field, in fact, I almost always ignored the pleas of anxious team-mates and coaches asking me to get back into my own penalty area to lend a hand at corners or free kicks, especially late on in games. I used gimmicks like tying my laces, adjusting shinguards or pretending not to hear, without doubt my favourite excuse. In truth, I wasn't interested in defending these situations.

The pregnancy was anything but simple. Things were going on, but not always with the right result. On one occasion we visited the hospital for yet another ultrasound, and the outcome was sad beyond belief. Just one foetus had survived, and although I can't say for sure, I have the belief that the one who didn't make it was a girl. I had fantasised about life with our princess, but sadly it wasn't to be. The feelings that came over me that afternoon were of great sadness, despair and bitterness. Instinctively I put my hand on Monica's stomach and began to caress her. I didn't know whether to comfort her or myself. At the same time, however, I felt a burst of positive energy and also a breath of hope, as if my son was saying, 'Hey, I'm here, and I need you.' The anxieties and worries increased and we had to follow doctors' orders and, to be honest, I had no time to dwell on football regrets. I had to concentrate exclusively on the present.

Still, I recall that period with great pleasure: from the ultrasound to the time we were told we were having a little boy, from evenings spent discussing names to the long walks on the seafront in Cesenatico and the DIY disasters made in an attempt to assemble his room without following instructions, which made me thankful I had chosen to use my feet to earn a living! Then there was Monica's ever-expanding stomach, which I would caress day after day, feel the baby kick, and buy all the gadgets on the market in order to listen to his heartbeat. I read up on *How to be the Perfect Father*, and looked forward to the most difficult job in the world. I tried to tackle the job with the utmost serenity, although I admit to being a bit too anxious and apprehensive. The days, at least for me, flew by and, almost without realising it, nine months of waiting was over.

Once I became a dad, only a small piece of the jigsaw was missing. Christian's arrival could be complemented with one more shot at the beautiful game, and in the spring of 2005, I was able to make a brief cameo of three months at Perugia. Just like the actor who has slipped from fame and the limelight, but is called upon for one more shot at glory. The team – experiencing financial hardship – was battling near the top of Serie B, and president Alessandro

Gaucci, eldest son of 'Luciano the Hurricane', had phoned to ask if I could help them out, as promotion would solve many problems. I flew to the miraculous Chierici for a crash-course in fitness and prepared impeccably for the challenge ahead.

A warm welcome – and some excellent footballers – awaited in Umbria. They were all united in a common cause, despite the fact it was a few months since they had been paid. I had accepted the proposal mainly because of the special feeling that bound me to the city, and not for economic reasons. Also, I knew that my little family could follow me there without too many problems and I certainly wasn't looking to revive my career at the grand old age of 34. I played very little, but offered more of a psychological support than a player at the beck and call of coach Stefano Colantuono, however I did manage to bring the team some good luck and my arrival coincided with an incredible run of 11 wins in a row. We finished fourth in the table and qualified for the play-offs, where Torino lay in wait.

The first game was played in Perugia and we had been an unstoppable speeding train for more than two months. We were stronger than our opponents, both physically and in technique, but were also aware they had hit a bit of form. Mind you, Torino sacked coach Ezio Rossi just before the first game, which perhaps suggested they feared us. Surprisingly, though, they won 2-1, thanks to a superb display by Brazilian midfielder André Luciano da Silva Pinga, and loanees Massimo Marazzina and Federico Balzaretti.

I was angry at the loss and stormed out of the stadium towards the team bus. I heard someone call my name. It was Lorenzo Marronaro, an old team-mate at Udinese and a great striker. He was a good guy and always generous with advice. We exchanged a few words, then he said, 'Too bad, it was a game you could and should have won.' I was frustrated and angry, which is why that phrase had a strange effect on me. I ran the game over and over again in my head while sitting on the bus. It was clear we had allowed Torino, and especially Pinga, to dictate the pace of the game. We should have man-marked him.

While speaking to Marronaro, I had mentioned a player called Jamal Aliou, a fast and tenacious Moroccan but someone capable of man-marking Pinga in the second leg. My point was, to hell with tactics and formations! Our season comes down to one final game, and if we allow Aliou to negate Pinga, it makes it a very interesting ten v ten. I confided in him because I really believed in that team and felt we could do something good if we got to Serie A. Marronaro said very little and we parted. I climbed on to the bus to await my team-mates and moments later, I saw the Perugia coach emerge from the stadium, and he was talking to Marronaro.

Four days later, we showed up at the Delle Alpi, which was packed with enthusiastic Torino fans. They were confident that the one-goal advantage would be enough to see them promoted, while we were also confident we could rescue the situation in front of a pretty frenetic 60,000 crowd. We played well, kept good possession and even found ourselves in front after some good play. Due to the result of the first match, and also the fact that Torino had finished above us in the table, we needed to win by two clear goals. We attacked intelligently from the first whistle to the last, and restricted the home side to a single shot at goal, and the last few minutes turned into the siege of Turin!

Our hosts had all but raised the white flag and were unable to get out their own half. After running the first match, Pinga had been marked out of the game by Aliou, just as Claudio Gentile had done with Zico and Maradona at the 1982 World Cup. The talented Brazilian had barely touched the ball and finally left the field limping from a blow received during the first half. I still wonder if my suggestion was put forward to the coach by Marronaro, or whether it was just a coincidence. I never found out but the reality was our dream had been snatched from us at the final hurdle. Sadly, Perugia had failed in their centenary year and thus, it was a sad Sunday evening in late June that Marco Negri finally called time on his career. It had been a bumpy, but enjoyable, ride.

Looking back, I am proud at the career I made for myself. I acknowledge that I was never a leader. In fact, the only time I wore the captain's armband was as a 16-year-old and it was my second season in the Udinese youth team. As the oldest in the group, I claimed my right to be captain at a prestigious youth tournament in Jesolo. Mind you, the role was taken from me as a means of punishment, after some friends and I had taken the towels from our hotel room to the adjacent beach for a refreshing swim in the sea. The coach had surprised me on our return and hadn't considered it the behaviour of a captain. Nevertheless, it was midsummer, the sun was shining, and we were in a beautiful seaside resort with sandy beaches crowded with many female German tourists. We were only 16, so I thought we had set a 'good' example!

I had started my career when the games were still played strictly with man-marking and the defender followed the attacker until the post-match shower; when it was perfectly lawful for the goalkeeper to gather up a back-pass from a team-mate; when the numbers on the players' backs ran from one to 11; the teams in Serie A relied on a maximum of two foreigners; all matches were held at the same time on a Sunday afternoon and fans were able to enjoy every goal scored just before dinner, thanks to the *90° Minuto* TV programme.

I stopped 27 years later when zonal marking was king, and players wore multi-coloured boots and kicked balls with strange trajectories that were able to fool even the most experienced of goalkeepers. When Italian teams were full of foreigners, and not always the best of the bunch. When many of my countrymen moved to Europe, of which I had been one of the first, when surnames covered the shoulders of club shirts and the most unlikely numbers – up to 99 – were chosen by the players themselves. Even if the two of Gentile and Beppe Bergomi, the three of Antonio Cabrini and Paolo Maldini, the five of Paulo Roberto Falcao and Fabio Cannavaro, the six of Gaetano Scirea and Franco Baresi will never be forgotten, they are no longer in fashion.

Some new rules have been introduced to promote the show and fair-play; cameras enter the dressing room before the match and those sitting at home can see the players walking around in their underwear while eating their lasagne. But while football terminology has been revolutionised, fortunately the magical journey of the ball that nestles behind the goalkeeper is still called simply a goal. In short, I think I have experienced at first hand a real generational change and witnessed a radical modernisation of the football world.

Throughout my career I never once conspired or played to relieve a coach; nor spent the afternoon at the club spying on fellow pros, or ever got too close to a chairman or journalist in a bid to enjoy special treatment, or even advantages. I tried to always be available to play when a coach asked me, even in poor physical condition, and only thanks to anti-inflammatories. I never cheated in order to be competitive athletically, or bet on a game, and I'm proud that many of my goals proved important for almost all the teams I represented. And I wasn't the type who trained hard all week and disappeared on a Sunday afternoon. Playing football, and especially the big games, excited me, and the bigger the challenge the better. I am proud and flattered to have been judged, appreciated, loved, celebrated, whistled, scolded, punished and criticised for what I did on the field. I tried to be myself all the time and was never 'reading from a script'.

I feel privileged to have had a career in football, a world that I loved with such passion, and that I had marked out as my preferred choice since adolescence. It taught me a lot, handed me unique opportunities and allowed me to live a privileged life. As the great comedian Marcello Mastroianni once said, 'If I had not done this job, I would've had to work for a living.' Football gave me many magical moments, that lasted more than 20 years and which, given some of my injury problems, is quite incredible.

Fate would decree I started my career in the summer of 1982, when the Italian national team, coached by Enzo Bearzot, and led spectacularly on the field by Paolo Rossi, won the World Cup in Spain. Subsequently, I decided to call time just before July 2006, when my friends Gattuso and Materazzi, along with national coach Marcello Lippi, were crowned world champion in Berlin. I made some great friends and when my final whistle sounded, there were genuinely no regrets.

XXIII

RETURNING TO GLASGOW FOR FERNANDO

O N 23 January 2015, after almost 15 years in 'exile', I finally returned to Ibrox Stadium. The left side of my body, the side which plays host to the heart and emotions, was incredibly eager and curious to once again visit my adopted home city of almost four years. I was excited about returning to Ibrox and pulling on the Rangers top one more time, and also savouring the most exciting atmosphere I experienced in my career, thanks to the marvellous Rangers support. This time, though, Monica and I were accompanied by a special young man – our wee boy, Christian. I was desperate to show him where his dad had played and to let him see with his own eyes the home of one of the most famous and successful clubs on the planet.

Okay, so that was the left-hand side of my body. But the right side, the rational part, and the one with the brain, was sad and reserved about the reason for my return. I was coming back to Scotland to take part in a charity match for my former team-mate Fernando Ricksen, a born fighter, and a man going through a very difficult time battling Motor Neurone Disease. I strongly believe that once you have been team-mates and shared the joys and disappointment of winning and losing you are team-mates for life.

For me, it was an honour to be invited to play for the Rangers Legends for Fernando. To be honest, I have never felt like a legend – even if perhaps I did play half a season like one – and that's still the case today. It's not a status I'm comfortable with. I consider myself a good player who was very lucky to have had the privilege of playing for Rangers, and I mean that from the bottom of my heart. To have scored goals on the hallowed Ibrox turf, and to be considered a part of the Rangers family, for me, is gratitude enough.

If we're talking true Rangers legends, then we are talking players like Fernando, as well as many of those who played in his benefit game. If you appreciate, respect and love someone, you have to show it and stand up when that person really needs your help. It is the only reason that, after ten years of inactivity, and without any training or matches of any kind (except for a couple of charity games), as well as many strands of grey hair due to a significant number of birthdays, I decided to pull the boots on one more time. When I told Christian I had been invited to play at Ibrox, the first thing he said, no, requested, was a couple of goals! For the first time in a long football career, I felt real pressure.

Arriving in Glasgow, I met up with some old friends – Guerrino, Mariangela and Marco from Il Pavone restaurant – and we enjoyed wallowing in nostalgia. I then took a stroll through the city centre, recognising many streets and places from my earlier spell in the city. I noticed many changes around town, although certainly not with the weather. My schedule in Scotland was very intense and busy. First of all I met up with my friend Jeff to talk about the book you are reading right now, before attending a question and answer evening in Cooper's Bar, a Rangers pub in Wishaw. It was the first such event I had ever been asked to speak at and I was more than a little nervous. Naturally there will always be issues with the different languages, but I'm always keen to give something a go, and it was a great opportunity to raise funds for Fernando, with my fee and ticket sales going to his fund. I had absolutely no need to be nervous, as everyone was so nice to me. There were questions and there were answers, but mostly it was about meeting supporters, both young and old, very curious, respectful and with a great memory!

Of course I was asked the 'queen of questions' almost straight away, about that damned squash ball. I was invited to select my favourite goal, the best players I'd played with and, more importantly, the current state of the club I started loving in the late 1990s, and still do to this day. And I was asked about Fernando, who I was pleased to speak about publicly. At the end of a very pleasant Q&A session, I had dozens of pics taken with supporters, signed countless autographs, which took me back to when I was playing for Rangers. Oh, and the organisers auctioned off a pint of beer 'poured by Marco Negri' for Fernando's charity, and two kind gentlemen paid £30 each for this 'privilege'. I shuffled behind the bar and took my time operating the pump to make sure the guys got their money's worth. I was complimented on my technique by the owner and told there was a job for me at Cooper's should I ever want it! It was the perfect end to a great night.

The following evening, I was a special guest together with some of the other players at a charity dinner for Fernando in the Ibrox suite. It was an opportunity to see him in person for the first time after so many years. When I stepped out my taxi at the front door of Ibrox, the memories immediately came flooding back. I took a selfie at the entrance, and then my first instinct was to head straight into the dressing room. I opened the door, just a little bit, and felt like an excited, but shy, child. I had a little peek behind the door and the sight that greeted me produced instant butterflies in my stomach. The Fernando tribute match tops were already laid out on the wooden bench, just as our tops used to be when I played for Rangers.

Not a lot had changed. I walked into the dressing room and the smell was the same. I was home, and sat there for a few moments, just drinking in the atmosphere. I was alone but in the company of old memories and deep reflections. I soon became fully immersed in many emotions, so much so that when I told Monica later that night at the hotel, she started crying. So much time had passed but so many old memories, both good and bad, flashed through my mind. My moment of meditation was interrupted only by a member of staff informing me that the organisers of the dinner were waiting for me upstairs. As I walked out the dressing room, I turned and had one more look at the old place. It was so special.

I walked up the famous marble staircase and there at the top, waiting to greet me, was Fernando. He was looking incredibly smart in his black suit, and we had a long and meaningful hug, and that was the moment he told me he had just had a tattoo of a lion with a giant mane. By now, you are aware of my feelings on needles, and I cringed as though it had just happened to me. Fernando is quite some man. It was a fantastic night and I was very comfortable in the company of former Rangers stars such as Nacho Novo, Michael Mols, Stefan Klos and many more. Charlie Miller had us in stitches and I had some great conversations with many Rangers fans. The way they also offered their love and support to Fernando was just so incredible, although I shouldn't be surprised by anything that members of the Rangers family do.

The following day, it was time for the match. Was I playing in a World Cup Final in front of 100,000 supporters at the stadium, and a worldwide TV audience of several billion? No, I had just awoken in my hotel room, and the nerves had already started to kick in. I really was going to be playing at Ibrox one last time, and boy did my stomach know it. After breakfast, we headed to Ibrox and the feeling was slightly different from the previous evening. This time I was here to play. I had a look at the team sheet – 'Marco, your number nine shirt is over there.' It wasn't the best of days, weather wise (so what's new?), but almost 42,000 fans had turned out for Fernando, which didn't surprise me in the slightest. Fernando is a hero and these fans, well, what more can I say?

To tell the truth, from the moment I arrived at Ibrox, the place was buzzing. For starters, to see guys like Jorg Albertz, Rino Gattuso, Michael Mols, Arthur Numan, Stefan Klos, Tugay, Gordon Durie, Andy Goram, Barry Ferguson and Bob Malcolm was a bit too much and I was very emotional. It was great seeing the guys but we all knew why we were there. There were so many other Ibrox legends. Guys like Jimmy Bell, the kitman, who I ribbed to the end of the earth when I noticed that Rino's jersey had an extra 's' in Gattusso! People like Tiny, who for 47 years has looked after the players at lunchtime, like Peter at reception with his charming white moustache and infectious smile and so many more. It really was like a homecoming.

Soon, it was time for the match and we all lined up in the tunnel as we used to before kick-off. And the nerves started again. The Rangers Legends were on the right and Fernando's All Stars on the left. We were asked to walk out with individual mascots and when we moved out on to the turf the noise had reached fever pitch. It was the loudest I had heard in a long time. And then it got even louder, honestly, when Fernando walked out and into the guard of honour created by both sets of players and mascots. Fernando walked with difficulty, but a determination that had characterised his time as a player. He has the heart of a lion and wasn't going to let anything stand in the way of getting out to the centre of the pitch to embrace the supporters with mutual love and affection.

As he walked up the centre of the guard he nodded to every single player. I felt a lump the size of a golf ball forming in my throat. The hairs on my arm stood to attention, and next to me Teddy Sheringham looked incredibly emotional. To my right, Rino had tears streaming down his cheeks. Nobody spoke. It was simply a tsunami of emotions, but each and every one of us was proud of our former team-mate. That level of emotion was prevalent throughout the entire match. Inside Ibrox there was a cocktail of sadness, happiness, smiles, memories, tears and hope, and I felt every single one of them inside.

During the match I had a couple of chances to score. I tried hard, and it would have been a great pleasure, but unfortunately the legs simply don't follow the instinct any more; they don't obey the brain, but at 45 years old, they are in charge. I went very, very close with one chance, a sitter almost, and once again I heard the cheers and the whispers of the fans – pure adrenaline for the striker. At the end I wasn't too unhappy at failing to score because the day wasn't about me, I wasn't there for myself. The joy of a goal would have been beautiful but it wasn't to be. Instead, until the last second of the game and, more importantly, until the final lap of honour with Fernando on our shoulders, I was filled with all kinds of emotions, which in many ways were unique.

I am absolutely devastated for the state of Fernando's health. It's a massive blow for him, and makes you think deeply about your own health and condition. Whenever I hear or read bad news, I'm saddened and very sorry, but then, the next day, life goes on. Not this time, though. Fernando and I have a lot of things in common – our passion for football, the fact we grew up playing football; the similar sacrifices we made to became professional football players, and the very fact we fought to win for the clubs we represented. I suppose this is the moment to understand life must be lived in the best way, every second. Sometimes we get angry for stupid reasons, while the most important things in life, the real ones, are staring us in the face. I want to thank Fernando for showing me exactly what true fighting spirit is. Fernando was a warrior on the pitch, while off it he continues to be an indomitable fighter. All the best pal, and God bless you.

It was soon time for me and the family to return home to Italy. In my suitcase I took home some unbelievable memories, and a container-load of overwhelming emotions. More than that, I can assure Rangers FC they have a new, special supporter. His name is Christian. My son simply fell in love with Glasgow, with the Gers supporters, with Ibrox, and spent more than £300 on Rangers tops, Rangers jumpers, Rangers hats and a mobile phone cover, although perhaps his urge to shop came as a result of his mum's DNA!

It was a strange experience flying home from 'home', and it took me back to a conversation I'd had many years previous with a dear friend. He told me that when he was young he had met the girl of his dreams. The only problem was, he didn't realise it at the time. He broke off the relationship for foolish and trivial reasons, perhaps mistakes made due to immaturity or youth. Many years had passed when my friend saw again his perfect women, and his feelings for her had remained intact. She was definitely the one, but sadly the right time had gone and her heart was now with another.

I know exactly how he felt, because Rangers Football Club was the one for me: it was the big team I had dreamt of playing for as a child. You know, the one that 99 times out of 100 remains a dream. It was the special opportunity that comes around just once in a lifetime. I would have to say that due to that damned squash ball I didn't manage to take advantage of my big chance. If only I hadn't played that day, but I did, and that moment has gone. But I want to make a promise to our great supporters, and can say without fear of contradiction, that it won't be another 15 years before I see my Ibrox – and Rangers – again. I won't allow that to happen – but neither would Christian!

EPILOGUE

ONCE A RANGER, ALWAYS A RANGER

SITTING at home one night and the phone rings. Close to the telephone is a framed copy of this book, which offers a constant reminder of my football career. Through time, we all get older and injuries catch up with us and an imaginary referee blows the final final whistle. The brakes go on and you believe they will be fixed in that position for the rest of eternity. But even though the football boots may remain untouched in your kit bag in a darkened cupboard, nothing can change the illuminating love you have always had for the beautiful game.

Sorry, the phone! On the other end of the line was Victor Morgan; one time agent of Fernando and now co-manager of the Rangers Legends team with Stan Gordon, another true blue Rangers man. What could they possibly want with me?

A few weeks later I was pulling on the Rangers top one more time; an act that remains to this day one of the most pleasurable of my career. Although I always try, I can't describe in words how much of a privilege this is. Every morning of your life you pull a shirt over your head, but it's very different when the Rangers crest is on that shirt. The crest weighs heavy and only a privileged few are granted the honour.

The legends games might be for charity, whether the benefactor is Fernando or the Lee Rigby Foundation, but believe me, the spirit of competition and challenge that pushed me and all the other former players to reach a very high level during our careers is always there. That Rangers team plays to win. So, both before and after the 90 minutes, charity is foremost in our minds, but during the game: no prisoners.

A common problem we share is that our minds still work perfectly. We think like we did in the golden days, when we were both young and fit. Nowadays, though, the legacy of 90 minutes is the 'chicken' legs, where you can't walk properly for many days! Even still, it's a small price to pay for the pleasure of knowing you can help someone that needs you because they are struggling, and of course there is the joy of meeting up again with former team-mates and the spirit of camaraderie that goes hand-in-hand with all of that. Mind you, same old stories, same old jokes, and the same players making fun of the same faces, but it's still very special.

And then there is the warmest hug from the most passionate fans on the planet. Every single time I get the same feeling. Rangers supporters, after 20 years, make me feel as though I'm still playing for the club and for them; they make me feel special, loved and like a part of the family.

In May, 2016, I was taking part in another charity match, this time for Fernando in Elgin, which is way up in the north of Scotland. It just happened to be Scottish Cup Final weekend and Rangers were playing Hibs at Hampden. After knocking out Celtic in the semi-finals, hopes were high of capturing a major trophy, but we had a match to prepare for ourselves on the Sunday. Imagine my great delight though when the organisers booked us on a supporters' bus travelling from Elgin to Glasgow. With the match a 3pm kick-off, an early departure from the hotel was necessary, but I was in great company, with Jorg Albertz – already asking after just five minutes of travel if we could stop the bus for a fag – and Nacho Novo. And accompanying us on our journey south were around 50 fervent supporters, who were more than ready to transform a 'sensible' bus into something I will remember until the end of my days. Three full hours of singing every Rangers song in the book (and perhaps a couple that haven't yet made it into the book!), the consumption of hundreds of beers, and enough jokes and stories to keep you entertained round a campfire for an entire night. Thank goodness I didn't understand them all completely. But the atmosphere on the bus was special, and always very friendly. I feel fortunate to have been a part of something so incredible. When you are a player, you are completely focused on your career and trying to do the best you can on the park, to impress the very supporters that were sharing the journey with Jorg, Nacho and I. It's only when you are part of something like that bus journey that you begin to understand the type of sacrifice every supporter makes to follow their club through thick and thin. Because of their location, the guys I travelled with from Elgin are up early on their day off and face a four-hour journey in all kinds of weather. They save up for a season ticket and spend a lot of money on club merchandise and other things to help make their day out an enjoyable one. All they ask in return is for the players to show commitment, loyalty, effort and respect for the badge, which is certainly not too much to ask.

Supporters are the most important part of any club and Rangers are a massive institution with a massive fan base. There is blue blood coursing through the veins of each and every supporter. Chairmen, managers and players come and go, but fans are for life, and the club is passed down from generation to generation like a precious family heirloom for siblings to cherish and follow.

ORSA (Oceania Rangers Supporters Association) and NARSA (North American Rangers Supporters Association) host conventions that attract hundreds, and sometimes thousands, of supporters every year. The fans spend the best part of a week together in an attractive location and eat, sleep and breathe Rangers. Thanks to Craig, a massive bluenose, I was invited to Phuket for my first convention. The city was invaded by a noisy, but good hearted troupe of Rangers supporters who were able to show the people in that part of the world exactly how supporters should follow their football team, and of course, how Scottish fans like to enjoy a beer or two.

Phuket is a wonderful place, but while I was there a legend was born, and sadly that legend centred on me. I was relaxing in the hotel after a game involving Rangers supporters and a local team – which we won – and after dinner a bunch of us decided to explore the centre of town. In Italy, we have many beautiful museums, but in Thailand there is a different type of culture, particularly their 'special' type of bars. After being a spectator at a very strange ping-pong game, we moved to a bar where an assortment of beautiful ladies were dancing around half naked. The music was very loud, but the spirit of our group was high. After a few minutes, and a nice cold beer, I felt a soft touch on my shoulder, which I thought was someone trying to attract my attention. As I turned round, I saw a very small animal – perhaps a mouse – walking on my t-shirt. I began to scream like a big girl and I was shaking my shoulder in an effort to dislodge this little intruder. The 'poor' hamster was clawing doggedly at my shirt with its sharp nails, flapping right and left like the sail of a boat caught in a dreadful storm. I was truly alone in feeling desperate. Everyone else was focused on having a good laugh (at me) and determined not to miss out on the evening's real entertainment. Suddenly there came a scream louder than all of mine put together. A young pole dancer was shrieking and pleading with me to stop shaking my shoulder as the tiny hamster was her pet!

Over the next few days, the story of the hamster became the main talking point of the convention, and all of a sudden I wasn't Moody Marco any more, but 'Hamster Boy!' Let me tell you, I have been called much worse.

Mind you, one of the greatest things for me is the manner in which I have been accepted by the Rangers supporters. Sure, I'm a former player, but that shouldn't be a guarantee that you should always be welcomed back into the 'family'. I believe everyone has to earn that right.

And while I'm on the subject of fan gatherings, please don't ask me to recount any stories from the NARSA convention, as, thank goodness, what happens in Vegas...

The relationship between myself and the Rangers support has certainly developed since I attended fan conventions at ORSA and NARSA. In Italy we have big clubs such as AC Milan, Juventus and Inter. They have millions of fans around the world, but this is still nothing compared to Rangers. There are a lot of people that life took away from Scotland many years ago, but their passion for the club, even more so now – if that is possible – is powered by a pride to support the blue jersey abroad.

On one occasion I was invited to Greece by a very special Rangers man who has started a supporters' club in Athens. Each Saturday – or whenever the Gers are in action – around 80 guys meet up in the club to watch their favourites play, and I'm assured the atmosphere is always electric. While I was there we played a five-a-side match against a team of Aston Villa supporters. We won the game and were celebrating in the bar afterwards when I asked George how a Greek guy could possibly fall in love with the most successful team in Scotland. He said that when he was a young lad, his father brought him home a present one day. He ripped open the wrapping paper to reveal the table soccer game, Subbuteo – and one team. Those 11 players were kitted out in a neat blue strip and George's father told him it was Glasgow Rangers. It was love at first sight and it never left him. It mattered not that Ibrox was almost 2,500 miles from George's Athens home. This is one long-distance love affair that has stood the test of time.

Another event which caught my imagination was a visit to the Erskine Home for ex-members of the Armed Forces. It was arranged by Tom Clark and Murray Roxburgh from the Rangers Supporters Erskine Appeal, a charitable group which has raised more than £750,000 for the old soldiers. I was privileged to go to Erskine and meet some real heroes, and also donate a couple of copies of my book to their library. It was a true honour to meet so many brave men and women. While there, I became engaged in conversation with one of the nurses, who told me all about an initiative they have started for those residents who struggle a little bit with their memory. The staff host a therapy session for residents with dementia, and the hope is that when the resident picks up a photograph of a former footballer, it will help to train the mind and he might remember the player and the associated memories that brings. I was told they very seldom fail to recall the names of the old Rangers players. The power of football and Rangers is amazing.

A few weeks after visiting Erskine, my co-author, Jeff and I were on our way to London for the British Sports Book awards, which were held at the iconic Lord's cricket ground. My book had made it on to the shortlist for Best International Autobiography, and even though we were pipped at the post, it was a fantastic experience which I was glad to share with my wife, Monica and Christian, my son.

Not long after that, another invitation came my way and left me with a huge smile on my face. I was asked on to Rangers TV by commentator Tom Miller to act as a matchday pundit at Ibrox and I had no hesitation in saying yes. It was an incredible experience, although trying to walk from the Ibrox car park to the main reception proved tougher than anything the match threw up. That day it took me at least an hour to walk the 100 metres because I was stopped by hundreds of fans asking for a photograph or an autograph, or even just to recall one of the goals I scored while a Rangers player. It was a great honour, and it's a walk I will never tire of making. I thoroughly enjoyed chatting to our supporters and it just made my perfect day complete.

It is always a great honour and pleasure to be back at Ibrox, although if I'm being honest, I do get a little envious of the current players as they are living the dream by getting to play in an incredible stadium in front of the greatest fans in the world, but I console myself by remembering that we are all part of the same Rangers family.

In February 2017, thanks to Derek, Diane, Nicky and Rodney, I attended the ORSA convention in Sun City, South Africa. I was looking forward to heading out on safari and along with 30 other Rangers supporters we ventured out in an open truck, and were instructed to keep our eyes peeled for the residents of this wonderful nature reserve. There were very few rules from the tour guide; just watch and wait. During the first 30 minutes all we managed to clap eyes on was a lazy coyote running through the wild savannah. On the other hand, there were plenty of beers in the truck so nobody was complaining. All of a sudden, luck was with us and we got to meet an elephant's family on the right, and a few giraffes on the left. Sadly, by the time we got our phones out to take some pictures, the animals were off. Someone in the truck screamed 'Oh my god!' and with that, the animals were gone!

When the tour finished, we were heading back to the main building when someone sitting close to me lit up a cigarette. Obviously he couldn't wait the few minutes till we got back and was hiding it behind the seat in front of him but after just a couple of puffs, the alert tour guide stood up at the front of the truck and, shaking his head in a very disappointed manner, walked purposefully to the back of the truck. Once there, he repeated one of his original instructions, 'SMOKING IS NOT PERMITTED.' The guilty-looking Rangers fan apologised and immediately tried to stub out the fag, before flicking it out of the truck. What's the big deal? We are only in the middle of a nature reserve, where it doesn't rain for most of the year, there is plenty of dry grass everywhere and animals in danger of extinction are living all around us. No big deal!!

Immediately, like a young Nacho Novo, the poor tour guide sprinted to the front of the truck, slid down the stairs like Batman and immediately took care of the fag, which was still lit. In doing so, he had prevented a pretty big disaster. Later, the tour guide calmed down (after a big tip) and was very happy to say 'adios' to the group.

Our day at the nature reserve ended with a fantastic dinner under a clear blue sky full of beautiful stars, the brightest I have ever seen. We enjoyed an amazing buffet around a 'controlled' fire that everyone embraced fully. The evening was perfect thanks to the live music from a local tribal band. Unfortunately the concert finished after just half an hour as the bongos were 'borrowed' by some Rangers supporters and a little spot in the middle of the savannah became like Ibrox during a home match. Everyone around me was bouncing and singing 'Follow Follow'!

At the end of last year I was offered a role with Serie A side, Udinese as full-time striker coach. Of course I snapped it up as it is something I have dreamed of doing since I retired. So I am now embarking on an exciting new career with Udinese manager Massimo Oddo and am back at the club where I made my debut more than three decades ago.

I am truly excited by this opportunity, but if you believe in the circle of life, then maybe one day my dream, to be back working at Rangers, will come true.

Arrivederci, my friends...

MY TOP TEAM

MARCO'S ELEVEN

IT was a privilege to play alongside so many great players during my career – players from all positions; including match winners and great defenders as well as a special goalkeeper or two. As you can imagine, it wasn't easy to restrict my top team to just 11, so something had to give. I took great care while selecting those who should represent 'Marco's Eleven', and just like the film with a similar name starring Brad Pitt and George Clooney, we were chasing our own personal pot of gold.

In my XI I decided to reward pure talent, as well as that fierce determination – and ruthless desire – which all players need if they want to make it in a tough profession. Then, of course, I could have picked a team made up solely of the players with whom I became great friends away from the drama of the football pitch. However, if I wish to one day pursue a career as a coach, I really need to start somewhere, so I reckon my team would play a 4-3-3 formation, with the emphasis definitely on attack. We would give most teams a real run for their money and, of course, we would play our home matches at Ibrox Stadium.

Mind you, Marco's Eleven might be 'slightly' unbalanced with a leaning towards the opposition goal, but goals will continue to fascinate me until the day I draw my last breath, although one thing is for sure, to play alongside these guys was a real pleasure and they gave me enough memories to last a lifetime. Nevertheless, it was just as enjoyable to play against hundreds of other great professionals and a real pleasure to know so many good people.

During my career I also had the opportunity to study and savour many interesting personalities. In fact, the mere idea of Luciano Gaucci struggling to cope with Gazza makes me smile. And I could count on one hand the number of former colleagues I wouldn't be happy to meet on a street corner these days. So, with these thoughts in mind, here is the eleven I have chosen.

Campione (Bologna) Balbo (Udinese) Laudrup (Rangers)

Dell'Anno (Udinese) Gattuso (Perugia & Rangers) Gascoigne (Rangers)

Prodan (Rangers) De Marchi (Bologna) Pasian (Italcantieri) Materazzi (Perugia)

Giuliani (Udinese)

MARCO NEGRI

CAREER
TIMELINE

A.R. Italcantieri Monfalcone – youth team 1982–1984

Udinese – youth team 1984–1988
Udinese – Serie B, 1988/89. Appearances 3, goals 0.

Novara – Serie C, 1989/90. Appearances 27, goals 0.

Udinese – Serie B, 1990/91. Appearances 5, goals 0.
Udinese – Serie B, 1991/92. Appearances 0, goals 0.

Ternana – Serie C1, 1991/92. Appearances 24, goals 4.
Ternana – Serie B, 1992/93. Appearances 9, goals 1.

Cosenza – Serie B, 1992/93. Appearances 24, goals 4.
Cosenza – Serie B, 1993/94. Appearances 0, goals 0.

Bologna – Serie C1, 1993/94. Appearances 24, goals 8.

Cosenza – Serie B, 1994/95. Appearances 34, goals 19.

Perugia – Serie B, 1995/96. Appearances 34, goals 18.

Perugia – Serie A, 1996/97. Appearances 27, goals 15.

Rangers – Scottish Premiership, 1997/98. Appearances 29, goals 33.

Rangers – Champions League, 1997/98. Appearances 4, goals 3.

Rangers – Scottish Premiership, 1998/99. Appearances 0, goals 0.

Vicenza – Serie A, 1998/99. Appearances 9, goals 1.

Rangers – Scottish Cup, 1999/2000. Appearances 1, goals 0.

Rangers – Scottish Premiership, 2000/01. Appearances 1, goals 0.

Rangers – Champions League, 2000/01. Appearances 1, goals 0.

Bologna – Serie A, 2001/02. Appearances 3, goals 0.

Cagliari – Serie B, 2001/02. Appearances 4, goals 2.

Livorno – Serie B, 2002/03. Appearances 20, goals 8.

Perugia – Serie B, 2004/05. Appearances 3, goals 0.